FACETS
of UNITY

Other books by A. H. Almaas:

The Elixir of Enlightenment

Essence
The Diamond Approach to Inner Realization

Luminous Night's Journey
An Autobiographical Fragment

DIAMOND MIND SERIES

Volume I: The Void
Inner Spaciousness and Ego Structure

Volume II: The Pearl Beyond Price
Integration of Personality into Being:
An Object Relations Approach

Volume III: The Point of Existence
Transformations of Narcissism
in Self-Realization

DIAMOND HEART SERIES

Book One: **Elements of the Real in Man**

Book Two: **The Freedom to Be**

Book Three: **Being and the Meaning of Life**

Book Four: **Indestructible Innocence**

FACETS
of UNITY

The ENNEAGRAM of HOLY IDEAS

A.H. Almaas

Diamond Books  Berkeley, California

The Enneagram of the Passions, Nine Holy Ideas (Holy Perfection, Holy Will, Holy Harmony, Holy Origin, Holy Omniscience, Holy Strength, Holy Wisdom, Holy Truth, Holy Love), Psycho-catalyzer, Ten Divine Holy Ideas and Trialectics are service marks of Arica Institute, Inc.

Cover illustration: Andre Avdoulos
Cover design: Chris Molé

First published in 1998 by
Diamond Books
Almaas Publications
P.O. Box 10114
Berkeley, CA 94709

ISBN 0-936713-14-3

Library of Congress Card Catalog Number: 98-071513

Diamond Approach is a registered service mark of the Ridhwan Foundation.

Typeset in 12 point Adobe Garamond by Byron Brown
Printed in the United States by Thomson-Shore

TABLE OF CONTENTS

Dedicated
with love and gratitude
to
Dr. Claudio Naranjo

who initiated me into spiritual work,
introduced me to the Enneagram knowledge,
and, through his pioneering work of integrating
psychological understanding and spiritual practice,
inspired my interest in that direction.

ACKNOWLEDGMENTS

This book would not have become one without the invaluable and dedicated work of several individuals. The editors, Sandra Maitri, Alia Johnson, and Byron Brown, have managed, with commitment and intelligence, to turn the original lecture transcripts of teachings I gave some years ago into a readable and accessible book. They have done an invaluable service for which I am grateful.

I also want to thank Sue Clarry for her important assistance in the original editing, Sheri Harms for her skillful and necessary copy editing, Byron Brown for his organizing and layout, and Sara Norwood Hurley, Diamond Books production manager, for her indefatigable commitment and support for the project and all individuals working on it.

I also want to acknowledge my debt to Claudio Naranjo, from whom I learned the transmitted knowledge of the Enneagram, and Oscar Ichazo, the source of transmission of this particular knowledge, who was most gracious in providing a preface for the book.

A.H. Almaas

FOREWORD

A.H. Almaas presents in this terse and skillfully written book another study on the main thematic of his series of inquiries, which he most appropriately names the Diamond Approach, which essentially consists of examining the totality of the mind in a journey toward the transcendental state of Pure Mind, also known as the Diamond Mind, most especially in the *Diamond Sutra*. It can also be found in the Platform of the Sixth Patriarch, and the same examination and discovery is found in the Platonic, Stoic, and Neoplatonic doctrine of *anamnesis* (Gr) or the "doctrine of the remembrance of the eternal Ideas or Forms." The mystical and transcendental point of this doctrine is that we know the eternal Ideas prenatally and that we can re-discover them only by tracing our mind back to its natural origin, which is unborn and whose supreme quality is its ability to reflect itself in the eternal Ideas or Platonic Forms.

Almaas was at one time a student of Claudio Naranjo, who studied with me in 1969 in Santiago, Chile, and in 1970 in Arica, Chile. Naranjo is one of the best theoreticians of our time, and he has shown his proven ability, along with his scholarly presentation and intellectual integrity, by passing to his students an accurate transmission of what I taught and to what precise point my teachings had implied a structure that was logical, metaphysical, and psychological, and in general, a spiritual structure. This spiritual structure is the one that sustains our entire cycle of experiences that are the treasures of our psychic life. At that point in

1969, I was presenting the structure of the mind in a ladder of seven distinct levels, each of which produces a pattern of behavior that functions like interconnected gears, resulting in an organic scheme where the inferior level is contained and explained by the superior one. This, of course, is pure Platonism, but as it is well known by all my students, the sevenfold ladder was only part of a much larger structure of my theory that I refer to with the code name of the Scarab, which is another ladder that has seventeen distinctive and interconnecting levels. The content of this larger scale, as well as the synthesized sevenfold scale, has been developed as an integral part of my theoretical proposition, where each level and its content is part of a structure that explains the basis of things, conforming to the inherent laws of the sevenfold ladder (the "Law of the Seven" as found in Plato's *Timaeus*, the *Chaldean Oracles*, and the *Hermetica*). Because of the interconnectedness of the levels of the Scarab, they have a direct interrelation and influence that is described in the Pythagorean "doctrine of the sound of harmonics": When a certain tone sounds, it produces an immediate reaction in the same notes of the other scales. This larger schema I am presenting in a book that I am now in the process of finishing. It is necessary to say very distinctly that the sevenfold structure is complete in itself and reflects the totality of the system in a condensed form. The necessity of passing a synthesized schema in 1969–1970 was important because of the need of my students to assimilate the method quickly and clearly in order to put it into practice, since the entire teaching has to be understood in terms of an "alive philosophy" that cannot be embodied unless it is practiced. An even deeper level of embodiment occurs through group processing, teaching, and passing the method of analysis to others. Because the teachings are well rooted in logic and rhetorics, they are explained with direct propositions and scientific clarity.

Following Plato, Neoplatonists condensed the structure of the psyche into ten principles based upon the Pythagorean Numbers, which are interpreted as Universal Principles, and in my system as the Ten Divine Holy Ideas, the tenth being the Unity of the pleroma of the One. In Proclus the ten Pythagorean Numbers are analyzed in his

"Platonic Theology," which indeed is the supreme seminal theology of all theologies from then until now. In the same way, we owe to Plotinus, who elaborated upon Plato's "doctrine of the One," his "doctrine of total transcendence of the mind in its pure and absolute transcendentality of the One." We also recognize his most important "doctrine of the trinity," where all monads have inside of themselves a manifestation of their own internal Unity in the form of an interconnected and interdependent triad, and since there only exists monads, all reality is a consequence of the inside movement of a triad (the "Law of Three" found in Plato's Timaeus, the Chaldean Oracles, and the Hermetica). In my system, the doctrine of the trinity is analyzed in logical terms by the logic of space, time, and cycles as proposed by *Trialectics*, which is basic for deducing the different levels of the system and its structure.

As I said before, Naranjo passed the sevenfold structure as proposed by me to his students, and immediately after working with me, he furthered his own investigations, mainly on the psychology of the system with a perspective of Gestalt Psychology, Depth Psychology, and Cognitive Principles. Naranjo worked mostly with the Enneagram of the Passions which, of course, is the psychological level of the system. Then Naranjo produced excellent psychological insights into the passions and the fixations, and their relationship to the entire psyche. In this way he produced a totally valid perspective of his further inquiries of the nine psychological types or as Naranjo named them appropriately the "Ennea-Types." He has also investigated the system as a theory of knowledge or as an epistemology. He has directed his inquiries as well into a semantic view of the true meaning of the names of the Holy Ideas and he hints at an ontology based upon them. In fact, my own ontological explanation of the problem of *being as such* and the *being* that is unstable and in constant *becoming* is established upon the exposition of the nine Holy Ideas, which have the innate power of transforming and transmuting our entire self by the means of meditation and contemplation or as the way of the "theoretical life" or contemplative life and its actualization in the *Entelechy* or the *Primordial Force* as found in Book Lambda (XII) of Aristotle's metaphysics. In my system the transformative power of the Holy Ideas receives the technical name of *Psycho-catalyzers* that function in the same way as simple chemical elements, known as catalyzers, which produce chemical alterations by their presence without being altered themselves. The Holy Ideas have to be envisioned as nine rays projected by the Divine One and Holy Mind, and when they are present together, the pleroma is produced and their original, natural, unborn, and immortal state is unveiled and realized. This takes us straight into theology, theogony or the origin of the Divine, and into philosophical anthropology that posits the question "What is man?", which is answered with the proposition that man is complete in himself only while in a state of enlightenment and self-realization that can be attained by working with the Nine Holy Ideas.

And now Almaas presents in this book an ontological analysis of the Holy Ideas, investigating with his methodology of the Diamond Approach the search of deeper answers, visualizations, and vistas of the Holy Ideas. As Naranjo saw the system from the perspective of psychology, Almaas produces, with the same validity, this book of scholarly inquiry from a perspective of ontology, with an acute eye of not losing the ultimate goal that every Holy Idea is, in fact, a direct and perfect path into the recognition and, most importantly, into the anamnesis that includes the three metaphysical parts of self-remembering, self-discovery, and self-realization. Almaas gracefully and expertly presents valid inquiries into the Enneagram of the Nine Holy Ideas with an approach of analysis and practice that no doubt will benefit and enhance the understanding of the transcendental nature of the Holy Ideas. This book is certainly directed toward an immense audience that is increasingly showing their attraction to working with the system of the enneagrams and, as a matter of fact, the readers of this work will find value and knowledge from being exposed to the guidance of Almaas's hermeneutical interpretation and mode of inquiry that is conducive to the existential experience of the Divine Holy Ideas.

Oscar Ichazo
September, 1998

INTRODUCTION

Most of us believe that spiritual realization is a matter of becoming happier, freer, and more noble, while retaining the basic outlines and categories of experience of our familiar view of reality. This attitude underlies the popular conviction that "growth work," including psychological work, can lead to spiritual transformation. That conviction reflects a lack of understanding that the basic paradigms of our world view, which determine our everyday experience, are an intrinsic part of the web of ignorance that binds us tightly within egoic experience.

Until we directly experience spiritual transformation, we do not truly understand that this transformation involves such radical changes in our experience of ourselves and our world that it is not a matter of becoming a transformed individual; we recognize, rather, that the reality that is realized is something that cannot be limited by such notions as "individual" and "world." The very principles and categories of experience that we take to be incontrovertible truths are transformed. What goes through a radical transformation is specifically our view of what truly exists, and the mode of this existence. In other words, spiritual liberation is a matter of one's experience and perception moving to another dimension of existence that has its own perspective, and further, of this dimension becoming the center and foundation of experience.

Our sense of self is transformed when it attains its essential nature, the ontological presence that is pure Being. No amount of psychological growth work is sufficient to bring this about, because the psychological realm, as it is known in ordinary experience, is a distorted and incomplete experience of our interiority, since it is out of contact with Being. Psychological observation and processing are necessary for the work of transformation, but if this transformation is to become truly spiritual, we need access to the dimension of Being.

Human beings typically live in a state of arrested development in which the psychological domain rules our consciousness. Reaching the fullness of our potential entails resuming our development, which leads beyond the psychological to the realm of Being or spirit. Our experience in traveling this path is that psychological understanding and spiritual experience are so interwoven and interconnected that they can best be viewed as forming a continuum of realms of human experience.

With this understanding, I decided to publish this book, which is a study of the types of the Enneagram from the perspective of the Holy Ideas. These Ideas are objective views of reality; their realization brings freedom from the deluded views of egoic experience and therefore, from the realm of the fixations. Our approach to the Enneagram of Holy Ideas is grounded in our perspective and methodology of spiritual development, the Diamond Approach.

Newcomers to the work of spiritual transformation will find this book an opening through which to perceive and perhaps experience previously unfamiliar domains. Those who have done a good deal of work on themselves using the Enneagram, and who have identified the main features of their psychological character, will find that this work provides a way to contact what lies beyond the fixated structure. Those who have been genuinely engaged in the work of spiritual transformation for some time, and who have had some deep experiences of their true nature, will discover a body of knowledge which facilitates broader access to the various dimensions of Being.

The body of knowledge in this book is most useful to the student who has done a great deal of self-observation and study, and has experienced many manifestations of Being. In this book, we will address the transitional stage between personal and boundless realization of

Being. The personal level involves the actualization of Being as the essence of the individual soul; the latter involves recognizing Being as the true nature of the cosmos as a whole. This transition, then, is the shifting of the identity from the personal to the universal.

This book elaborates our view of the truth of the cosmos, the truth of the human being, and the relationship between the two. It explores the spiritual path in relation to God, the world, and the soul—the three primary elements in any spiritual teaching. The objective or enlightened view of the cosmos can be elaborated upon using many systems or terminologies, such as the Sufi system of the divine names or the Buddhist system of the Buddha qualities and families. I will elaborate on this view here using the system of the Enneagram, specifically the Enneagram of Holy Ideas.

PART ONE

PERSPECTIVE

CHAPTER ONE

A Brief History
of the
ENNEAGRAM

To understand what the Enneagram is, it is necessary to know something about its history. The nine-pointed symbol of the Enneagram first made a significant appearance in the modern West through the teachings of G.I. Gurdjieff, an Armenian mystic, around the turn of the century. Gurdjieff appears to have learned it from a secret school in the Middle East, a school steeped in a spiritual tradition that is at least two thousand years old. He did not, as far as we know, teach the Enneagram of personality fixation, which is currently the most widely known Enneagram. This Enneagram, which has become popular in recent years, came mostly from Claudio Naranjo, a Chilean psychiatrist and teacher, who learned it from Oscar Ichazo, a South American spiritual teacher. It is not clear which parts of this Enneagram teaching originated with Ichazo and which were added to or elaborated upon by Naranjo in the context of his extensive knowledge of depth psychology. Naranjo, from whom we learned the body of knowledge associated with the Enneagram, related it to the Middle Eastern school with which Gurdjieff was associated, but clearly stated that he received the basic knowledge of the Enneagram from Oscar Ichazo.

According to Naranjo, the idea that the figure of the Enneagram embodies an objective map of reality in its various manifestations and dimensions originated in this ancient school. Using the map of the Enneagram, one can acquire detailed understanding of any dimension of experience. Two categories of Enneagrams refer to inner experience: one pertaining to egoic experience (reflecting fundamental spiritual ignorance), such as the Enneagrams of Fixations and Passions, and the other pertaining to essential experience (reflecting spiritual enlightenment), such as the Enneagrams of the Virtues and the Holy Ideas. Not only are there inner connections within each Enneagram, but there are also very specific relationships between the various Enneagrams.

Several books on the Enneagram have appeared in recent years, addressing mainly the Enneagram of Fixations, or ego-types. The ideas in these books derive from Naranjo's teachings in the early seventies. Most of these publications present the Enneagram as basically psychological, and use it primarily as a method of typology. While the Enneagram is very useful as a method of identifying and clarifying psychological functioning, its possibilities are far more powerful than this limited application.

Our view on the higher uses of the Enneagram is in accordance with that of Ichazo and Naranjo. In his book, *Ennea-type Structures* (Naranjo, 1990), Naranjo presents the Enneagram as a means for self-observation and study as part of the larger work of spiritual realization. He elaborates upon how the personality characteristics of the nine ego-types (which Naranjo calls "ennea-types"*) are expressions of the loss of contact with Being, our essential nature, and in so doing, shows that the true value of this knowledge is to help us to reestablish this contact. For example, describing the Passions, the emotional underpinnings of each ennea-type, Naranjo states that they ". . . arise out of a background of ontic obscuration; that the loss of a sense of I-am-ness sustains a craving-for-being that is manifested in the differentiated form

---

* An enneagrammatic type refers not only to a particular fixation or a particular set of behavior patterns, but also to the associated passion, idealized essential aspect, virtue, and so on. For this reason, we find "ennea-type" to be a more useful term than the traditional "ego-type" or "fixation" as it expresses this multi-dimensionality; therefore, we will use it in this book.

of the ego's nine emotions." (Naranjo, 1990, p. 30) This view of the ennea-types' fixated passions, as related to the loss of contact with Being, reflects the perspective of the Enneagram-transmitted body of knowledge, as in Ichazo's understanding: "Every person develops a style of compensating for the lack, the ontological emptiness which is at the center of the ego. We say there are nine basic styles or points of ego fixation." (Bleibreu, 1982, p. 13) Although this is also Ichazo's view, Naranjo's study is the first published account of how each character type is related to the loss of contact with Being. Naranjo's work, as well as Helen Palmer's work connecting the types to modes of intuition, and Don Riso and Russ Hudson's discrimination of the psychological structuring of the types (Palmer, 1988; Riso and Hudson, 1996), makes it possible for us to present this study of the higher Enneagrams without providing a teaching on the Enneagram of personality type.

As our work, the Diamond Approach, developed, we observed that one's self-understanding can be simply and systematically organized with the help of the Enneagram. This enabled us to understand some of the Enneagrams in a new and sometimes deeper way, and also led to the formulation of new Enneagrams. Our understanding of the Enneagram, then, is the product of experiential integration of the commonly understood body of knowledge of the Enneagram, learned primarily from Naranjo, along with our own discoveries.

The transmitted view is that the Enneagram knowledge is an objective knowledge of reality. We find this to be true. We understand the objectivity of the Enneagram to mean, among other things, that it can be perceived directly by anyone with the necessary capacity, who inquires effectively into the nature of reality. And since it is a true model of reality, one cannot exhaust its knowledge. Knowledge of reality is both unlimited and inexhaustible: Each teaching has a specific way of describing reality and none of these ways exhausts all possible experience. The Enneagram is a structure which facilitates the revelation of truth about Being and about human beings as part of this Being. We view the present book as a new contribution to the knowledge of the Enneagram.

CHAPTER TWO

Overview
of the
HOLY IDEAS

Each Holy Idea represents a particular direct perception of reality as a specific characteristic or facet of the unobscured perception of what is. The nine Ideas, then, provide us with a comprehensive view of objective reality. The transmitted view of the Enneagram is that each ennea-type fixation is the expression of a limited mental perspective on reality, and that each of the nine egoic perspectives is the direct result of the loss or absence of the enlightened perception of one of the Holy Ideas. The Enneagram of Fixations reflects the deluded or egoic view of reality, expressing the loss of the enlightened view, which is represented by the Enneagram of Holy Ideas.

The notion that each fixation is the result of the loss of a particular unconditioned perception of Being implies that ultimate freedom from this fixation is possible only through the experiential realization of the corresponding Holy Idea. This is reflected in Naranjo's definition of Holy Ideas: "aspects of reality that have the virtue of dissolving the individual's fixation or implicit cognitive error." (Naranjo, 1990, p. 1) The teaching that the fixations arise as the consequence of the loss of the Holy Ideas goes far deeper than the conventional psychodynamic understanding which relates psychological patterns to early formative experience. Working with the Enneagram only on the psychological level leaves us stuck on the psychological level. Working with the Enneagram as part of a larger spiritual work, however, leads to a much deeper realization of truth and thus, a freedom from personality patterns that is literally unimaginable from the perspective of ego.

Ichazo views the work on the Enneagram of Holy Ideas as necessary for freedom from the fixations. He calls the Holy Ideas the "psycho-catalyzers" needed for the work of "psycho-alchemy." He believes that the ego develops because of the loss of contact with Being: "When we turn away from our primal perfection, our completeness, our unity with the world and God, we create the illusion that we need something exterior to ourselves for our completion. This dependency on what is exterior is what makes man's ego." (Bleibreu, 1982, pp. 9–10)

Loss of Being and the Holy Ideas

Naranjo does not discuss the view that the ennea-types reflect the loss of our contact with Being from the perspective of the Holy Ideas. His treatment of the relation between the ennea-types and the loss of contact with Being focuses on the Enneagram of Passions, explaining how the particular passion which rules each ennea-type reflects and perpetuates the loss of contact with Being. This is a significant and useful teaching, and is quite an advance, in terms of spiritual orientation, over the Enneagram publications that do not emphasize the relation of ego to the loss of contact with Being. Yet Naranjo's view leaves the relation between the ennea-types and Being rather general. It does not show why and where the differences between the ennea-types originate. Naranjo uses the concept of Being or Essence in a general sense, without reference to the different objective ways of experiencing it, such as the Enneagram of Holy Ideas.

We are not aware of any published study showing the details of how and why the ennea-types and their mental fixations develop in a way that connects developmental factors to the loss of the Holy Ideas. We are aware that Ichazo has an understanding or theory about this process, but he has not published it, and we have only gleaned some limited and general fragments from various sources regarding his view.

In this book, we explore how contact with Being is lost and how this is reflected in the loss of the perspective of the Holy Ideas. The central premise of this study is the transmitted view, discussed above, that the fixations are reflections of the loss of the Holy Ideas. We discuss each of the Holy Ideas in detail and how the loss of each leads to the development of the corresponding fixation. Each loss manifests as the development of a particular delusion, an incorrect view of reality, the center of what Naranjo terms an "implicit cognitive error."

A Holy Idea is a particular unconditioned, and hence objective, experiential understanding of reality. For example, from the perspective of one Holy Idea, reality is experienced as a nondual unity of Being, and the loss or absence of this Holy Idea leads to the delusion of duality, which manifests in the conviction that there are ultimately discrete objects in reality. There are nine specific delusions reflecting the loss or absence of the nine Holy Ideas. These delusions function as the primary principles of egoic existence. Each delusion forms the center of a psychological complex, which we view as the core of that particular fixation.

C.G. Jung's notion of complexes, each of which is a psychological constellation with an archetype at its center, is similar to our notion of the core of each fixation. His notion is stated succinctly by the Jungian analyst Nathan Schwartz-Salant: "Complex: An emotionally charged group of ideas or images. At the 'center' of a complex is an archetype or archetypal image."(Schwartz-Salant, 1982, p. 180) The Holy Idea can be seen as the archetype at the center of each type. Jung, of course, did not discuss the Holy Ideas as archetypes, but his definition of archetypes would include the Holy Ideas:

> . . . the archetype represents the authentic element of spirit, but a spirit which is not to be identified with the human intellect, since it is the latter's *spiritus rector*. The essential content of all mythologies and all religions and all isms is archetypal. (Jung, 1959a, p. 76)

Elsewhere, Jung elaborates,

Thus in *De Diversis quaestionibus LXXXIII* he [St. Augustine] speaks of *"ideae principales"* which are themselves not formed ... but are contained in the divine understanding. Archetype is an explanatory paraphrase of the Platonic *eidos*. For our purposes this term is apposite and helpful, because it tells us that so far as the collective unconscious contents are concerned we are dealing with archaei or—I would say—primordial types, that is, with universal images that have existed since the remotest times. (Jung, 1959b, pp. 4–5)

Whether or not we view the fixation cores as complexes and the Holy Ideas as archetypes, the core of each ennea-type functions as its central psychological constellation, forming the nucleus of the fixation. The various characteristics of each ennea-type are simply the naturally arising manifestations of these core complexes, constituted by various self-images, object relations, ego defenses, psychological patterns, modes of behavior and cognition, and so on. So these cores determine the differentiating characteristics separating each ennea-type qualitatively from the others.* More accurately, the characteristics of each ennea-type reflect its inner core, and the different characteristics of the nine types reflect the different complexes of the cores. And since the defining center of each core is a particular delusion that uniquely reflects the loss of the particular Holy Idea, it becomes clear that it is the Holy Ideas that are ultimately responsible for the variations of the ennea-types.

---

* The characteristics of the external part of the fixation—its shell—can be more fully understood by exploring the determining influence of another higher Enneagram we use in the Diamond Approach. This Enneagram reflects the Holy Ideas in the realm of the essential aspects.

CHAPTER THREE

The Diamond Approach
and the
HOLY IDEAS

As we have noted, the present work expands on the under-standing of the Holy Ideas as it has unfolded in the context of the development of the Diamond Approach. At the same time, the per-spective of the Holy Ideas actually provides a context for understand-ing some of the underlying basis for the method of inner work that constitutes the Diamond Approach. The Diamond Approach devel-oped in a context that included the understanding of the Enneagram as a map of reality and a sacred psychology.

Reality as Unity

The Holy Ideas constitute a map of the view of reality as unity. Each Holy Idea is a view of reality which reflects an understanding of the wholeness and unity of the world or universe, of human beings, and of the functioning of reality. The understanding of unity—the non-duality of the various elements and dimensions of existence and man-ifestation—is an element of every traditional spiritual understanding. Both Eastern and Western teachings that include a method of inner work toward realization of reality inevitably lead to the perception of the nonseparateness of human and world, physical world and con-sciousness, divine and mundane. Many of these teachings understand human suffering to arise from ignorance of this truth, that is, separation or alienation from awareness of the sacred or the real.

In the Diamond Approach, we find several dimensions of Being which involve a perception of nonduality. Many seekers who approach or read about the understanding of unity or nonseparateness associate the idea of unity with a kind of homogeneity. For example, on one level of perception the seeker sees directly that all of manifestation is made of one medium. In this perception, the emphasis is on the awareness that everything is made of one something, one substance, and discrimination of different aspects of manifestation is not part of the experience. This is what we call *unity*. Another level that involves a perception of nonduality is the nonconceptual, that is, direct awareness of reality more fundamental than or prior to conceptual thinking. Here, too, there is a sense that there is "one thing" which constitutes all of reality, and from this perspective it is clear that there are no separate objects. Reality on this level can appear as one solid "block" which cannot be separated even conceptually.

Another level of perception which includes awareness of nonduality is what we call *oneness*. In this perception, the awareness of nonseparateness is clear, but within that whole, unified reality, discrimination is present. One sees the different colors, forms, and movements within manifestation, without those differences appearing as separating boundaries. It is clear that the whole of the universe is one living, harmonious manifestation. Discriminated form and movement are seen as occurring within a whole, not as the movement of separate parts.

A particular contribution to the process of inner work made by the understanding of the Holy Ideas is the idea that the principles or laws governing manifestation can be understood, and that this understanding can lead us to a realization of unity. There is a particular, specific order to all levels of manifestation, and there is a continuity between what Ichazo calls cosmic order or laws and all levels of reality, including the physical and psychological. The Holy Ideas address the objective understanding of the relationship of the individual to the greater whole. We use the knowledge of the Diamond Approach to develop a particular view of how the Holy Ideas relate to the fixations, exploring for each ennea-type the specific effects of losing touch with awareness of unity. Losing touch with unity is losing the sense that one is part of Being, part of the manifestation and flow of the whole of manifestation. In other words, the delusion of separateness from the whole takes nine forms, representing the loss of the nine Holy Ideas.

As will become clear in the course of this volume, the method of the Diamond Approach is based from the outset on the perspective of unity, as revealed by the Holy Ideas. At the same time, the student is not expected at the beginning to understand or appreciate this view; on the contrary, students begin by working with the actual, limited egoic identifications they find themselves in. Truthfulness about, and openness to, the limitations of the deluded ego state are central to the method. Thus, for example, a central attitude encouraged in the student's exploration into her character is the attitude of *allowing*, that is, attempting to take a nonjudgmental, noncontrolling position with respect to whatever arises in her inner experience. Thus, the perspective of the practice reflects the Holy Ideas of Holy Work and Holy Will. The understanding of Holy Work is that the ego self does not know what is supposed to happen, and that only by addressing what is true in the present moment can one participate in the Holy Work of the whole. The understanding of Holy Will is that the functioning of the whole of reality is proceeding in one's process of unfoldment, and the easiest path is to surrender one's personal effort or will to this functioning. Another way that the perspective of the Holy Ideas is reflected in the method of the Diamond Approach is the systematic exploration of the particular patterns governing one's egoic character. This method contrasts with various others that encourage the student to meditate directly on the ground of Being or awareness, ignoring or putting aside the distracting content of thoughts and feelings, which are seen to be relatively unreal. The Diamond Approach differs, also, from methods that attempt to make specific changes in a particular belief or character trait of students.

It is not easy to appreciate the depth to which both our everyday functioning and our efforts to work toward realization of the truth are governed by the delusion of the separate existence of the self. This delusion renders completely impossible the true transformation of one's view of self and world, since the root of ego suffering is that sense of separation. Working with the perspective of the Holy Ideas and with the specific issues and difficulties that arise out of the loss of unity is a powerful tool for opening the possibility of true transformation, beyond anything imaginable by psychological or growth work.

Understanding Early Development

In the course of discussing each core in detail and how it results from loss of contact with the particular Holy Idea, we also explore how early childhood experience causes this loss. The chapters in Part Two focus on the conditions in early life that make an individual turn away from, or become disconnected from, the dimension of Being. We explore D.W. Winnicott's work on the influences of the early holding environment on the development of the self (Winnicott, 1965), and extend his understanding to encompass the dimension of Essence or Being. We clarify the manifestations of Being—the essential dimensions—that are needed in a child's early environment to hold the experience of the self or soul such that its development is a "continuity of being," as Winnicott would say. We see how an environment lacking such manifestations of Being causes the soul to react in such a way that it loses contact with its Beingness, its essential core and nature. Inadequacy in the holding environment leads not only to the loss of contact with Being in general, but specifically to the loss of one's particular Holy Idea.

It is part of the transmitted theory of the Enneagram that each person is born with the capacity to recognize all the Holy Ideas, but with one of them particularly sensitive, strong, or dominant. This is the one that is most strongly affected by the inadequacy of early experience. This means that one's ennea-type is determined at birth, and hence is independent of one's early life circumstances. This is bound to be a controversial notion. We have no data to prove or disprove it, and for our understanding, it does not particularly matter. We would have the same understanding if we posited that early experience determines which Holy Idea is most strongly affected. This would bring up other questions, such as what kind of early environment leads to the loss of a particular Holy Idea, but this question is not significant for this study.

The inadequacy of the early holding environment leads not only to the loss of contact with Being, as reflected in the loss of a particular Holy Idea, but also to the loss of *basic trust*, which is an innate, unquestioned, and preverbal confidence in reality. This loss leads to specific distrustful reactions determined not only by the inadequacy of the holding environment, but by the particular delusion that results from the loss of the particular Holy Idea. The *specific delusion*, the *specific reaction* of distrust, and the particular way in which the self experiences the inadequacy of the holding environment (the *specific difficulty*, which is again qualitatively determined by the particular delusion), form the elements of each fixation's particular core. These three elements develop simultaneously as a consequence of the loss of Being, which results, at least partially, from the inadequacy of the early holding environment.

The second part of this book, then, discusses basic trust, the early holding environment, and the specific manifestation of Being related to an adequate holding environment, *Living Daylight*. Part Three is a detailed discussion of the Holy Ideas and the development of the fixations as the Ideas are lost.

Integration of the Enneagram into the Diamond Approach

There are a few points that we would like to make about the body of knowledge in the Holy Idea chapters. First of all, our understanding lays no claim to orthodoxy. We do not claim that it is part of the transmitted knowledge about the Enneagram, whether from Naranjo, Ichazo, or any esoteric school in the Middle East. We began with the transmitted premise that the loss of the Holy Ideas is responsible for the development of the fixations, and with the names of the Holy Ideas and their definitions by Ichazo, but the detailed understanding we give of each Holy Idea and its relationship to the corresponding ennea-type comes from the teaching and personal experience of the author. As a reference point, each chapter begins with Ichazo's definition as it was presented through the Arica Institute in 1972. Our understanding of the Holy Ideas began with these definitions, but we have subsequently developed our understanding of the Ideas on our own, sometimes remaining near to his view and sometimes not. We do not claim that our perspective reflects Ichazo's view, for we do not know his view beyond the definitions. The understanding we give of how loss of Being and loss of contact with the Holy Ideas occur in relation to the early holding environment, the resulting *specific delusions*, and the elements comprising the nine cores, are original to our understanding. This does not mean that similar or comparable accounts do not exist in other places, but if they do exist, we are not aware of them.

We stress this point in order to clarify that the information in this book reflects our integration of parts of the Enneagram into our own perspective, the Diamond Approach. In this approach, we use theories and concepts from various spiritual and psychological schools, and develop them as they correlate with our own personal experience. Our integration of elements of the Enneagram knowledge into the perspective of the Diamond Approach is similar, for instance, to our integration of Margaret Mahler's theory of separation-individuation, which extends her theory to encompass the essential realm, as described in our book, *The Pearl Beyond Price, Integration of Personality into Being: An Object Relations Approach* (Almaas, 1988). It is also similar to our integration of elements of the Sufi knowledge of the *lataif*, the inner subtleties, as well as the five awarenesses of the Buddha from Mahayana Buddhism.

It is important to keep in mind while reading this book that we view the Enneagram from a particular perspective which might differ from other perspectives of it, even those of the sources of the transmitted knowledge. The Arica teaching of Oscar Ichazo, in particular, views the Enneagram within the perspective of his own system. His formulation of its utilization, its significance, and its relationship to the larger question of spiritual work is unique to his perspective and seems very different from ours. Many of the books in circulation written about the Enneagram use it as a system of typology, and at best as a tool for psychological observations and processing. Helen Palmer focuses on using the Enneagram as a tool for developing intuition, or inner wisdom, while Dr. Naranjo seems to view it as a tool for psychological observations and processing as part of the work of spiritual transformation. Don Riso's books add a lot of discrimination about Enneagram types and their psychological sources and manifestations.

We use the Enneagram as a tool and a map at specific junctures in our work of spiritual unfoldment. Initially, we use it as a psychological map that aids self-observation and study. Students also work with our theory of holes (see *Essence*, Almaas, 1986), which describes the loss of Essence and the consequent development of the personality. Then the work of uncovering the essential aspects proceeds. The theories of depth psychology on object relations, narcissism, and the like, constitute a major portion of the tools used to access the various essential dimensions. The Enneagram is then used at particular points as a map of certain levels of reality, in order to facilitate spiritual transformation. For example, work on the Passions and Virtues helps students in the process of purification of the soul. The Enneagram of Holy Ideas is most useful at the juncture between personal and cosmic realization of Being, as previously mentioned.

As with other concepts from various schools, our approach utilizes the Enneagram for the purpose of direct, experiential understanding. It is not used only for psychological observations and typology, nor only for guiding various spiritual practices, but specifically for guiding and supporting open inquiry into one's experience. This guidance and support of open and intelligent inquiry is the primary purpose of the present book.

Freedom from the Fixations

While it is useful to know and to have explored one's ennea-type, this is not the basic orientation of this study. Our orientation is that the nine Holy Ideas are representations of one reality, each highlighting a different facet of its direct perception. The nine delusions are principles inherent in all egoic structures; they underlie the totality of egoic existence. Understanding the delusions inherent in one's experience is useful not only to penetrate and understand one's own fixation, but more importantly, it is useful for understanding the principles that form the foundation of egoic experience. Regardless of one's particular ennea-type, it is important to observe all the nine cores in one's experience, and to penetrate experientially into all nine delusions which keep one's egoic experience going. In our experience, this is more important than recognizing one's particular delusion, because the deeper we penetrate into what determines our experience, the more the universal principles and the barriers to realizing them are recognized in their entirety. At that point, one's particular ennea-type becomes less significant.

All nine delusions make up the obscured or conditioned experience of egoic existence, and all need to be recognized and seen through if one is going to transcend that existence. One's work on oneself must lead to accessing the realm of Being, for it is the alienation from Being that is the fundamental cause underlying egoic experience. While psychological processing is a necessary part of the work, no amount of psychological processing can release the soul from the ego fixation. Ultimately, Essence must emerge and transform the consciousness. For this reason, work on the Enneagrams of the egoic dimensions, like those of the Fixations and Passions, cannot be fully completed except by penetrating to the delusions underlying them, and these delusions cannot be penetrated except by direct experience of the Holy Ideas. Only this direct experience of the dimension of Being, and its integration in such a way as to illuminate the delusions *as* delusions instead of as incontrovertible truths, can fundamentally free the soul from its fixations.

The initial enthusiasm that one experiences through learning the Enneagrams of the Fixations and Passions, and the clarity it adds to one's experience, must not be allowed to obscure the fact that freedom from the Fixations and Passions is not an easy matter. It is not enough to see one's psychological patterns for one to be free from them, and, moreover, it is not possible to see oneself completely and accurately without the presence of the experience of Being. Knowing the map of the Enneagram of Fixations, regardless of how deeply and in how much detail, is not sufficient to bring about transformation, let alone liberation.

The work on the cores and their central delusions is difficult, and deluding oneself about its accessibility will lead to frustration. It requires a great depth of experience, a certain degree of spiritual transformation, and, most likely, precise guidance. The direct experiential realization of the Holy Ideas is necessary, and this is no easy task. It cannot be attained by leisurely engaging in some kind of path that feels comfortable and nonthreatening to one's view of reality. Deep commitment, total dedication, and an ever-expanding openness to what is possible are some of the necessary ingredients if one's path is going to lead to transformation.

Hopefully, this gives us an appreciation of the immensity of the task of true spiritual realization, without which any notion of liberation is mere daydreaming. It is with this in mind that we hope this book will contribute, in some small measure, to the efforts of those who are seriously engaged in their spiritual transformation, and those supporting the transformation of others.

PART TWO

LIVING DAYLIGHT

AND

BASIC TRUST

CHAPTER FOUR

BASIC TRUST

W̲e will begin our exploration of the Holy Ideas by inquiring
into a particular condition or orientation of the soul that is their basis.
The relative presence or absence of this condition in our individual consciousness, or soul, has a significant effect on our orientation toward
or away from Being. When this state is present, the development of
the soul moves toward Being; when it is relatively absent, the soul
develops more toward ego. The soul always develops an ego and an identification with it, due to the nature of infant helplessness, physical
embodiment, and conceptual development (see Chapter 22 in *The
Pearl Beyond Price*, Almaas, 1988); however, the degree of fixedness
and completeness of that identification will be greatly influenced by
the degree to which this state is present. By understanding it, we can
see why spiritual development seems relatively easy for some people
and more difficult for others, as well as why that development seems
to happen on its own for a few people but not at all for most people.
The amount of presence or absence of this quality does not explain these
differences in development entirely, but it is a strong determinant.

To understand the significance of this condition, we need to understand what happens in the process of spiritual transformation. The ego
is a psychic structure that is based on crystallized beliefs about who we

are and what the world is. We experience ourselves and the world through the filter of this structure. Spiritual awakening involves connecting with those dimensions of experience obscured by ego structure. In our work, the Diamond Approach, this development is a gradual process of moving through the various facets of this ego structure—particular beliefs and images that we have identified with and taken to be true.

The Importance of Basic Trust

The first step of this process in dealing with any sector of the ego has two parts. The first is becoming aware of—actually perceiving and experiencing—the particular belief or identification that constitutes the structure. The second is the dissolution of that facet of the ego structure. The latter is the most difficult one in the process of transformation, since it means letting go of part of one's identity, and this surrendering can be experienced as a dissolution, a disintegration, a fragmentation, or a sense that you are falling apart. This juncture can be very painful or frightening because the old sense of your identity is crumbling and falling away and you don't know what—if anything—will take its place. What you've held on to has felt real to you, and now you're letting it go and heading into what feels like unknown and uncharted territory. It feels like jumping into an abyss and it can be terrifying.

If this jumping into the abyss is easy, one's transformation tends to happen easily. But if this letting go of past identities is difficult—very painful or excessively fraught with fear—one will tend to hold on to the old, staying aligned with one's ego. What makes the difference is the presence of a certain kind of trust that we call *basic trust*. It is an unspoken, implicit trust that what is optimal will happen, the sense that whatever happens will ultimately be fine. It is the confidence that reality is ultimately good; that nature, the universe, and all that exists are of their very nature good and trustworthy; that what happens is the best that can happen. Basic trust is a nonconceptual confidence in the goodness of the universe, an unquestioned implicit trust that there is something about the universe and human nature and life that is inherently and fundamentally good, loving, and wishing us the best. This innate and unformulated trust in life and reality manifests as a willingness to take that plunge into the abyss.

When this trust is deep, it manifests in how you live your life, not necessarily in what you feel or what you think. Basic trust is experienced as an unquestioned sense of safety and security that is intrinsic to the way you act and live. When deeply present, this trust is so much a part of the fabric of your soul that it is not something you think about—it is preconceptual, preverbal, pre-differentiation. Furthermore, it is so basic that events and circumstances in your life cannot disrupt it.

For this reason, basic trust is different from our usual psychological sense of trust. Our ordinary confidence in people and situations is highly conditional and dependent on familiarity and reliability. Painful experiences or personal betrayals can disrupt our trust in the external and internal elements of our life. So ordinary trust is of little value for stepping into the unknown because those elements are always subject to change.

Basic trust, on the other hand, is not a trust in some thing, some person, or some situation, and so is not readily diminished by life circumstances. Instead, it gives you an implicit orientation toward all circumstances that allows you to relax and be with them. You feel in your bones that you are and will be okay, even if the events at the moment are disappointing or painful, or even completely disastrous. Consequently, you live your life in such a way that you naturally jump into the abyss without even conceptualizing that you will be okay, since you have the implicit sense that the universe will take care of you. Your life itself becomes a spiritual journey, in which you know that if you stop trying, stop efforting, stop grasping, stop holding on to people, objects, and beliefs, things will be okay, that they will turn out for the best. This doesn't mean that letting go or allowing structures to dissolve will necessarily feel good—that's not what you trust. Even if it doesn't feel good, even if you are frightened, you somehow know that this dissolution will be okay. The capacity to accept the most problematic phase of spiritual transformation—the dissolution of familiar structures and identities—arises from this innate sense of safety and security.

Basic trust is difficult to discuss because doing so makes it explicit, while it is fundamentally implicit. Those who have it never think about it, never question it, never even know that there is such a thing. When they see someone who doesn't have it, they wonder why he is having such a difficult time, why he doesn't know that things will be fine. In those who have never lost basic trust, there is an innocence. Only when you have lost it and go through consciously developing it again, do you understand what it's like not to have it.

The Presence or Absence of Basic Trust

Basic trust is the soul's way of attuning to a fundamental law of reality, the fact that our sense of existing as a separate and isolated entity is false, that our ego experience of isolation and helplessness is an illusion based on identification with the world of physical manifestation. Knowing that we are all part of one reality means that our true nature is not defined by ego experience or the physical body and cannot be fundamentally hurt or destroyed. If the individual soul is in touch with this reality of non-separateness, then it will reflect that by functioning in a way that expresses this knowledge. However, to someone who has lost touch with nonsep-arateness, the first person's actions will appear trusting in a way that seems unjustifiable. Even to the conscious mind of the first person, her own actions may appear mysterious if she is not in touch with the experience of nonseparateness. For this reason, she can only feel that she simply trusts things will work out, but trusts so implicly that she almost feels she knows. When the soul's experience is consciously that of being a separate individual, it can only experience the contact with implicit non-separateness as the sense of the benevolence of life, as basic trust.

Most people do not have a lot of basic trust; they feel that it's okay to trust in some situations and not in others. Certain conditions have to be met in order for them to trust. This is not an inherent trust in life. This is conditional trust. When basic trust is prominent, it affects one's life globally.

Each of us has some degree of basic trust; it isn't something we either have or we don't have. Without it, we wouldn't be able to function. Its manifestation in everyday life is the way you trust your body based on the physical laws of nature. For instance, unless you are blind, you trust that if your eyes are open, they will function and you will see. It is so basic an orientation that it's hard to call it trust; you just take it for granted. When you go to sleep at night, you take it for granted that you will wake up the next morning. You don't have to tell yourself, "I trust that it will be okay if I fall asleep"; you just close your eyes and go to sleep. Beginning the work of spiritual transformation indicates that you have a measure of basic trust well beyond what you have in the functioning of your body, and in the course of doing the Work, this trust deepens and becomes more integrated.

Basic trust gives us the capacity to surrender, the capacity to let go, the capacity to jump into the unknown. With it, you don't need assurances that things are going to be okay because you implicitly know things are going to be okay. It isn't a trust in something in particular since it is preconceptual—it is prior to your differentiated ideas about what you trust. So basic trust is even beyond trusting in God, because feeling that you trust in God means that you already have a concept of God.

The presence of basic trust indicates that you have the innate sense that life is fundamentally benevolent, and that that benevolence exists independent of you and your actions. You will have this sense to the extent that your grounding in the universe has not been disturbed. The relative presence or absence of basic trust is a belly quality, something one's whole being is either grounded in or not. The disturbance of basic trust is a significant factor in ego development because the perspective of ego is diametrically opposed to the sense of basic trust. The ego's perspective arises out of a lack of this trust. It is based on distrust, on paranoia, on fear, on the conviction that you're not going to be adequately taken care of and that the universe is not there to hold and take care of you in the ways that you need. This conviction causes you to believe that you have to engage in all kinds of manipulations and games to get your needs met and to make things work out.

Unfoldment of the Soul

Now we can see how the presence or absence of basic trust is crucial to the initial step in the process of the transformation of any sector of the ego. This step is only completed by giving up the particular structure we have been holding on to. Basic trust gives you the capacity and the willingness to let go of the images, identifications, structures, beliefs, ideas, and concepts—the remnants of the past that make up the ego.

Implicit in this initial step is the second one: If you are able to surrender, then you are willing to be. You are willing to not try to change things, to not manipulate them, to not push and pull at them. You are willing to just be present, which is a sort of realization itself. First, then, is the death of the old; second is the realization of Being. If you don't have basic trust, you will react to what arises in accordance with your conditioning and will want your process to go one way or another. You won't let yourself just be present; you'll be tense and contracted. So basic trust is needed for you to be able to allow the ego to die, and also for you to be willing to just be, without reacting.

The third step of transformation also requires basic trust. The third step is to allow things to develop spontaneously and naturally the way they want to develop, without trying to channel them in ways that you think they should go. This means not trying to determine the course of your development or push it one way or another. So if you have basic trust in your process, you not only are willing to jump into the abyss, you not only are able to be with whatever arises, but you also trust that wherever things take you will be okay. This allows the natural unfoldment of your soul, opening to your inner nature.

So if basic trust is present, the soul will more easily let go of old structures, will more easily settle into simply being, and will tend to let its process unfold without interference, which will lead naturally toward essential development. Without basic trust, the attitude of ego will predominate; the soul will lack implicit confidence in her life and process. The ego will try to take things into its own hands and manipulate, pushing things one way or the other, resulting in the further isolation and entrenchment of ego.

Basic trust is an inherent condition of the soul. Your soul has basic trust like your bones have calcium. It is that fundamental, that basic to the nature of the soul. It is beyond nonconceptual; it is not even an experience. Rather, it gives our experience a sense of ease, of safety and security, with a carefree state in the mind. A lack of basic trust is evident in all the insecurities of ego. Like all qualities which involve a sense of support, the presence of the quality which underlies basic trust tends to remain unconscious or implicit until its absence is felt. And since ego structures and activity are connected with the sense of the lack of trust, the focus of the personality will be on this lack, on fear, on worrying and planning and compensating for the perceived lack of support. This is why we can say that this quality is inherent in the soul while at the same time the sense of a lack of support predominates in one's conscious experience.

The more that basic trust is present, the more the process of realization and transformation can proceed smoothly. If we lack basic trust, it becomes important for us to develop it. Development here does not mean building up some new experience of self. It means experiencing the factors which brought about the original profound disconnection from reality and, in particular, experiencing repeatedly the fundamental truth of nonseparateness to the point where the soul can again rest in the knowledge of that truth. Each new experience of essential truth deepens the soul's contact with her own basic trust.

Ease and Freedom in Living

In a sense, basic trust is a bedrock for the process of spiritual development, but it also affects the quality of the whole of our lives. It gives us the sense that our lives are evolving naturally, moving and progressing in ways and directions that we may not yet know or understand but that we feel confident will be okay. If basic trust is present, our lives have a sense of freedom. Then the desire to know where things are going arises, not out of wanting to control the unfoldment, but out of simple curiosity.

When you are functioning from basic trust, it is implicit in how you live, how you interact, how you act in the world, how you go about your life. It is a fundamental quality for human living, as well as a necessity for the work of transformation. We can see to what extent it is present or not in observing the way we live our lives. Basic trust manifests through our actions rather than through our thoughts or feelings, since it is knowledge in the belly and belly knowledge shows through action. So it is a type of knowledge that we don't usually think of as knowledge.

To understand basic trust in action, we need to distinguish it from the ego's tendency toward inertia and inactivity. To have basic trust does not imply that you don't act. It does not mean that if someone is pointing a gun at you, you don't do anything to defend yourself. It means that you trust your impulse to run—you trust your inherent intelligent functioning. Likewise, trusting that the universe will take care of you does not mean that you stay in bed all day. The universe will take care of you by making you get up and tend to your business. The universe unfolds in an optimal way, and part of that unfoldment happens through you and your actions.

When you have a lot of basic trust, you are courageous and authentic. You take risks. You don't sit on your capacities. You engage in life wholeheartedly, doing what feels appropriate to you with the confidence that it will work out. Without much basic trust, you are paralyzed with fear of failure and fear of rejection. If you're looking for a mate, basic trust means taking the risk of talking with someone you're attracted to. You may be a little frightened, but the fear is not a big deal and you act anyway. If she rejects you, so what? You feel resilient. After all, there are millions of people in the world. But without basic trust, rejection can feel like the end of the world. You feel hopeless. So basic trust implies *real* hope, which we will discuss when we get to the Holy Idea of Holy Hope.

When your basic trust deepens, you have an inner sense of relaxation that allows your soul to unfold spontaneously and naturally. The trust affects your mind in such a way that you begin to see that whatever happens is right even if it's painful, and things that you had thought were bad turn out not to be bad. You have a different outlook, seeing a more fundamentally true view of the universe. You see that everything that exists in the world is just right and that whatever happens is just right, that what is can't be added to or subtracted from. This is the Idea of Holy Perfection. To see this truth, you have to trust the universe. When there is a depth of basic trust, you perceive the universe through the Holy Ideas. If there is little basic trust, you see the universe through a closed mind, through the filter of the fixated structure of the ego.

Without feeling the loving holding of the universe, we can have no basic trust. How can you really let go and let yourself be if there isn't trust that things are fundamentally okay, that whatever happens is appropriate? If you don't have this trust, you are constantly scared, constantly tense, constantly fighting reality—inner and outer. So we need to reclaim our basic trust. All work on oneself is necessary because one's basic trust is not complete. If it were, you would feel completely relaxed and you would spontaneously grow to become what you are supposed to be.

Since our basic trust is not complete, we fight, resist, and struggle; and then we need practices and teachings to see that our struggle is fruitless and is actually the problem. We all want to be at peace with ourselves, with our lives, with whatever situation we find ourselves in. We don't know how to do that, so we are always struggling and fighting with our reality, trying to bring about some harmony and relaxation, some lessening of worry and fear. But all we need to do is to quit struggling with ourselves and with reality. When it is said that suffering ceases when one is realized or enlightened, what is meant is that the struggling ceases. Enlightenment is not a matter of not feeling pain, but of not fighting it.

Basic Trust and Realization

Basic trust, then, is synonymous with being realized, with being settled, with not struggling. When we say not struggling, we mean not struggling with yourself. This doesn't mean that you don't need to make efforts. If you need to chop wood, you chop wood, but you don't hesitate and wonder if it is the right thing to do or judge yourself for how you do it. You simply chop the wood. Most of us can't simply do that because we are fighting with ourselves. When we investigate, we find that we fight ourselves because we don't trust. We don't trust that if we relax, we will have the capacities, we will have the intelligence, we will have the strength, we will have the compassion that we need to deal with our lives. We don't trust that reality as it is is fundamentally fine and will work for us and support us without any interference on our part. Basic trust is learning that life is manageable, is workable; that we can relax into it and just let it be. It is the trust that the universe itself supports us and that we have the inner resources to deal with whatever life presents us.

So basic trust means trusting enough to let your mind stop, to be silent within, knowing that if there is something you need to know, the knowing will come. It means trusting that if you need to do something, you will be able to do it. It means accepting and trusting the silence, the stillness, the Beingness. If we don't trust, we can't let our minds be silent and we can't let ourselves be still. We think we always have to be on the go, always making one thing or another happen or not happen, so we don't let our minds or our bodies rest. We believe that if our minds are quiet, when we need certain information, it is not going to be there. We believe that if our bodies are still, when we need to act, we won't be able to.

Without basic trust, we don't have trust in our nature, our inner resources, and in the universe that gave birth to us and is constantly supporting us, constantly providing for us, and will continue providing for us whatever we really need. Without that trust, we don't experience ourselves as the children of the universe that we really are. We experience ourselves as abandoned, outcast, left on our own—and not only on our own, but lacking and deficient in capacities. We experience ourselves as alone, isolated, separated, not being provided for by the universe, and at the same time, small, unable, and without what it takes to provide for ourselves. So we live in a constant state of fear. This is the basic position of ego.

To experientially understand basic trust and to develop it, to let ourselves surrender, let go, and relax into what is, is not simple because our minds have become so complex in our attempt to deal with our ignorance and distrust. Our minds are split into so many fragments that are constantly fighting with reality and with each other. Because our minds are so complicated and disharmonious, it takes a lot of work, intelligence, and energy to penetrate the thick complexity and darkness, to discover what the actual truth of reality is. Reality itself is very simple and straightforward, but we can't see that simplicity, we can't see the normality of our natural state.

Let's look at some examples to understand what we mean by simplicity and complexity. How often is it that you feel hungry and eat a meal and are really at peace and not in some kind of conflict with yourself about it, worrying about whether it is the right time to eat or not, whether you are eating too much or too little, whether you are eating only because your stomach is empty and you want a little food? The mind complicates the experience by thinking about it, reflecting on it, judging it, telling you that you shouldn't eat now or you're bad for eating what you want. Or you are tired, for instance, and you want to just relax and maybe read the newspaper or watch a little TV, but does your mind leave you alone? "How can I rest when there are things I haven't done? How about my responsibilities? Am I wasting my time or not? Am I being indulgent? I should have rested before—I'm tired because I don't give myself time to rest."

If you observe yourself, you will see an almost continuous commentary going on inside. One part of you is always critiquing what you are doing, feeling, and thinking, telling you that you are wrong for what you're feeling or thinking, you aren't doing it right and you never will, you're basically a bad person anyway, you shouldn't do it this way, you should do it that way, and so on. What about just resting when you are tired? What about just sitting down, reading your book, having a cup of tea, watching TV without doing anything else? Can you do that?

When you start working on yourself, the situation gets even more complicated. You are sitting there watching TV, and you start thinking, "I shouldn't be watching television—I should be meditating or reading some holy book instead of wasting my time watching this dumb television program." You bother yourself, criticizing your state: "I should be more cosmic, not enjoying this stupid sit-com."

This is our suffering; this is our pain. We don't leave ourselves alone to just be. Even when we meditate, it's rare that we just sit there and let ourselves be. "Am I doing it right? Nothing is happening. I'm wasting my time." Seldom do we just sit and allow whatever happens to happen. This is what we mean by the discord that arises because we have no trust.

If basic trust informs your experience, your psyche is relaxed. Your soul is at peace with itself and with your situation, resting in the unquestioned confidence that the universe provides, that you have, and will receive, what you really need, and that things are workable. If we really have this trust, this deep inner relaxation, it becomes possible to live our lives out of love, out of an appreciation of life, out of enjoyment in what the universe provides for us, and out of compassion and kindness for others and ourselves. Without it, we live our lives defensively, in conflict with others and with ourselves, becoming self-centered and egoistic. To find our basic trust is to reconnect with our natural state that we have become separated from. When we are innately infused by reality, our soul or consciousness is completely transparent to the truth that we and the universe are one, that we are supported by reality and that that reality is by its very nature good, and that what happens is inevitably right since it emerges out of that inherent perfection. When you understand this, it becomes obvious why it is so difficult to relax and let go, and why it is so important to regain our basic trust.

CHAPTER FIVE

LIVING DAYLIGHT

What determines whether a soul has basic trust? Basic trust is the effect on the soul of a particular aspect or quality of Being that we call Living Daylight. We call it this because if one's perception is subtle enough to visually see and kinesthetically feel the substance of one's consciousness, it actually looks like daylight, and is felt as an alive consciousness. It is experienced as something boundless, in the sense that it is not bounded by one's body but rather is experienced as something that everything is made of. It is a universal sense of presence in that it pervades everything and is everywhere. The first level of experiencing it is to perceive that it is everywhere; the second level is to see that everything comes out of it; and the deepest level is to know that everything is made of it. At this deepest level, everything in the universe is seen to be originating in, bathed in, and constituted by, Living Daylight.

This quality is called by many different names in different spiritual traditions. It is called divine love, conscious presence, universal love, Christ consciousness, or Christ love. In the Hindu tradition, it is called *satchitananda*, which expresses the experiential qualities of this aspect of Being. *Sat* means presence or truth, *chit* means consciousness or awareness, and *ananda* means bliss, pleasure, or love. These three qualities are the experiences of Living Daylight in each of the three centers.

When it is experienced through the mind, it is experienced as light and consciousness. When it is experienced through the heart, it is experienced as universal boundless love. When it is experienced through the belly, it is experienced as a pervading conscious presence. When you feel it in the belly, you feel that you are held, contained, enfolded by a loving presence, and that this presence is what really exists in the world.

Boundless Dimensions of Being

Living Daylight is the most accessible of what we call the boundless cosmic dimensions. We call them dimensions in that although they are each experienced as one medium, each contains within it all the qualities of our True Nature, the essential aspects. Living Daylight is the first of these boundless or universal dimensions, meaning that it is the beginning of seeing that the whole universe is animate and conscious—pervaded by an intelligent consciousness. It is sometimes experienced as a sense of blessing, which in Sufism is called *baraka*. Because Living Daylight is a boundless dimension and at the same time the source of basic trust, it functions as the appropriate holding for the soul in the transition from individual experience to the boundless unity of Being. The dimensions are boundless and universal in the sense that the experience of the associated consciousness is not limited to one's individual experience but, rather, is seen as true about everything, pervading the whole of the universe. The other boundless dimensions are each progressively a step closer to, or a subtler differentiation out of, what we call the Absolute, the ultimate reality, which is the farthest dimension from ordinary human consciousness. Because of their increasing closeness to the Absolute, the other boundless dimensions become more difficult to discuss and to relate to, while Living Daylight is the boundless dimension most available to human consciousness and most easily understood. The boundless dimensions are coemergent and inseparable, structuring the unity of Being. The Living Daylight dimension expresses Being's goodness, abundance, beauty, and loving quality.

This idea of the universe being conscious and animate, alive and intelligent, comes from very early in the history of human consciousness.

It is one of the oldest and most basic ideas in religion, spirituality, and philosophy. In the Hermetic tradition of ancient Egypt, for example, the universe, or *cosmos* as they called it, was seen as a living being. This notion was developed in the various monotheistic traditions that originated in the Middle East, and was part of Hellenistic understanding as far back as Pythagoras. It is only since the scientific revolution of the last two hundred years that we have seen the universe as fundamentally physical.

We can experience Being in any of its boundless dimensions, each dimension revealing an aspect of its timeless truth and providing a necessary ground for experience and life. So the experience of this alive consciousness at the level of Living Daylight is that the universe is pervaded by love, that it *is* love, and that everything within it is an expression of love. It is the experience of the universe as an expression of intrinsic goodness or positivity. For human beings, good means loving. If someone wishes you well or feels positively about you, we say that that person likes and loves you, and so we call this quality love. The universe is experienced here as fundamentally loving, functioning universally in such a way that life unfolds in a positive way, functioning personally in such a way that you become more of what you can be—fulfilling your destiny.

Basic Trust and Living Daylight

Living Daylight, this tender and loving presence, is experienced as the origin of all states of consciousness, as well as the origin of everything. If this loving presence is seen as the true nature of everything that exists, the universe is seen as benevolent since it is made up of benevolence, and is therefore something you can trust. The soul feels held by the universe, taken care of in a loving, appropriate way, provided for, supported, and loved.

This universal conscious presence is experienced not only as loving but also as soft, sweet, gentle, and delicate, giving you the sense that you are held in a loving embrace by the universe. If the universe as a whole and everything in it is pervaded by, is composed of, and is an expression of, this fundamental loving presence, it is natural that you would feel relaxed and trusting, with the sense that you will be taken care of and that things are going to turn out okay.

Basic trust is the implicit confidence in reality that results from experiencing this quality, this dimension of Being. It is the trust that even if you fall, you will be held. If you let go, things will be okay. If you let yourself not know, you will be guided. If you do not manipulate, you will be taken care of in a way that is appropriate for you. And as we have said, it manifests in the way we live, the way we conduct ourselves, the way we relate to our lives and to the universe in general. It colors our relationship to everything. If you are really feeling trusting, you are relaxed and all your energies are flowing; you can become very creative, you can become courageous, you can initiate all kinds of things, and you can live fully. There is surrender, relaxation, a carefree attitude about being and about life, a sense that the way things are is fine and the way they will progress will be okay. This allows things to unfold appropriately for a human being, without the interference of the mind, which really doesn't know how we are supposed to unfold. If your basic trust is deep, you trust that you will unfold to be what you ought to be without having to direct that unfoldment.

CHAPTER SIX

The HOLDING ENVIRONMENT

We will focus now on the primary barrier to fully experiencing basic trust—we want to understand what it was that scared the Living Daylight out of you! As we have described in detail in earlier books (*Essence, The Pearl Beyond Price, Diamond Heart Books 1, 2, 3*), each differentiated quality of Being, or essential aspect, becomes disconnected from our experience and arrested in its development as we move through the various developmental phases and subphases of early childhood. Whatever environmental factors were problematic in these stages contribute to the psychodynamic issues related to the particular aspects that predominate in each stage. The essential quality of Strength, for example, becomes more or less lost to our experience depending on what transpired during the period when we were separating from mother. Issues related to merging, associated with the essential aspect of Merging Love, are shaped largely by what happened during the symbiotic phase, when we felt united with mother. So the psychodynamic issues that we have in relation to any aspect of Being are determined by what we experienced during the associated developmental period. However, when it comes to the essential quality of Living Daylight, which gives the soul basic trust, the situation is different. The specific issue associated with this quality has more to do with the overall container for the whole of our childhood development, rather than with one particular period. Our connection with Living Daylight is affected by the overall ground or background for the entire process of maturation and development.

The actual experience of Living Daylight can help us understand this ground and the issues associated with it. When you become aware of the quality of Living Daylight that gives rise to the sense of basic trust, the feeling is that everything is okay in a deep, intrinsic way—not that there aren't difficulties or pain, but that things are workable. You have the sense of being taken care of and of being held, as we have said, and if this experience deepens, you will feel that you are enveloped and comforted by a soft, loving, gentle presence. It feels as though the environment around you is soft, supportive, protective, and understanding. You might experience it literally as the sense of being held by a wonderful light love. You might also have the sense that all parts of you are held together so that they can grow and develop to become all that they can.

Basic Trust and Holding

From the direct experience of Living Daylight, we can see that the situation in childhood that contributes to the sense of basic trust is what is referred to in the psychological literature as the "holding environment." The person most responsible for this concept of holding is D.W. Winnicott, an important figure in the British object relations school. What he calls the holding environment is the environment during the first year or so of life, the period of infancy before the child begins to develop a separate sense of self. Initially, the environment is the womb; later on it is the arms that held you, mother's lap, perhaps father and other people, the environment of your crib, your bedroom, your house—the whole situation. So "holding environment" here means the totality of the surroundings and the general feel of it through the formative years. Mother is central to this environment but it isn't limited to her.

The child can experience the environment as more or less holding. If the environment is a good holding environment, it makes you feel taken care of, protected, understood, loved, and held in such a way that your consciousness—which at the beginning is unformed, fluid, and changeable—can grow spontaneously and naturally on its own. The soul in this respect is like a seedling. A seedling needs a particular holding environment in order to develop into a tree: the right soil, enough water, the right nutrients, the right amounts of light and shade. If it doesn't have the proper holding environment, it won't grow steadily and healthily, and it might not grow at all.

A good holding environment, then, is the environment that is needed for the human soul to grow and develop into what she can become. It needs to provide a sense of safety and security, the sense that you are, and can count on, being taken care of. Your soul needs an environment that is dependable, consistent, attuned to your needs, and that provides for you in a way that is empathic to those needs. This is the ideal environment for human growth. If the environment has a good sense of holding, you will experience basic trust. When there is no extreme disruption and no intense unresolved frustrations or problems, insecurity is not generated and you rest in a fundamental sense of well-being. Your world feels secure, safe, continuous, and dependable in a loving way, so you develop with a fundamental trust and confidence in reality. You feel supported in your sense of connection with the universe, and your inherent trust in it is strengthened by a good holding environment. Your trust in reality has not been challenged, so it doesn't even come into consciousness; the holding environment is integrated into your sense of the world.

Basic trust is inherent in the sense that if everything is going well with respect to the holding of the environment, the child doesn't even think of trust or confidence. Quoting Winnicott,

> It is axiomatic in these matters of maternal care of the holding variety that when things go well the infant has no means of knowing what is being properly provided and what is being prevented. On the other hand it is when things do not go well that the infant becomes aware, not of the failure of maternal care, but of the results, whatever they may be, of

that failure; that is to say, the infant becomes aware of reacting to some impingement. (Winnicott, 1965, p. 52)

It is only when there is some disruption in the holding that the lack
of trust or confidence begins to be experienced. In other words, before
things feel like they are going wrong, the child doesn't register that
things are going okay. If there is some disruption and then it ends, the
child forgets about it and goes back to taking the holding environment
for granted. However, if some lack of holding remains constant, or
consistently intermittent, the child will not take the holding for granted,
will become apprehensive, and will begin to lose the sense of basic trust
in reality.

Holding

The sense of the holding environment is an overall experience. Winnicott
describes it as follows:

> Holding: Protects from physiological insult. Takes account
> of the infant's skin sensitivity—touch, temperature, auditory
> sensitivity, visual sensitivity, sensitivity to falling (action of
> gravity) and of the infant's lack of knowledge of the existence
> of anything other than the self. It includes the whole rou-
> tine of care throughout the day and night, and is not the same
> with any two infants because it is part of the infant, and no
> two infants are alike. Also it follows the minute day-to-day
> changes belonging to the infant's growth and development,
> both physical and psychological. (Winnicott, 1965, p. 49)

Physical holding is the most obvious instance of the holding environment. Infants like being held by the mother or father, but they need
to be held in the right way. Anyone can carry a baby, but not everyone can hold a baby in such a way that the child senses that it is loved,
it is being communicated with, it is understood, it is merged with, it
is secure, its body is molded with. As Winnicott says,

> It should be noted that mothers who have it in them to pro-
> vide good-enough care can be enabled to do better by being

> cared for themselves in a way that acknowledges the essential nature of their task. Mothers who do not have it in them to provide good-enough care cannot be made good enough by mere instruction.
>
> Holding includes especially the physical holding of the infant, which is a form of loving. It is perhaps the only way in which a mother can show the infant her love. There are those who can hold an infant and those who cannot; the latter quickly produce in the infant a sense of insecurity, and distressed crying. (Winnicott, 1965, p. 49)

When a baby is held in a way that is holding, it feels held in a way similar to how it was held inside the womb, and there is less discontinuity in the holding from its life inside mother's body to outside of it. This sense of holding will not disrupt the child's sense of basic trust, and the effect will be that Living Daylight—the loving and supportive dimension of Being—remains an intrinsic part of its sense of reality. The holding becomes integrated into the depths of its consciousness, and the result is a sense of basic trust in reality. The child's sense of basic trust will begin in relationship to mother and the holding environment, and will extend to the world and the whole universe. This will allow the child to grow and develop into its full potential.

A good holding environment is not just a matter of the mother loving and providing physically for her child; the emotional climate in the family is a part of the holding of the environment as well. If there is tension between the parents, for example, the child will feel it and the sense of holding will be somewhat disrupted. The presence or absence of other siblings and their interrelationships also affects the holding of the environment, as do the environment's actual physical qualities. Whether it is chaotic or dreary, too noisy or lacking in stimulation for the child, all affect the amount of holding he or she experiences. What the family as a whole is going through will affect it. If the family is going through a difficult financial period and there is a sense of fear and insecurity in the parents, this will not only affect the parents' relationship to the child directly, but will also create an anxious environment full of expectations of difficulty or danger. If the child grows up during war-time, the holding will also be compromised. Physical traumas, such as the child getting sick, or one or both parents becoming ill, will be experienced as disruptions in the sense of being held and therefore in the sense of basic trust. The effect of whatever disruptions occur will be cushioned and mitigated to the degree that the environment is generally holding.

The holding environment includes the psychological, the physical, the emotional, the spiritual—the totality of the world the child lives in. To the extent that the environment holds the various manifestations of the soul, the soul feels supported by the environment and therefore, intrinsically connected to the universe. The soul can then experience its Beingness in a continuous way, without disruptions from the environment, and that sense of Beingness can develop and mature. The child feels himself to be an inherent part of the universe as a unique expression of it.

Although his concept of the continuity of being is slightly different from ours, Winnicott's understanding is close:

> With 'the care that it receives from its mother' each infant is able to have a personal existence, and so begins to build up what might be called a *continuity of being*. On the basis of this continuity of being the inherited potential gradually develops into an individual infant. If maternal care is not good enough then the infant does not really come into existence, since there is no continuity of being; instead the personality becomes built on the basis of reactions to environmental impingement. (Winnicott, 1965, p. 54)

The holding environment, then, is fundamentally important for the infant's continuity of Being, for his sense of *isness*. This continuity allows the child to develop into a mature human being; this is what we call the process of *individuation*. When the environment is not holding enough, not providing enough of what is needed by the child, there is a disruption in the child continuing to be himself. This disruption appears as an actual disintegration of the sense of Beingness, and that then manifests as a reaction to the disruption in the environment. As Winnicott puts it,

> As a result of success in maternal care there is built up in the infant a continuity of being which is the basis of ego-strength; whereas the result of each failure in maternal care is that the continuity of being is interrupted by reactions to the consequences of that failure, with resultant ego-weakening. Such interruptions constitute annihilation, and are evidently associated with pain of psychotic quality and intensity. In the extreme case the infant exists only on the basis of continuity of reactions to impingement and of recoveries from such reactions. This is in great contrast to the continuity of being which is my conception of ego-strength. (Winnicott, 1965, p. 52)

The Loss of Holding

When the child does not have the support to be herself, she reacts in such a way as to try to establish or reestablish the holding environment. If impingements continue, the child will keep reacting in an attempt to deal with the situation, trying to make things work such that she feels held. The reactivity in response to the impingements or disruptions in the environment is the child's attempt to bring about what she needs so that she can survive and develop. If the holding isn't there or isn't dependable, the child will try to manipulate herself, her parents, and/or the environment to bring it about. The child might develop all kinds of ways to please the parents by doing things for them, entertaining them, or hiding her needs. On the other hand, she might try to distract them from their problems, throw tantrums to get attention, or become manipulative or even deceitful to try to get the holding to return.

By having to react to the loss of holding, the child is no longer simply being, and the spontaneous and natural unfoldment of the soul has been disrupted. If this reactivity becomes predominant, the child's development will be based on that reactivity rather than on the continuity of Beingness. If her development is based on reactivity to an unsafe environment, the child will develop in disconnection from Being and therefore, her ego will be what becomes most developed. If her development unfolds out of the continuity of being, the child's consciousness will remain to some extent centered in her essential nature, and her development will be the maturation and expression of that nature.

The less holding there is in the environment, the more the child's development will be based on this reactivity, which is essentially an attempt to deal with an undependable environment. The child will develop mechanisms for dealing with an environment that is not trustworthy, and these mechanisms form the basis of the developing sense of self, or ego. This development of the child's consciousness is then founded on distrust, and so distrust is part of the basis of ego development. The child's consciousness—her soul—internalizes the environment it is growing up in and then projects that environment back onto the world.

Ego Development and Basic Distrust

Implicit in the ego, then, is a fundamental distrust of reality. The failure of the holding environment leads to the absence of basic trust, which then becomes disconnection from Being, which leads to reactivity, which is ego activity. The Enneagram maps the various ways the ego develops to deal with the absence, disruptions, ruptures, and discontinuities of holding. The reaction for Point One is to try to make the holding happen by improving oneself. For Point Two, it is to deny the need for holding but, nonetheless, be manipulating and seducing the environment to provide it. For Point Three, it is to deny the need for it but pretend to oneself, "I can do it on my own. I know how reality can be and how I'm going to develop and I'll make it happen." For Point Four, the loss or absence of holding is counteracted by denying that there is a disconnection from Being, while at the same time trying to make the environment be holding through attempting to control it and oneself. For Point Five, the reaction is to not deal with the actual sense of loss and not feel the impingement directly through withdrawing and isolating oneself, avoiding the whole situation. For

Point Six, the strategy is to be more in touch with the fear and distrust, being defensive and paranoid about the environment. For Point Seven, it is by planning how to make it good, and fantasizing what it will feel like, rather than feeling the pain of the loss of holding. For Point Eight, it is to get angry about the loss of holding and to fight the environment to get it back, to try to get justice, and to get revenge for the hurt. For Point Nine, the reaction is to smooth the whole thing over and act as though everything is fine, living one's life in a mechanical and dead way. This is how the nine ennea-types develop: out of reaction to the loss of basic trust.

To the extent that the environment provides adequate holding, the child can develop in the context of a continuity of being which allows and supports the individuation of the soul—one's unique embodiment of Being. Because there are degrees of holding and of impingement, and because no holding environment is without failures, we typically develop a real (essential) and a false (egoic) self in varying proportions. Basic trust is usually not totally missing, but it is seldom complete. To have absolute basic trust is to be completely realized.

The more we are identified with the false self, the personality, the more we are identified with the absence of basic trust. In order to develop basic trust, and consequently more contact and identification with Being, we need to experience the lack of holding imprinted on our souls. As with any other aspect or dimension of Being, we must first work through the resistance to experiencing the absence or "hole" of it, and then when we fully experience this hole, the missing quality will arise. The effect of the hole of Living Daylight in early childhood is experienced in adulthood in many ways. Emotionally, it will be felt as the need for holding and the sense that no one and nothing is holding you. The feeling of the need itself might be defended against by a lack of trust that anyone will be there for you. This need for holding might be experienced as the desire to be taken care of, the need to be actually physically held, the need for someone to see you and support you. This can lead to the physical sense that there is a kind of emptiness in the belly which makes you feel as if you are suspended in a cold and inhospitable space. This emptiness carries with it the sense that you want to be held, but nobody and nothing is holding you. As we have seen, the central element of the holding in infancy was physical holding and care, but the sense of holding is also global, including the sense of being held emotionally and mentally. Ultimately, it is the sense that your soul is being held.

Allowing ourselves to experience the hole of holding is a crucial step in reclaiming contact with the holding dimension of Being, Living Daylight. Your sense of basic trust is also increased each time you experience the environment responding to you in a supportive way and each time you experience yourself being held in one way or another. In the process of spiritual work, each time you move beyond your usual sense of reality and of who you are—each time you jump into the abyss with its sense of disintegration or fragmentation and accompanying fear—and you experience Being coming through, giving you a sense of support, a sense of relief, of satisfaction, of meaning, your basic trust is strengthened. The more experiences you have that involve dealing with painful states and memories, and resolving them, allowing you to connect with various aspects of your fundamental nature, the more that sense of trust is created. The more your soul is held and the more basic trust is developed, the more you will unfold. Providing this holding for who you really are is one of the functions of a spiritual teaching and a teacher. So the whole of the Work ultimately builds basic trust.

CHAPTER SEVEN

LOVING LIGHT and the BEAST

As we begin to get a sense of the universe as a loving intelligence whose function is to support us and hold us in such a way that we develop and unfold with ease, and we begin to feel the nonconceptual and nonverbal trust that arises from it, a particular psychodynamic issue is likely to arise for us. This issue is a specific barrier to experiencing Living Daylight, especially on the level of the heart, where we refer to it as *Loving Light*. The barrier is a kind of resistance that often takes the form of a profound skepticism about the existence of such a loving intelligence: "This sounds like a lot of new age bullshit to me!" Or it may take the form of anger: "If there is such an intelligence, where has it been all my life? Where was it when I needed it?"

Your Relationship with God

These reactions are manifestations of disbelief in, distrust of, lack of faith in, paranoia about, suspicion of, a sense of betrayal by, anger at, or even hatred of, this intelligence. The issue here is your relationship to this intelligence, which—if you conceive of it theistically—is your relationship with God. If your mind is more impersonally oriented, you'll think of it as your reactions to whatever intelligence or presence infuses the universe—which is functionally the same thing as the concept of God. These reactions have a history of hurt, frustration, and a sense of betrayal by God, and they are universal in the sense that everyone who is identified with an ego experiences them in one form or another.

As we have said, the ego structure is based on experiences in early childhood that leave an imprint on the soul of a lack of holding, leading to a loss of contact with the loving and supportive dimension of Being. Repeated experiences of physical and/or emotional pain, as well as impingements from or neglect by the environment, lead the soul to react in an attempt to bring the holding about. The soul experiences itself as cut off, alone, separate, isolated, and it feels that it has to fend for itself and help itself in order to survive. This is how the fixations develop.

The distrust that is fundamental to the egoic perspective is based on not experiencing the goodness of the universe. From this distrust arises what we call the Beast, the part of the ego that is not only frustrated and angry, but also hates what is good and positive. When you are experiencing the Beast, if there is any love, you hate it and want to destroy it. "Where has it been? Where was it when I needed it?" or "God is supposed to be all-loving, all-merciful, all-compassionate, but if that's true, why am I suffering so much and why is the world such a mess?" This part of the ego has the consciousness of a young child and it can't rationalize these things as adults do, consoling and explaining to themselves that, "God is testing me." Even though a child might not conceptualize it, the thinking is something like, "If God isn't here when I really need Him, God is no good. If I stay open and vulnerable, I'll get clobbered again, so what good is He? I don't want Him—I hate Him. He just makes more trouble for me—I trust and then I get hurt. I had better just depend on myself and forget about Him. No more trusting—that's it."

Our relationship with God is deep and unconscious. It is not what our conscious minds tell us it is or ought to be; it is how we feel about God in our guts. Unless you have worked it through, everyone has anger toward God or the universe, however you conceive of it. Everyone has suffered, felt abandoned and hurt, and has wondered in anger at God—where was the help, where was the support, where was the holding, where was the love, where was the blessing? Such feelings are hidden in many people behind their sense of themselves as God-fearing or God-believing. For such people, allegiance to God often covers more hatred of God than that of nonbelievers, since there is more reason to be angry at Him: "I believe in you—I know you're there, so where are you? Paying attention to other people?" These feelings need to be brought to consciousness and worked through before we can consistently experience this loving presence as a force in our lives. Doing this means putting aside what the church told you your relationship with God is or should be, what you were told in the mosque or at temple, in order to really find out what your soul in its depths believes and feels about this intelligence we call God.

The issue of the Beast arises when Living Daylight is experienced through the heart as a quality of light that is loving and holding. The Loving Light is what some call Christ consciousness: universal, boundless, unconditional love and light. As the Loving Light arises and begins to affect ego activity, what it does specifically is erase egoic hope. Love is action in the now, while hope is for the future. So, as the love arises, it affects the egoic hope, and the more you let go of the hope, the more ego activity ceases. Loving Light arises as a result of seeing the hope as a central part of ego activity. However, the Loving Light provokes the Beast, the structure of hatred which originated in reaction to the loss of this Christ love. The Beast is felt as a resistance and opposition to Loving Light. It is not surprising that the Beast or the devil is a starring character in many mythological stories.

Hatred and the Beast

In fact, when you experience the Beast, you might even experience yourself as a kind of devil, with horns, red eyes, a tail, and so on. Many people actually experience this structure explicitly. You feel as if you sprout horns and a tail and you're full of fury and hate. You just want to annihilate.

If you do act out your hatred, of course it is destructive. But many people believe that just *feeling* the hatred will be destructive. Feeling the hatred can lead some people to act out physically and to be destructive, and that needs to be avoided. But most people—unless they have difficulty knowing what behavior is appropriate—tend to resist acting out the hatred even as they begin to directly experience the Beast.

It is difficult to say why the specific experience of the devil arises. I think that the image of the devil that we see in books comes from the actual experience of hatred. It's not that you get an image of the devil only because you've seen it somewhere. That image comes from an original experience, although what makes the original experience take that particular form is hard to say. It might have to do with the tension patterns of the body, or the energy flow in the system during such a state. But it appears to be an archetypal image.

The Beast is a very specific issue related to the essential quality of Power. The essential Power of the soul is caught up in, and distorted by, the hatred and pride in the Beast structure. When you allow the black hatred is when you may feel yourself become the devil—a giant, black and powerful demon with tremendous pride and destructive hatred. You might tower over the city, looking at it and laughing. You might be filled with a powerful, destructive, cold, calm, and calculating hatred. You might experience the absolute insignificance of everything you see. Allowing this energetic structure to arise, and understanding its origins, illuminates deep issues about early levels of the soul's disconnection from love.

If you are able to feel the hatred without resistance or acting out, the hatred will transform into essential Power. This Power can penetrate the delusions that keep the ego's reactivity in place and it can allow the soul to become still enough so that the quality of love can affect its state and its perception.

This Beast structure is connected with another primitive structure in the soul which results from frustration about early nourishment and love; this structure we call the *Jackal* and it has to do with the experience of *negative merging* (see Chapter 20, *The Pearl Beyond Price*, Almaas,

1988). The Jackal state is a more animal-like sense in which the quality of the soul is deep suffering, burning frustration, and aggression. When this is happening, you are experiencing the actual negativity in the soul that appeared partly in response to frustration and also in response to being merged with mother in the symbiotic stage when she was in a negative state. These structures of negativity become illuminated when the deeply relaxing and opening effect of Loving Light touches the soul. In this way, the structures can be seen and understood, although they are not easy to work through because they have such early, primitive roots.

Another reason that the need for dealing with hatred naturally arises when working with the quality of Living Daylight (or Loving Light) is that you see so much frustration and suffering in others around you and do not usually perceive directly God's love and mercy, which is supposed to be there. Especially if you live in a theistic tradition, you are told that God is merciful, God is good, God will help you. Yet, for most of your life, since you were a child, there was always pain and suffering. Where was God's love? According to the perception of the child, you don't see God interfering at all because, as a child, you think God is some kind of person who will help you. But you don't see anyone like that showing up to take away the suffering. So you feel disappointed and hurt by God and then, of course, anger and enmity towards Him. That anger is directed toward the Loving Light because you're disappointed in it. It didn't help. You felt abandoned by God.

The issues of negativity, reactivity, hatred, and particularly the devil-like structures we are discussing here, are often neglected in spiritual paths that involve an emphasis on love. Our experience in the Diamond Approach is that when these structures are not hidden or rejected, but are illuminated and understood, the actual truth of the loving nature of the universe becomes accessible and can be integrated into the ongoing experience of the soul.

CHAPTER EIGHT

The
REAL WORLD

As the ego develops, a self-image associated with a sense of identity takes shape. This sense of self forms relative to, and in conjunction with, your internalized images of your parents—of the most important people in your life—and your image of the world. You know yourself and the world around you through your internal representations. (See *The Pearl Beyond Price,* Almaas, 1988, for a detailed discussion of this process.) For those living in theistic cultures, an internal representation or image of God also develops. As you encounter the concept of God, you develop an idea of what God is, and a relationship to that idea, which includes your self-representation in relation to God. So we form a God-representation, a self-representation, and a relationship between the two. In psychological language, this is our "object relation" with God.

The God Representation

Your unconscious image of God determines how you relate to the intelligence of the universe, that which is beyond you as an individual and beyond your parents as individuals. Thus, to some extent, this unconscious image of God affects your sense of the world, which is the entirety of the holding environment. To have a correct relationship with what actually exists, with the Intelligence beyond all appearance, you have to rend the veils that obscure your vision of it. One of these veils is your projected images, and the primary one is your unconscious God representation. From the beginning, God is usually presented to us as whoever or whatever it is that is taking care of and looking after us and the whole universe, so our sense of basic trust and of holding are intimately connected with our idea of God. The image that we have formed of Him determines our degree of basic trust. The more that that image is loving and holding, the more we are able to relax, resting in the knowledge that we will be taken care of. The less our image of Him has those qualities, the more frightened we are, believing that we have to struggle, that we have to be good or somehow different, and that we have to manipulate others and ourselves to get what we need.

Your God representation is an amalgam formed from your early experience with your mother, your experience with your father, what the culture around you said about God, what you were taught if you went to church or temple, what you heard about God in school, on television, and in other places, and pictures you saw related to God or religion. Your relationship with God is particularly affected by your relationship with your parents, since in the beginning they were gods to you in the sense that they took total care of your life. From your perspective as a very young child, your parents appeared omnipotent and omniscient. Also, because in the early months of infancy your sense of self was fused with mother and you were still abiding for the most part in Being, your sense of mother contains many aspects of the experience of Being. All of these experiences with mother and father and whatever religious ideas you came in contact with form your unconscious image of God. In theistic cultures, the image of God is usually anthropomorphic, taking on human or super-human characteristics; but even if your parents were atheists or Buddhists, you probably formed an image of God.

We are not talking about your direct experiences of God here, but rather what your mind thinks of as God. Many people, especially those who come into the Work, have experiences as children that they later understand were direct experiences of God. These experiences, for the most part, do not affect our beliefs about the intelligence we call God, nor does what our rational, conscious mind tells us about Him. It is the concept about Him that we hold in our unconscious and deeply believe in emotionally, that we project onto the objective, universal force that exists.

Duality of God and the World

Now we will turn our attention to the other aspect of that which is the universe—the world. The world, ourselves, and God are not different things, but they become separated out from each other in our minds as we grow and develop. Concurrent with losing our true connection to, and innate oneness with, reality in childhood, many kinds of divisions, dualities, splits, and separations form in our minds. In a predominantly Christian culture like ours, one of the main divisions is the separation of God from the world. There is the kingdom of heaven and there is the earth. There is the spiritual and there is the physical.

So when we embark on a spiritual path, we unconsciously believe that we are setting out for heaven. We think that the path is a matter of going to a spiritual universe that we somehow see as separate from physical reality, from the here-and-now, from the world we live in. This deep split is implicit in Western culture, and Western religions actually support it. All theistic religions basically look at things through this dichotomy: There is God and there is the physical world. Their religious formulations are based on it, and only when you get into the mystical elements of these religious traditions can this split be seen through.

This split in which heaven and earth are two different things is not the fault of Western culture but rather, a reflection of a characteristic of the development of ego itself: its loss of contact with reality. As we develop, the environment inevitably fails to hold us completely. The spiritual element—our essential nature—is rarely fully or even partially held, while our physical nature, our minds, and our emotions receive much more holding. Because we gradually lose touch with what is not held within us, the spiritual recedes from our awareness and becomes split off. While we are by nature spirit manifesting in a body, as our ego develops, we become blind to that reality. It is analogous to becoming color-blind, seeing only part of the spectrum. We see the physical world but we do not see the fundamental or spiritual component of it. We could call this seeing and experiencing of only part of what we are and what is around us *essential blindness*.

If we see the whole spectrum of what exists, we see things as they are; but if part of our vision is blocked, if we have this blindness, we see only one part of what is but assume that what we see is all that there is. So when we are essence-blind, the world is only physical to us, and we assume that if there is a spiritual reality, it is somewhere else. This belief is supported by our God representation since, with rare exceptions, God is seen as separate from the world. This is one of the things that disturbs our basic trust and in some sense destroys it: How can you have basic trust when you don't see the true reality of the world, when what you see is a physical world of random or meaningless events, when you don't see its spiritual nature, when you don't see what gives it goodness, what gives it perfection, what gives it meaning? We see an empty world, a world devoid of God, a world devoid of Being, a world devoid of love, a world devoid of consciousness, and we think that that is how the world really is. So how can we trust? We naturally believe the world is not going to give us what we need, and that if we want to survive, it is all up to us. But because we don't see the spiritual dimension in ourselves either—in fact, our ego is built on this sense of lack—we don't see that we actually have the capacity to take care of ourselves. This sense of deficiency is the psychological manifestation of our lack of contact with our spiritual depths.

As we have seen, our image of God is determined by our early environment, developing out of our relationship to our parents, to other significant people in our early childhood and whatever we learned from friends, church, school, and other influences. All of these were synthesized into an image of God, along with our relationship to that image. So our relationship with God reflects our relationship to our early environment.

The World Representation

The same thing happens with the world. The way that we see it is a reflection of our early environment, and we see it pretty much according to how we experienced our environment early on. Just as we formed a God representation, we formed a world representation, generally referred to as the *representational world*. And just as you develop an image of who you are that is essence-blind and therefore incomplete, the same thing happens with your internal representation of the world. In actuality, your image of yourself is closely related to your image of the world, since they form out of your experience of yourself in your early childhood environment. We see ourselves and the world through these images that formed many years ago, and so we experience ourselves and the world according to images from our childhood.

This is related to the well-known psychological phenomenon of transference, in which we project images of people from our early childhood onto people in our present lives. We unconsciously see this person as mother and that person as father, with the corresponding image of ourselves in relation to them, recreating these early relationships. Likewise, we project an image of the world onto our present-day experience of it, based on our early experience. This world representation is a synthesis of many images. It is based primarily on our early experience with mother, since she was the central figure in that environment, but also includes the totality of the environment that we experienced as a child. Because of our essential blindness, our world representation is almost inevitably that of a world devoid of depth, devoid of consciousness, devoid of presence, devoid of God, devoid of truth. It is an empty shell, a projection of mother's empty breast.

As long as you see the world as separate from God or devoid of Essence, you cannot really recognize, experience, or embody your essential nature in a permanent way. We are not something separate from the world—the sense of separation is only a mental construct—and so it is impossible to recognize the fundamental nature of one without seeing that of the other. When we see through this dichotomy, when we perceive beyond our world representation, we see that the physical world has a reality that is similar to our essential nature in the sense of its presence and consciousness, and we perceive that world to be perfect and good. We see, in other words, that the physical world is made out of conscious, loving presence, and this recognition underlies the sense of basic trust.

World as Theophany

There are many flavors to this perception. We might experience it as heaven and earth becoming one, bringing the kingdom of heaven to earth, seeing the world as a manifestation of God's love, the world as a manifestation of God Himself, or the world having true existence. What is common to all these varieties of the experience is seeing that the world, people, physical reality, actions, and phenomena are all reflections or manifestations of a loving nature. It is the perception that the intrinsic nature of everything is a loving, conscious quality, whether we're talking about physical objects, human beings, actions of a human being, or physical phenomena. All are seen as manifestations of that loving, conscious presence. If we really see this, we are already in heaven. Wherever you turn, there is harmony, beauty, and love. Regardless of whether something looks ugly or beautiful, its intrinsic loving quality transcends all appearances.

This is the most fundamental mystical experience. In contrast to other spiritual experiences, such as an inner experience of Essence or the sense of grace descending onto you, the mystical experience is the recognition and experience that everything, with nothing excluded, is a loving, conscious presence. This consciousness can be experienced at different levels and dimensions like other essential qualities, but its central characteristic is an aliveness, a reality, a truth, a profundity.

When you have this mystical experience of seeing the loving nature of the universe, you see that what will bring about peace on earth is not politics. You see that there is no way to bring true harmony to the world except through seeing the harmony that is already there. You see that external harmony has to be an expression of inner harmony; otherwise, it will never manifest because one's view of the world would remain a projection of the inner delusions of separateness and conflict.

Basically, everyone has this projection and is at odds with it, trying to change it or improve it, fighting with it inside one's mind, making little changes here and there, but not fundamentally resolving it. If you really recognize the inner nature of reality—that it is loving, that it is joyous, that it is abundant—you will live from that recognition and you will act so as to bring about in others the same recognition.

This is why spiritual teachers rarely get involved with social reform. They aren't against it, but they recognize that it will not solve the world's problems since those problems are based on cognitive distortions. This is why some Buddhists take the vow to forestall personal enlightenment until all sentient beings are enlightened—if all sentient beings are enlightened, it would mean true peace and harmony everywhere on earth. From the standpoint of the Kabbalist path and the Sufi path, working on oneself is not a matter of liberating oneself; rather, it is a matter of helping God live, helping God manifest in the world. Other traditions see working on oneself as helping reduce God's suffering; since God *is* the world, its suffering is His suffering. The more we see that the true nature of the world is harmony and love, the less there will be general suffering and the more God will live consciously through everyone. When you see this, you see that the theistic and the Buddhist approaches are working toward the same thing: Whether you talk about the enlightenment of all sentient beings or God existing consciously through all sentient beings, you are talking about all the eyes of the universe seeing the same harmony.

As you understand the issues and barriers we have been describing as being within yourself, and work with them one by one, they gradually begin to fall away. Then the external images, external beliefs, external structure, the whole external shell of the experienced world softly and gently dissolves into a wonderfully soft, fluffy, sweet, holding presence. The more we feel held by the universe in this way, the more we can let ourselves relax inside and the more our fundamental nature can inform our experience.

CHAPTER NINE

The HOLY IDEAS
and
BASIC TRUST

W e can now talk about the Enneagram of the Holy Ideas in relation to the question of basic trust. The nine Ideas can be understood as differentiated ways of seeing what makes basic trust possible—nine different ways of perceiving the fundamental ground and reality of love. Basic trust is nonconceptual, as we have said. The Holy Ideas are in the conceptual realm, discriminated enough for us to put basic trust into language. Another way of putting it is that the Holy Ideas are nine different perceptions or views of God, if you are speaking theistically, or of our fundamental nature, if you are speaking nontheistically. They are the unobscured perspectives of the enlightened mind, universal ways of experiencing reality in the sense that they are unchanging, since they are the perception of what objectively is.

Enlightened Mind

The perspective of the Holy Ideas is the view that arises when there is freedom from any fixed position. This is what we mean when we speak of liberation and enlightenment. Enlightenment is not seen as a specific experience, but rather as an experience and understanding of how things are. This includes basic trust, that is, the condition of the soul when it is in contact with Being in its various dimensions, including the quality of Living Daylight. The view of the enlightened mind also does not imply being in any particular state; rather, it is what is perceived when one is free from the need to be in any particular state. It is the perspective of what is sometimes called the "natural condition"—how reality appears before the ego clouds one's perception.

The Holy Ideas, then, are nine different facets of the enlightened view of reality, nine different explicit perceptions that can be discriminated when basic trust is predominant. The fixations described in the Enneagram of Personality are nine different facets of the distorted view of the ego. When we are working with the Enneagram, it is not a matter of seeing what's missing in our consciousness, as we do in the theory of holes, but of seeing how our consciousness is twisted such that reality appears a particular way. One's fixation is not one's ego structure, so we are not looking at a particular psychic structure. Rather, we are focusing on a particular twist that the whole of the ego has, a particular distortion that affects all of its parts. All of your ego is twisted in a certain way that affects all the structures within it, giving them all a particular feel, a particular flavor, a particular style, which colors and filters the totality of your experience. The distorted view of the ego twists the state of consciousness of the soul in a way that gives it a certain posture, a certain outlook that affects the totality of the consciousness, giving the identity of the ego its particular support and flavor.

In studying each Holy Idea and its accompanying fixation, we will expose the central twist, the primary distorted view of reality that makes one's soul continue to be structured by the ego rather than abiding in its natural condition. The ego has affected the soul such that it has strayed so far from its natural condition that it has created a whole outlook, a whole life, a whole universe which is illusory.

Objective Reality

To truly understand the Holy Ideas is to look at reality with unobstructed eyes, to experience and live and act without distortion. To experience in this undistorted way means understanding what it is to be a human being, and what life and the universe are about. It means finding out what the natural condition of a human being living a life in this world is. It means discovering how we can live in a natural condition without even thinking about what our state is or whether we are enlightened or not. It is to see reality as it objectively is—a reality independent of your experience of it.

There is a Sufi story in which three blind men are touching an elephant without being able to see it. Each concludes what the elephant is like based on which part he is touching. As in the story, your experiences might be snapshots or glimpses of various parts of objective reality, or they might be distortions of it. Your various experiences can lead you to think that you understand the elephant, when, in fact, you are only touching its trunk or knee or tail, and making inferences about the whole of it. Objective reality is the totality of the elephant, not various experiences of it. Our unobscured experiences of reality corroborate the view of objective reality, with the view being the integrating factor, the ground for all of these experiences.

The fruit of the path is the capacity to live in objective reality. With the understanding of the view of objective reality, you can discriminate how each of your experiences is a reflection of this reality, a distortion of it, or an approximation of it. The view in its totality cannot be completely grasped until an individual arrives at a deep realization of it, but that does not prevent us from trying to understand what that view is. This attempt helps us to orient our work on ourselves because our understanding of what reality is determines our minute-by-minute and day-to-day approach to our own consciousness. In fact, the methodology and actual practices of the various spiritual paths are determined by the particular understanding of reality out of which they arose. Because the view of any genuine teaching is an elucidation of the one reality, the various teachings are similar; where they vary is determined by the particular view of reality that is emphasized on each path. When you are engaged in a path, you need to understand the view of that teaching to be able to fully engage in its work—to be aligned with its path and to have the right attitude about its practice in your life. Understanding the enlightened view as revealed by the Holy Ideas helps us see the basis of the specific methodology of the Diamond Approach: the unfoldment of consciousness through the clear and precise understanding of consciousness. This understanding will also reveal a way of life that supports this way of working on oneself.

The Holy Ideas, then, are objective views of reality, reality seen through the eyes of our natural condition. We call them Ideas because they are the perspective of the awakened center in the head, the higher intellectual center. They are nine different perspectives of reality seen without the subjective filter of the ego, and these views are only possible if basic trust is deeply integrated in one's soul. From a monotheistic perspective, to understand the Holy Ideas means to perceive God in a particular way, to perceive things from the perspective of God, or to perceive things from the point of view of the soul in relationship to God, depending upon which Holy Idea one is working with.

Differentiations of Basic Trust in the Holy Ideas

Here we will discuss each Holy Idea briefly, focusing particularly on its relationship to basic trust. We will explore each in depth in Part Three. We will begin with the Holy Idea for Point Eight, Holy Truth. When basic trust is dominant, the head center opens and we perceive the *fact* of reality. We see that the universe in its totality—all levels, including the physical—exists in a fundamental way and that that existence is the true reality. We see that all of existence is the manifestation of God, the Divine Being, True Nature—whatever name you wish to give it. So Holy Truth is the perception that God exists as the totality of existence—that He is what exists and the existence of what exists—and God is not something separate from the universe. When basic trust is deeply integrated, we see that everything is pervaded by the living presence or consciousness that we call Living Daylight or Loving Light. It could also be called God, love, consciousness, presence, or Being. This perception of existence is the perspective of Holy Truth.

The next Idea is that of Point Nine, Holy Love. This is the perception and the understanding that this true reality is the existence of love, it is love, and its action is loving. Another way of putting it is that the universe functions according to benevolent laws. Seen from the perspective of Holy Love, the whole universe is pervaded by, held by, created by, and constituted of, a consciousness that is loving. So at Point Nine, the nature of the Living Daylight dimension of Being is perceived.

When basic trust is prominent in the soul, you not only perceive the fundamental existence of the universe as a presence whose nature is inherently loving, but you also see that it is perfect. This is the perspective of Holy Perfection, the Holy Idea of Point One. Not only is existence seen to be perfect, not only is everything in it seen to be just right, but whatever happens is also seen as right. Being is seen to have a rightness about it, and the way it functions is also seen as right. So the presence of basic trust makes possible not only the acceptance of what is, but also a sense of the perfection of what is.

Holy Will, the Idea of Point Two, is the perception that whatever happens is the functioning of this true consciousness. Out of this perception follows an acceptance of what transpires, an acceptance of the will of the universe, which leads to Holy Freedom, another name for this point's Holy Idea. If you are in touch with the presence of Being, pervaded by the Living Daylight, you see all that happens as its functioning, and so it makes sense to surrender to whatever happens. You know that whatever happens is fine and, in not resisting it, you realize a sense of freedom, a sense of flow. So Holy Freedom has to do with the relationship of the soul to reality.

The Holy Idea for Point Three is Holy Hope, Holy Law, or Holy Harmony. Holy Hope is the perception that because all that happens is the functioning of a benevolent reality, things naturally move in the right direction. There is trust that the natural unfoldment of the universe functions according to inherently optimizing laws, and so things evolve correctly; therefore, you don't need to take matters into your own hands to make them happen. There is an implicit hope, rather than a hoping that the right things will happen.

Holy Origin is the Holy Idea for Point Four. This is the perception that we as individual souls, as well as all that exists, come from and are part of the loving presence of Being. Being is our origin, our substance, our nature. From this perspective, we see that implicit in basic trust is the sense of connection with our Source.

Holy Omniscience, sometimes called Holy Transparency, the Holy Idea for Point Five, again deals with the relationship of the soul to reality. Omniscient means all-knowing, so the perspective here is that in the presence of basic trust, the soul knows reality—but it knows it specifically as a oneness. This is the perception, the realization, the understanding that everything that exists is interconnected and makes up one thing. The boundaries experienced by ego are not ultimately real, so separation and isolation are illusions. The view of Holy Omniscience is the perception that you cannot truly separate yourself since we are all one thing, and any sense of boundaries between ourselves and anything that exists in the universe is not ultimate. Omniscience is the way God knows things—as a totality, as one thing with no separations. From this perspective, we see what God sees: Everything is one.

The next Idea, that of Point Six, is Holy Faith or Holy Strength. It tells us that implicit in basic trust is the faith or confidence that reality or God will come through, will support us, is fundamentally there for us. Holy Faith is the closest Idea to basic trust itself; it is a differentiated perception of basic trust. As we said, basic trust is not differentiated enough to be a feeling or an idea; when it becomes explicit, we call it Holy Faith.

Holy Wisdom, Holy Work, or Holy Plan is the Idea for Point Seven. When there is basic trust in reality, we not only perceive that things are fine the way they are and that what happens is optimal, but we also get a sense of how things are unfolding. We have a sense of what the evolution of a human being toward completeness is about, what the natural, spontaneous evolution of the human soul looks like. The Holy Plan, then, is God's plan—the perception of the direction of the soul's unfoldment when it is in contact with Being—the blueprint of what a human being is meant to become. From the perspective of Holy Plan, we see that the universe functions in such a way that human beings can become complete. A human being becomes complete when God is fully replicated in that human life, when the macrocosm is replicated in the microcosm. This is what is meant in some spiritual traditions by man becoming the image of God.

Holy Work is the actual evolution, the process of that unfoldment itself. Holy Work is God's work, which is the unfoldment of the consciousness of the soul into the perception of the whole universe and whatever efforts we make in that direction. So the Work is part of Holy Work, and in it we are working to bring our souls into alignment with the Holy Plan through being present. Action in the present in reality is Holy Work, and such action evolves and develops the soul according to the natural laws of its unfoldment—according to the Holy Plan for how a human being develops.

Basic Trust and the Fixations

As we have seen, basic trust is both implicit in these nine Ideas and engendered by them. The Holy Ideas, on the other hand, are the differentiated perspectives about the universe, about reality, about ourselves and life, that are present when basic trust is well established. In the language of the transmitted knowledge of the Enneagram, when the belly center is open and connected with the center of the earth, the head opens in heaven amongst the stars and you then perceive the world through the nine Ideas. While perceiving the world through all of them, each individual will perceive the world most strongly through the Holy Idea associated with his or her ennea-type. Each of the ennea-types, with its fixated views of reality, is constellated around the absence of the associated Holy Idea. We can say that the fixated mental perspective of each ennea-type is simply a blind spot, and the specific blindness is the lack of perception of the Holy Idea for that type. Thus, each fixation's central blind spot is the absence of basic trust, which is caused by the disconnection from the basic ground of Living Daylight, experienced in a differentiated way. So the loss of basic trust is experienced by each fixation inseparably from the loss of one of the Holy Ideas.

One's fixation, then, is due to an incorrectness or a distortion in how reality is perceived. According to the transmitted teaching of the

Enneagram, this incorrect view will be corrected if you understand and experience reality through the undistorted perspective of the Holy Idea associated with your ennea-type. This is probably why the Holy Ideas are referred to as "psycho-catalyzers" by Ichazo; they catalyze the process of transformation in the soul from identification with ego to identification with Being as who and what one is. This is one way of going about the process of transformation. From the perspective of the Diamond Approach, however, we see that basic trust needs to be re-established through contact with the quality of Living Daylight, and resulting from that, we will spontaneously experience the Holy Ideas and, therefore, see reality objectively. We have seen that as one works through the psychodynamic issues around basic trust, one naturally begins to perceive the Holy Idea of one's fixation. As the Holy Ideas become understood, we learn to experience and live in reality, with its essential qualities and boundless dimensions. Basic trust opens the higher intellectual center, allowing us the view of the Holy Ideas, which liberates us from the delusions of ego and helps us to establish our consciousness in the unity of Being.

PART THREE

WORKING

WITH THE

HOLY IDEAS

CHAPTER TEN

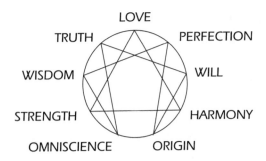

Orientation to the HOLY IDEAS

In Part Three of this book, we will work on understanding as objectively as possible how reality actually is. This means confronting the basic, fundamental, universal mistaken views and beliefs about how things are. As we have said, it is not a matter of confronting a lack within oneself, but rather of exposing one's delusions. A delusion is something which you take to be true but which is not true. It is a twist in your mind that distorts your perceptions. Its resolution is not a particular state of consciousness, but rather, a corrected view of reality through which all states are experienced. So working through this perceptual distortion is a matter of changing your mind, changing your perspective, changing your philosophy about reality, life, and yourself.

Obviously, this is not a simple matter, and much resistance will be encountered along the way as this understanding becomes experiential and not simply intellectual. Most people don't want to change their minds. They might be willing to experience difficult emotional states, provided there is the promise of some wonderful state at the end of the tunnel. But to actually change one's frame of mind might not seem so desirable.

Because the Holy Ideas are differentiated ways of viewing what is, they are conceptual and so are related to the higher intellectual center. To understand them on an experiential level is to open the head center. The perspective of the Holy Ideas that we are going to be working with is the view of reality that arises when the head center is open, active, and functioning. When this center is closed, one's perspective on reality is filtered through the nine delusions of the fixations. Getting a taste of how reality objectively looks confronts the delusions in a systematic way. Each delusion is a very specific and deep belief about oneself and reality, crystallized into a conviction, which is incorrect in a specific way. So our work with the ennea-types is not a matter of going into the details of how each one operates, but rather of seeing how their cores are the result of basic delusions about reality, which can be corrected through truly understanding and perceiving the corresponding Holy Idea.

Ego Delusions

If one actually sees the nine Holy Ideas accurately, it will allow objectivity about what is, and thus automatically reveal the delusions. On an experiential level, the delusions are certain manifestations in the personality that don't seem to change, regardless of how much you have worked on them, regardless of how many times you have addressed the issues involved, and regardless of what essential states you have experienced. For instance, you might believe that there is something wrong with you. This belief can't be relieved by the presence of any essential aspect because it is not the result of an inner lack of contact with Being. It is, rather, a delusion that arises from not understanding the Idea of Holy Perfection, and as long as you don't understand it—

that you are, by your very nature, just right—that sense of wrongness will remain. It is not a matter of some aspect of your True Nature being unavailable to your consciousness; it is that there is a particular distortion, a particular twist in how you think, how you perceive yourself and reality, that needs to be untwisted.

Our focus, then, is not oriented toward any particular state of consciousness, but toward correcting our deluded points of view. We are addressing our fundamental, overall view of reality—our understanding of it and our perception of it. The quality of Living Daylight is the grace or blessing needed for this process, but it is not the outcome. The outcome is a letting-go of a fixed cognitive position about reality.

The Enneagram is a map or design to help you understand and attune yourself to reality. It is like a prism, separating out nine different objective perspectives on reality with their nine corresponding deluded perspectives. The nine delusions of the ennea-types are simply different ways of expressing the same distorted point of view about reality—that of the structured part of the soul, the ego. Although your particular fixation gives your whole experience a specific flavor, you cannot have one delusion and not have the others since they are all intertwined and are simply nine different ways of expressing the same thing. In the system of the Enneagram, the ego is symbolized as a nine-headed dragon, meaning that although each fixation is a specific delusion, each is part of the same creature.

So we will study the specific details of each Holy Idea. We will explore what each means, what the perceptual experience of it is, and what delusion results from not having it. We will get into the core, the depth of each of these delusions, each of these heads of the dragon, which is the twist in the soul itself out of which mushrooms the whole ennea-type. Each of these core convictions about reality is the opposite of its corresponding Holy Idea, and so is an unholy idea, a corrupted idea. The delusions lead to estrangement from reality, away from the harmony and richness implicit in Being.

We will see how the loss of each Holy Idea leads to a particular delusion about reality, although the delusion does not reveal the experiential core of each ennea-type. It is more like the seed, in a sense, of each fixation, in that it is a distorted idea about reality, something mental, a conviction. This conviction implies the missing Holy Idea but does not fully explain how the ennea-type forms.

Fixation Cores

The actual formation is a specific pattern followed by all the ennea-types. To understand it, we need to go back to our understanding of basic trust, how it is related to the holding environment, how the holding environment is related to Living Daylight, and how objective reality manifests in differentiated form in the Holy Ideas. We have seen that the sense of holding in the environment allows the integration of, and uninterrupted contact with, Living Daylight in the soul, and that when this dimension is part of one's experience, the sense of nonconceptual, nonverbal basic trust arises. When this trust is experienced conceptually, it manifests the perspective of the Holy Ideas.

The loss of the sense of holding will lead to the loss of contact with Living Daylight, and this will result in a sense of deficiency particular to each ennea-type. The absence of holding is experienced in a certain way that is determined by the particular Holy Idea that is lost, and it is then experienced as a specific painful, deficient, and difficult state we call the *specific difficulty* for that ennea-type. The *specific delusion*, the distorted view of reality resulting from the loss of the Holy Idea particular to each ennea-type, shapes the specific sense of deficiency. That sense of deficiency is the embodiment, as it were, of that conceptual formulation. The delusion also shapes how each ennea-type reacts to its *specific difficulty*. We have seen how the absence of holding leads to a lack of trust, which in turn causes the soul to react rather than to continue its spontaneous unfoldment, and each ennea-type has a particular way of responding to its deeply painful sense of deficiency. We call this the *specific reaction* of each ennea-type. Out of the interaction of the *specific difficulty* and the way it is responded to, which is the *specific reaction*, the core of each ennea-type is formed. Out of that core arise all of the emotional and behavioral patterns associated with that type.

We discussed in Part Two how the Holy Ideas are basic trust made explicit. The embodiment of basic trust is more important than understanding the Holy Ideas because it transcends our perception of what is and what is not reality. The Holy Ideas serve as nine doorways to basic trust because if they are understood, the head center opens, Living Daylight descends into the body, and as it reaches the belly, it is integrated into the belly center as a fundamental trust in reality. While working on the Holy Ideas is a way of developing basic trust, from another perspective the Holy Ideas are basic trust maturing in the process of human development and growth.

The Three Corners of the Enneagram

The Enneagram has traditionally been divided into three corners, each made up of one of the points that form the inner triangle (Points Nine, Six, and Three) and the two points on either side. This division helps elucidate the Holy Ideas. The Holy Ideas of the top corner, formed by Points Eight, Nine, and One, correspond to objective perspectives about the totality of reality—the cosmos as a whole. They are the understanding of reality in terms of its totality. In other words, using theistic terminology, it is understanding what God is. From a non-theistic perspective, it is understanding what total completeness is. These three Ideas are the most important for basic trust. Holy Truth, Holy Love, and Holy Perfection are the three ways that, when combined, tell us how reality is in its wholeness, whether you call that totality God, Divine Being, the Divine Mind, or Oneness.

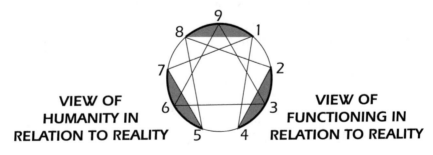

VIEW OF TOTALITY OF REALITY

VIEW OF HUMANITY IN RELATION TO REALITY

VIEW OF FUNCTIONING IN RELATION TO REALITY

The Ideas of the corner formed by Points Five, Six, and Seven are views of the human being from the perspective of the whole: how this reality is reflected in the human soul, what the true relationship is of the human being to this overall reality, and how the totality of reality appears in the individual person. In other words, these Ideas explicate how that reality manifests as a human being. The Ideas of the top corner are independent of the human being, while those of the Six corner are the awakened or objective perspectives of that total reality as it is reflected in a human being. When you experience yourself through the Holy Ideas of the top corner, you experience yourself as God, not as a human being. But when you experience yourself through the Ideas of the Six corner, you experience yourself as a human being who is a reflection of the overall reality.

This understanding of what the total reality is, and what a human being is from the perspective of this total reality, gives us an understanding of what doing is, what functioning is, what living is, and that is what the Holy Ideas of the corner formed by Points Two, Three, and Four refer to. They are views of functioning in relation to these perspectives, and they provide a true understanding of what it means to act. They address how doing and functioning happen, who does it, and how one goes about it. This corner gives us an understanding of what living is like from a non-egoic perspective, and so helps us put spiritual practices in perspective. Because these Ideas show what functioning and living actually are and how they occur, if you understand them, you will know in what direction a particular practice leads and whether or not it will take you to what is real.

We could study each of these corners separately, but to make the Ideas easier to understand, we will divide them up another way. We will make three triangles, each formed by one Holy Idea from each of the three corners, thus representing a view of the universe, a corresponding view of man, and a view of functioning. The three triangles are composed of (1) Points Eight, Five, and Two—Holy Truth, Holy Omniscience, and Holy Will, (2) Points One, Seven, and Four—Holy Perfection, Holy Wisdom, and Holy Origin, and (3) Points Nine, Six, and Three—Holy Love, Holy Strength, and Holy Harmony.

CHAPTER ELEVEN

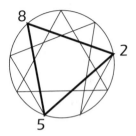

Point Eight
HOLY TRUTH

The awareness that the cosmos objectively exists now; that this existence is its own definition, and continues whether an individual understands it or not; and that the individual experiences the truth of Reality most completely when he views each moment fresh, without preconceptions about what should be happening.
— Ichazo, 1972

The Holy Idea for ennea-type Eight is Holy Truth. It refers to the unity of existence, and includes and goes beyond Essence and the Absolute. To understand what the Holy Truth is, we need to first investigate what truth is.

Truth

The first type or level of truth that we encounter is what we call *relative truth*. Relative truth is the fact of what is happening, and we call it "relative" because it is specific to the person, the situation, and the time in which the experience is taking place; this means it is constantly changing. For example, the relative truth right now is that you are sitting reading this book, and a while ago the truth was that you were doing something else. The relative truth depends on the situation, and tells us the facts of what is happening now. These truths are the most obvious ones, and are the points of departure for contacting a deeper level of truth.

If you inquire more deeply into the relative truth of a situation, you will find that the psychodynamic and existential bases of it begin to reveal themselves. Then, at some point, you might start to experience what we call the *essential truth*, which is the presence of Essence itself. For example, let's say that you find yourself fantasizing about eating some ice cream. The relative truth is that this is what is going on in your mind. If you inquire into the desire for the ice cream, you might realize that you are feeling alone, and that this brings up a sense of missing a particular kind of contact. Then, as you stay with that, you see that you're wanting a certain kind of love that reminds you of your mother. You realize that your mother's love tastes a little like ice cream. This might lead you into experiencing a quality of love that is sweet and soft, and that makes you feel cared for and loved. As you contact this quality of love, you are in touch with the actual essential aspect that you long ago identified with your mother. This level of the truth of the situation is the essential truth. That truth is a quality of love that is present in you but is only felt on a relative level as the desire for ice cream.

On this essential level, the facts of your situation take on a sense of meaning, of richness and of depth, because they usher you into the realm of what truly exists, beyond the surface of things. An essential truth is not a thought, an idea, a reaction, or an action; its most important characteristic is that it is an ontological presence—it has a substantive existence. Although the relative truth of a situation can take us to the essential truth of it, the essential level is not dependent upon the situation. It is self-existing; it is its own realm existing independently of who we are and what we are doing.

The essential truth helps us understand what is really happening and what exists beneath the appearance of things. A fantasy of eating ice cream is simply an image in your mind, and even real ice cream disappears or changes form after it is eaten. The love that it may evoke or reflect, however, has an intrinsic and unchanging existence, although your awareness of it may come and go. It exists as a presence that is substantive and real; it has energy, affect, and potency.

If we continue pursuing the truth of the situation, the essential truth will continue to expand and reveal ever-deeper dimensions of Being until, at some point, we come in contact with the formless dimensions of Being. When we first encounter Essence, we experience it in the dimension of form, contained within us, in other words, "There is love in my heart, will in my belly, clarity in my head," and so on. At a deeper level, the presence of Essence expands and loses its boundaries, and we realize that it is actually boundless. This is the beginning of experiencing the formless or boundless dimensions. The first formless dimension that we usually encounter, as discussed in Part Two, is that of Living Daylight: a love that is not just within you, but is everywhere—pervading everything, penetrating all boundaries.

So we have moved from the fact of what is happening to what truly exists within you, and from there to what truly exists beyond your body—what exists in the whole cosmos. In the boundless dimensions, Essence still has the quality of being a presence, a fullness, and a richness. As our experience deepens, the boundless dimensions keep revealing themselves in continuing depth, one after the other, as we penetrate deeper and deeper concepts within our mind, and these dimensions will lead us eventually to the deepest, innermost truth—absolute truth. This dimension of the Absolute is beyond all concepts, including that of existence or non-existence.

It is not that there is a formless or boundless dimension that pervades everything or is the essence of everything, since seeing it this way creates a dichotomy that does not exist. It is not as though there is me and there is my essential nature. The formless dimensions bring in another kind of perception, which is of Being as a formless, boundless, real existence, a substantial presence that is not contained by any boundary. When you experience pure, translucent, self-existing boundless presence, you see that it is not only the fundamental nature of Essence itself, but also of everything that exists. It exists in everything, and everything exists in it. We see here that the universe is ultimately pure Being, and that this pure Being not only supports us, infuses us, and is our nature, but more fundamentally, that it constitutes us. It is completely inseparable from what we are. So it not only pervades and fills the universe, but it *is* the universe. This understanding that there is no universe separate from this pure boundless self-existing Beingness is a more complete level of the truth.

The perception that Being constitutes the totality of everything is what is generally called a mystical experience. Before this, you may have spiritual experiences, but when you experience the oneness and the unity of existence, you are on the level of the mystical. In the dimension of Living Daylight, you experience that everything is made out of love. When you look around you, everything might appear, for example, to be made out of a pink and sweet diamond-like taffy substance, and be pervaded with a wonder, a beauty, and a sweetness.

So the experience of boundlessness that arises as we move into the formless dimensions becomes the deepest level of truth that we perceive. On the level of the *Supreme* (the dimension of Pure Presence or Pure Being), for example, you realize that everything is a translucent Beingness. You see that it is not as though translucent Beingness is in everything or that everything exists in it, but that everything *is* the translucence. It is inside things, outside things, and in between them. There is no place that is not translucent Beingness. On this level of the Supreme, there is no separation between what we call appearance and reality, the form and the meaning. They are all one thing; there is a unity.

The perception of this unity arises through merely seeking to understand the truth of the situation. It is not a matter of generating a particular experience; you just open your eyes to what is here. When you experience this level of truth, you not only perceive this inherent unity, but you also see that as you stay with one boundless dimension, it reveals another, deeper one. Dimensions of formless Being reveal themselves until we come to the origin and source of all dimensions, the Absolute. Initially, you might experience the Absolute as the source of everything, but as your experience matures, you realize that everything *is* the Absolute—there is no separation. The full experience of the Absolute is that there is nothing *but* the Absolute. Just as you have seen that love constitutes everything on the dimension of Living Daylight, and Being constitutes everything on the level of the Supreme, here we see that the Absolute constitutes everything. So as our understanding of the nature of reality deepens, it becomes more and more mysterious and nonconceptual, until it arrives at this dimension of the Absolute in which the nature of reality reveals itself as a profound mystery.

Comprehensive Unity

However, none of the levels of truth that we have been describing is what the Holy Idea of Holy Truth refers to. Holy Truth is the perception that all these levels are actually one thing, that all the dimensions constitute a complete state of unity. In other words, all the dimensions of reality are completely inseparable from one another, and all are the same thing. This is the perception that there is absolutely no duality—either horizontally (between objects) or vertically (between dimensions). So although we experience ourselves moving progressively into deeper and deeper dimensions of reality as our inquiry becomes increasingly subtle, Holy Truth is the perception that all these dimensions exist simultaneously. They are all facets of the same reality, so the sense of a hierarchy is ultimately illusory.

To understand how all the dimensions exist as a unity, let's take the example of the physical body. At the level of relative truth, we first see the appearance of the body: we see its shape, we notice the limbs, the face, the expression. Penetrating beneath the surface, we realize that there are muscles, bones, organs, blood vessels, and so on. This level would correspond to the essential truth. If we investigate into the nature of these inner components, we will see that they are all made out of molecules. These molecules reveal themselves to be made out of atoms which, in turn, are made up of sub-atomic particles. These levels would correspond to the progressive truths of the formless dimensions. Investigating even more deeply, we discover that these are ultimately space, corresponding to the Absolute level. Are the sub-atomic particles or the organs separate from the outer form of the body? No. All these dimensions are present and interpenetrate each other. You couldn't take one level away and leave the others remaining. Although the Absolute is the ultimate reality that remains unchanged if you take everything else away, all levels of reality exist as a totality all the time. They form a unity.

Holy Truth, therefore, negates duality. It tells us that there is no such thing as discrete, separate existence. However, we know that for the consciousness of the ego-self, the sense of separateness is fundamental. So Holy Truth challenges and ultimately dissolves the ego's sense of separateness.

While one does experience the sense of unity when experiencing any of the formless dimensions, the perception here is of the unity of the dimensions themselves. The Buddhists call this "total completeness," while the Sufis call it the "all-inclusive state," or the "Divine Being," whose all-inclusive name is *Allah*. Allah, then, does not refer to any particular dimension or state, but refers to all that exists—at any time, on all its levels and in all its dimensions—as a unity. So you could call the perception of Holy Truth objective truth, reality, the universe in its totality, Divine Being, unity of existence, or total completeness.

Oscar Ichazo's definition of Holy Truth is: "The awareness that the cosmos objectively exists *now*; that this existence is its own definition, and continues whether an individual understands it or not; and that the individual experiences the truth of Reality most completely when he views each moment fresh, without preconceptions about what should be happening."

Let's break this down and see what we can understand. "The awareness that the cosmos objectively exists *now*." He is saying that the totality of all that exists, on all its levels (which is what he means when he uses the word *cosmos*), is the nowness of experience and that this totality objectively exists. It is "its own definition," meaning that it does not depend on our opinions about it; and "continues whether an individual understands it or not," meaning that it actually exists whether or not we understand it. To experience reality fully, one must view "each moment fresh, without preconceptions about what should be happening," meaning that if we are completely open and not filtering our experience of the moment through our subjectivity, we will see this unity existing right now, and that *now* does not refer to time, but to the immediately apprehended existence of the universe itself.

So everything that is conceivable and experienceable exists right now as one. The formless dimensions, the essential states, and physical reality are not separate from each other, nor are physical objects separate from each other; there is no division anywhere—only complete unity. The alchemical concept for this is the idea of the macrocosm, the totality of the universe.

The Sufi view of this Holy Idea is expressed in the following poem by Shabistari, from *The Secret Garden*:

> He whose great soul is never vexed by doubt
> Knows of a surety that there is but one
> Existence absolute. To say "I am the Lord"
> Belongs to God alone: his personality
> Is not with thee; fancy and thought lie hid.
> God's glory may by none be shared; therein
> I, thou, and we are not, for all are one.
> The person and the existence join in one,
> For unity admits no variance.
> He who is free from self, when he obtains
> That freedom, through his echoing soul resounds
> "Verily I am God,' and in eternity
> Is opposition overwhelmed, and then
> The pilgrim and his progress are but one.
> Concord and incarnation spring from variance,
> But unity is born of pilgrimage.
> So nature's order from existence springs,
> Nor God his slave, nor man his God becomes.

Concord and union here may never be,
For to see two in one is error's core.
Creator and created beings are
Alike a dream, nor is what seems to be.

. . .

What is that atom greater than the whole?

. . .

There is one atom greater than the whole—
Existence; for behold the universe
Is, yet that universe itself is *being*.
Being is various in outward form,
but in its being there is inward unity.
(Shabistari, 1969, pp. 48, 71)

Shabistari is saying that to understand and experience this unity, we have to experience Beingness. It is only in Beingness that we can perceive the unity. If we look at reality from the egoic perspective, we don't see unity; we see discord, opposition, and duality. But if we experience Beingness and allow it to guide us, it will lead us to the formless dimensions and the experience that things don't exist separately from each other. On this level, we see that separateness is not ultimately real, and that although objects may appear discrete, in reality all objects actually make up one thing.

This understanding is expressed from a Buddhist perspective in the following passage by the Tibetan lama, Longchenpa. It is taken from his text on the *mantrayana tantra*, which is written from the state of unity itself, as though it were expressing itself. You will notice that the language is very similar to that of some of the theistic approaches.

All experiences and life-forms cannot be proven to exist independently of their being a presence before your mind, just like a lucid dream.

All that is has me—universal creativity, pure and total presence—as its root.

How things appear is my being.
How things arise is my manifestation.
Sounds and words heard are my messages expressed in
    sounds and words.
All capacities, forms, and pristine awarenesses of the buddhas;
The bodies of sentient beings, their habituations, and so forth;
All environments and their inhabitants, life forms, and
    experiences;
Are the primordial state of pure and total presence.
(Longchenpa, 1987, p. 32)

Not realizing that everything we can perceive is nothing other than the manifestation of one's mind is called *samsara* in Buddhism. Samsara, the delusional state, is seen from Longchenpa's point of view as not recognizing the unity of what is.

What follows is another section from *You are the Eyes of the World*, in which the nondual doctrine of *Dzogchen*, or total completeness, is described:

[Because my creativity is beyond all affirmation and negation,]
I determine all events and meanings.
Because no objects exist which are not me,
You are beyond perspective or meditation.
Because there does not exist any protection other than me,
You are beyond charismatic activity to be sought.
Because there is no state other than me,
You are beyond stages to cultivate.
Because in me there are from the beginning, no obstacles,
You are beyond all obstacles; self-arising pristine awareness
    just is.
Because I am unborn reality itself,
You are beyond concepts of reality; subtle reality just is.
Because there is nowhere to go apart from me,
One is beyond paths to traverse.
[Because all buddhas, sentient beings, appearances,

> Existences, environments, inhabitants]
> Arise from the quintessential state of pure total presence,
> One is beyond duality.
> Because self-arising pristine awareness is already established,
> One is beyond justifying it; the transmission of this great
>   teaching provides direct entry into understanding.
> Because all phenomena do not exist apart from me,
> One is beyond duality. I fashion everything.
> (Longchenpa, 1987, p. 35)

So according to the Idea of Holy Truth, reality, when seen objectively, has no divisions in it. It exists, it is now, and it is nondual. There is no me, no you, no other, no universe separate from God; no universe separate from the Void; no you and Essence, no personality and Essence; no physical body and soul—all these distinctions are illusions and are not ultimately real. There is only one thing, and it cannot even be called "one" because if you call it one, you are comparing it to two, and it is not one in contrast to two. It is nondual, an indivisible existence, no matter how you look at it or think about it. While the different teachings may emphasize different qualities of this unity, seeing it from the perspective of love or awareness, for example, the assertion here is that fundamental to reality is the *fact* of unity. All the religions assert this sense of the all-inclusiveness of reality. Another way of saying it is that God is everywhere, omnipresent. Holy Truth is the way that the teaching of the Enneagram of Holy Ideas expresses this understanding.

We must remember that the nature of the whole of reality is not expressed by Holy Truth alone. It is described by all three Holy Ideas at the top of the Enneagram. If you really experience the unity of all things, you also recognize the inherently loving quality of that unity. The existence of Holy Love is the existence of a loving, gentle, positive quality. Plato referred to the ultimate reality as *the Good*, indicating that he perceived the intrinsic positivity of it. We will explore this in more detail in the chapter on the Holy Idea for ennea-type Nine. If you experience the unity described by Holy Truth, you will also experience its fundamental rightness, its Holy Perfection. You will see that everything that happens is perfect because all is happening exactly as it should. You will see the beauty and harmony of whatever happens because that is what is; it is the truth of the moment seen without the interference of the perspective of the ego. We will expand on this in the chapter on the Holy Idea for ennea-type One. These three Holy Ideas are interconnected, and together they describe the nature of reality.

In some traditions there is a debate about what the ultimate reality is: Is it the Absolute, or is it the state of total completeness? The Sufi and Kabbalistic traditions take the view that the Absolute is the ultimate reality. The Indian traditions are divided, with the Vedantists taking the Absolute to be ultimate, while some of the yogic paths take the state of total completeness to be ultimate. The Buddhists disagree: The Theravaden tradition believes the Absolute is ultimate, while the Tibetan Buddhists are divided. The Nyingmapa sect believes that the state of total completeness is ultimate, while the Gelugpa believe the Absolute is ultimate.*

In my view, there is no need to decide, since freedom has nothing to do with what state you experience or take to be ultimate. So the question is largely a matter of how you define "ultimate truth." If you define the ultimate truth as that which is left when everything that can be removed is removed, you are describing the Absolute. It is the state most devoid of any creation or concept, reality reduced to its simplest minimum. If you define ultimate truth as the actual state that is experienced if there is no manipulation or conceptualization of your experience, you recognize it as the state of total completeness, because

---

* When I mention other religious or spiritual traditions and their points of view, I am not saying that my understanding of them is authoritative. I am referring to their descriptions of various states and understandings in the light of my own experience, explicating their knowledge through my own understanding. Someone of a particular tradition might say that they mean something slightly different and that I am misinterpreting what they mean. In referring to a particular tradition, I am not sanctioning it, or even agreeing with its tenets. There are distinct differences between the Diamond Approach and other traditions, although there are also many similarities in perspective. I am simply using examples from other traditions in order to facilitate understanding of things that are difficult to explain in words.

there is no duality present in it. The state of total completeness is all-inclusive, with the manifest and the unmanifest existing in nonduality. Everything is present, including the Absolute, which is seen as its inner nature.

In either case, the perception of the unity of all of existence—Holy Truth—remains the same. It is the perception that there are no divisions and no duality between things, that everything is one Beingness, one existence. This is the reality beyond egoic reality, true existence independent of the personal mind. It includes everything without any separations, and it does not matter whether you call it God, the One Mind, the state of the Buddha, the Tao, or the Divine Being.

The most important understanding of Holy Truth is that physical reality and true existence are not separate. Physical reality is made up of objects which can be discriminated. If you perceive the world exclusively through the physical senses, you perceive only discrete objects, such as people, trees, animals, rocks, clouds, oceans, earth. If you experience this level only, which is the basis of the egoic perspective, the universe that you see is dualistic. But if your perception is unobscured by your beliefs, your inner perception becomes unblocked, and the universe looks quite different. If your perceptual capacities are clear, you recognize that other dimensions exist in addition to physical reality, such as love, Beingness, and awareness. At this level of perception, you see that there is only one existence, one homogeneous medium. This medium encompasses physical reality, which is one particularization of it. Objects are seen as objects, but they are not discrete—they are more like waves on the surface of an ocean, lacking existence without the whole of the ocean. So differentiations exist, but not ultimate divisions.

Physical Reality and Nonduality

Surprisingly, this perception of unity makes physical reality itself appear more concrete, not less. It appears more three-dimensional, with more sense of depth. Ordinarily, when experiencing the state of Oneness, physical reality is seen as the surface, with the boundless dimensions as the underlying depths. But when the boundless dimensions are perceived as interpenetrating the physical, the three-dimensionality is enhanced. Everything stands out, feels more real, more present, and more itself, in a sense.

In the experience of nonduality, it is not as though physical reality were a dream emanating from it—that perception would still be dualistic. When duality is seen through, physical reality is imbued with the essential dimension, and the two become one. This gives the physical more reality, more substance, more existence, more meaning, more depth, and more dimensionality. When you look at people, they seem more substantial, and even their bodies appear more physical, in a sense. Every object and person has a concreteness and a definiteness that makes each appear more defined, more present, and more complete, because your experience of them includes the depth of the true existence. When everything is perceived as the Absolute, each atom, each form, has its depth. The Absolute not only underlies everything, but penetrates all of manifestation. Depending upon which dimension you are experiencing, everything you perceive acquires the depth and beauty of that dimension.

Reality itself is seen as the beauty and the grace of that dimension. So the totality of the universe is the Absolute or the Supreme, for instance, manifesting as beauty. Your body, your thoughts, and your feelings, then, are not separate from the truth, but are part and parcel of it. They are the truth itself. And the truth is there in every atom, every thought, every feeling, everywhere. So it is not your inner nature; there is nothing else *but* the truth.

In nonduality, the unification is complete. This is very different from one's initial experiences of essential reality in which there is you and your body, and Essence is felt to be inside you. To understand the difference, let's suppose that the state of Essence you are experiencing is the *Pearl*, the *Personal Essence*. In this case, you feel as though a full pearl is filling your belly or the whole of your body. Now, imagine that instead of the pearl filling your belly or your body, each one of your atoms is made out of that pearl. The sense of each atom as a pearl is still physical, but it feels like the fullness of the pearly existence. This is what I mean by unity. The physical and the essential become one. It is not that the physical is filled by the essential, but rather that the physical *is* the essential. In the same way that your muscles are composed of atoms, so the whole of your body is made out of Beingness.

When this sense of unification is complete and there is no duality in your experience, physical reality itself is experienced as the ultimate reality. Then all of physical reality, including all its objects and all of its manifestations, is seen as that beautiful, substantial, and fundamental reality. It is not separate from it, it doesn't come out of it, nor is it filled by it—it *is* it. Grace doesn't happen to physical reality; physical reality itself is the grace, is the beauty, is God. This is what Buddhists refer to as the Great Seal, the *Mahamudra*, in which all that you feel and see are unified with true nature. It is the unity of appearance and emptiness. This is one way of understanding what I mean by unity without duality. There is no separation at all, no division at all, no distance between the surface and the depth—in fact, there is no surface and no depth. There is no inside and no outside. They are the same thing. The unity is the complete interpenetration, the complete intermixing of inner and outer. It becomes all of one quality, all of the same thing.

Experiencing this unity reveals to us that life is beautiful. Prior to this, when you experience yourself moving from the state of the physical or of the personality to the state of the essential or of the boundless dimensions, there is the feeling that life is a problem. The best option seems to be to get away from life, and one may long to disappear or die. From the perspective of unity, there is no such thing as dying, nor of being reborn. There is no such thing as ego death, and no such thing as enlightenment either, since you are already the unity. This is the state of affairs all the time and always—before you develop an ego, when it is dissolving, and after you are dissolved. All those parts are the unity itself, and so you are not going anywhere.

This is why Longchenpa indicates in the poem quoted above that there is no path to take, no state to attain, and no technique to use.

All you need to do is recognize that the state of total completeness is the state of everything right at this moment. If you don't interfere or manipulate things and just let them be the way they are, you will experience this state of unity, which I sometimes refer to as the *natural state* since it is allowing things to be as they naturally are. This is reality, this is enlightenment, this is God. You don't need to change anything or be anywhere other than where you are. Even if you are experiencing suffering, that suffering itself is the reality, and absolutely nothing needs to be done about it.

This understanding explains why reality is also called Holy Perfection, the Holy Idea of ennea-type One. Holy Perfection means that everything is perfect at all times because there is never anything or any experience that is not the reality of the Holy Truth. Even when you experience yourself as separate from the reality, that is again the reality. So from this perspective, there is no need for a person to do anything—you don't need to practice, you don't need to understand yourself, you don't need to do any work on yourself since everything, including yourself, is already in the state of unity.

It is from this perspective that some teachings, including the Buddhist Maha Ati teaching, say that there is no need to practice—you don't need to meditate, to sit in any posture, or to visualize any deity. The only practice is to relax, because you are already there and nothing needs to be done. So in that tradition, whenever you see any egoic manifestation, you just relax. If you are more advanced, you don't even need to relax, since you are already in the state of unity, so being relaxed or unrelaxed is irrelevant.

This is the foundation for the practice of Dzogchen, which is taught by the Nyingmapa sect of Tibetan Buddhism. It is a tradition that works in the nondual only, and is said to be for people possessing superior capacity. The idea is that the state of unity, the natural state, is not something to be attained; it is the state of affairs all the time. If you think that there is something to be attained, you are creating a duality, since you are implicitly saying that there is a natural state and an unnatural state. From the Dzogchen perspective, the natural state is always the state that is occurring; you are just not always recognizing it as such. Even when you are not aware of it, you are in it. The only difference is that when there is recognition, you suddenly see the depth, the concreteness, the reality, the beauty, the harmony, and the grace of how things actually are. You see how things are already perfect, and this is why another name for total completeness is the Great Perfection.

The perfection of reality includes even what we call imperfection from the egoic perspective. Reality is a perfection that cannot become imperfect. In the language of the Enneagram, this is the Idea of Holy Perfection. The moment you see that there is nothing but God, you recognize that everything is perfect at all times and at all points in space. If God is everything that is, how can there be imperfection? When you don't like some manifestation and you want things to be different, all it means is that you have not surrendered to the Holy Will. You have your own prejudices and ideas about how things should be, and these could form the basis of your own personal religion!

The Idea of Holy Truth is that nothing is excluded. The ego is not excluded, thinking is not excluded, reactivity is not excluded, neurosis is not excluded, and the physical realm is not excluded. This is because there is nothing but the One, so there is no other. Obviously, when there is one and no other, "one" is not being used in the mathematical sense. Pythagoras taught that numbers start with three: One is God, two is the Logos, and three is the beginning of creation. Since reality is one and there is no other, how could there be duality? So every time you experience a new dimension of Being, you realize that it is part of the One, which includes all numbers, so the two resulting from the new dimension is included within it. This is difficult to conceptualize, because this One is an infinite existence. Since it has no boundary and encompasses infinite space, you can't conceive of it as the mathematical one. When you demarcate one area of physical space and then another, can you say that there is more than one space? Both are subsets of, and included in, the all-encompassing space.

The state of unity, experiencing that everything makes up one thing, appears in all the boundless dimensions. The sense of it becomes progressively deeper, until one experiences that all the dimensions are unified. This is a progressive attainment and it doesn't happen all at once. You might, for example, experience the unity of the dimensions of Living Daylight and the Supreme, in which case the experience of unity would have the transparency and clarity of the Supreme, as well as the whitish-yellow hue and sense of delicate love and grace of Living Daylight. Or the sense of unity might be experienced between the dimensions of the *Nameless* (Nonconceptual) and the Supreme. But the experience of the complete unity is a much more difficult attainment.

Generally, most people initially experience unity while experiencing one of the formless dimensions by itself. So if one is experiencing the state of unity on the level of Living Daylight alone, it would be the sense that everything is love; or if one is experiencing it on the level of the Supreme by itself, it would be the sense that everything is pure Being, pure presence. Again, this is not the experience that everything is made out of love or of Being, which is the experience of these dimensions still infused with duality; but that the whole universe *is* Living Daylight or *is* the Supreme. This is the state of unification.

In any case, the level at which one experiences the unity is not relevant to the Idea of Holy Truth. The most important thing about the state of unification is that there are not two. Egoic consciousness is, by its very nature, based on division. If there is no duality in your perception, the ego is non-existent. The study of the Holy Ideas is not the study of the building blocks of ego—these are elucidated when exploring the essential aspects and the formless dimensions. Here, we are studying the principles that hold the building blocks of ego together.

Duality

So in this study of the Enneagram of Holy Ideas, the first principle that we encounter which holds the ego together is the belief in duality. This is one of the subtlest and deepest principles, without which the ego could not exist and function in the way it does. It arises as a result of the loss of perception of Holy Truth. When a direct perception about reality is lost, which is to say that when one of the Holy Ideas is lost to our experience, what arises is not a particular state, but rather a distorted, erroneous, mistaken idea about reality, which we call a *delusion*. In other words, the loss of each Holy Idea leads to a *specific delusion* associated with that point on the Enneagram. So one of the fundamental properties of reality, as described by Holy Truth, is its nonduality. When the oneness of reality is not perceived, the delusion of duality arises. This delusion is the perception that the differences and separations between things that exist are ultimate, that this is the true state of affairs.

Because of the way the mind functions, the loss of an Idea leads to a deluded idea about reality. You cannot just not have a principle of reality, because the mind can't function without one. So if there is no perception of the fundamental unity of all of existence, then there is the perception of duality. If there is duality, there is the loss of unity. The loss of unity is the loss of the condition of the natural state of total completeness. Basically, it is the loss of God Consciousness.

The belief in duality will remain in place as long as there is no understanding of Holy Truth. The ego by its very nature assumes duality: the belief that who I am is ultimately separate and discrete, and that all other manifestations are also separate and discrete. This results in divisions in our minds between ultimate truth and the world, spirit, and matter, Absolute Truth and relative truth, God and the universe, God and myself, you and I, ego and Essence. This belief in division as ultimate is a conviction so deeply ingrained in the soul that it is one of the last things we can even contemplate confronting, let alone releasing.

Even after a long time traveling the spiritual path, we cannot conceive that this might be an assumption about reality rather than the truth. We think, "This is how reality is—everyone knows that. My parents believed it, my teachers believed it, scientists write books on how things are fundamentally divisible, and everything seems to work according to this knowledge." This conviction is so deeply entrenched that it has become an organizing principle for the very particles of our souls. Like a magnet arranges particles of metal, this conviction arranges our souls so that we can't even imagine that things could be otherwise.

We are, metaphorically speaking, always pointing north, and so we think that this is how reality is. Letting go of the magnet would mean realizing that that orientation is not reality, and that things are actually much more free-flowing than we thought.

The sense of duality, then, arises through the loss of the Holy Truth; and the Holy Truth, as previously discussed, has the qualities of goodness, of positivity, of being loving. In Holy Truth, the multiplicity is in unity at all levels, and everyone and everything is holy. The word *holy* in the language of the Enneagram is not used in the usual dualistic sense: that which is opposite to the bad, the mundane, or the human. *Holy* means objective, how things really are beyond the cloud of egoic experience. So here, *holy* means objective truth. When you are experiencing the state of Holy Truth, everything becomes hallowed, filled with a sense of wonder, beauty, and grace. There is a sense of holiness to the experience, and those who live in this state are called "holy" in the spiritual traditions.

Original Sin

So the experience of duality is imbued with the loss of that holiness, beauty, and harmony, and therefore, has a negative tinge to it. This loss will be experienced as the sense that something is fundamentally wrong. The closest thing to this sense is the feeling of "original sin." You know something terrible has happened, but you don't know exactly what it is; you don't know it is the loss of your natural state. The term *Dzogchen* in Tibetan literally means the natural state of the human individual, the condition where everything is completely the way it should be—and this is what you have lost. This results in a very deep state of something that we call "sin." It feels like a disconnection, a loss, and a falling from grace; you no longer live in Holy Truth.

You sense that what is most true and precious has been lost and destroyed, and that someone or something is to blame. Through the filter of the delusion of duality, one thing becomes perceived as being in opposition to another, and one side is guilty. The loving and perfect truth has been lost, and so someone has committed a crime or a sin here, and must be found and punished. This is the position of the ennea-type Eight, which has been called Ego Venge. Ultimately, you blame yourself for no longer being divine, and later this blame is projected onto others in order to protect yourself from the self-hatred that would otherwise result.

When children experience that something goes wrong, they tend to blame themselves. Regardless of whose fault it really is, the quality of self-blame in the ego leads the child to take the responsibility. Even when children are sexually or physically abused, they always believe it is their own fault. From the perspective of the Enneagram of Holy Ideas, the depth of the sense of self-blame is not dependent upon what actually happens, but is due to the absence of the perception of Holy Truth. So, universally, children blame themselves for the loss of their sense of being divine, for their fall from grace. The result is a deep anguish and sense of guilt which becomes the primary source around which other guilts later accumulate.

The moment you place blame on yourself or others, you are not only experiencing the loss of the preciousness of the state of unity, but you are also reaffirming the sense of duality—of there being a you and an other. Blame, then, whether of self or other, indicates that the ego is already operating within the delusion of duality. If you are in touch with the inherent unity of all of existence, if it is all one thing, blame simply does not make any sense.

Self-Blame

Ultimately, all self-blame comes down to blaming oneself for not being enlightened. Universally, there is a core place within all ego structures where one feels guilty for not being a realized Being. The guilt, as we have seen, has to do with the fact that (in Christian terms) you have been thrown out of paradise—yet you don't blame God for this; you blame yourself. The deeper you go into understanding the sense of guilt, the more you realize that you feel guilty for not being real. This is particularly relevant when you have realized the essential aspect of the *Point*, the *Essential Identity* (see *The Point of Existence,* Almaas

1996). Here you see that you have carried within you a profound sense of guilt for losing contact with your true nature. A sense of great betrayal arises, not just because your parents didn't see your real nature, but that *you* stopped seeing it. You abandoned what is real in you; you abandoned yourself. Each ennea-type will experience this guilt in a slightly different way, as it is filtered through the lens of each one's *specific delusion*, but this guilt and self-blame for the loss of contact with Being is universal to all egoic experience.

The Bible tells us that Adam and Eve were thrown out of the Garden of Eden for eating the forbidden fruit. From this perspective, we can see that the fruit is the experience of duality, the first departure from the state of unity, the first division. So because you are not in a state of total completeness, you feel guilty and bad, and have an attitude of punishing and hating yourself. This gets projected, and you attempt to remedy the situation by getting revenge. This is the constellation or complex that results from the loss of Holy Truth.

Revenge is really the ego's attempt to regain the original state of unity. It is a way of trying to get rid of the guilt and the pain through a convoluted line of reasoning that goes something like this: Someone hurts you, and the pain involves loss of the sense of unity. So you retaliate by hurting him or her in exactly the same way, in the belief that doing so will enable you to rid yourself of your own pain and restore the sense of unity. This is the rationale behind the Biblical phrase, "An eye for an eye, and a tooth for a tooth."

The nine delusions arising from the loss of the nine Holy Ideas are the seeds around which the cores of the nine ennea-types develop, and while each is most dominant for the ego structures of that type, the nine are present in all ego structures. The delusions, then, form the nine principles inherent in all ego structures and lives informed by ego. We have seen how the loss of Holy Truth leads to the delusion of duality, and how out of this loss of true reality—this state of "the fall"— arises the painful sense of badness, guilt, and original sin. Self-blame ensues for not being divine, which becomes self-punishment and the attempt to avenge oneself. This constellation forms the core, the major psychological constellation related to this point of the Enneagram, out of which the whole ennea-type develops.

The Holy Ideas are different forms of the perception of the soul in a completely open and transparent state, that is, the soul in touch with Living Daylight. The loss of this state of openness and wholeness—whether it results from normal egoic identification with a separate sense of self or from the contraction away from contact with experience that is involved in reacting to a sense of the loss of holding—inevitably results in the loss of the sense of unity, connection, perfection, love, flow, and so on.

The *core constellation* is actually one unified process with three facets: 1) As we saw in Part One, the loss of an Idea is the same process as the loss of a sense of holding in the environment and the loss of basic trust. So the loss of Holy Truth leads to the *specific delusion* of duality. 2) Loss or inadequacy of the holding environment results in the painful egoic state that we call the *specific difficulty*. Here, the loss of holding, filtered through the delusion of duality, results in the *specific difficulty* of a sense of badness, guilt, and fundamental sinfulness. 3) The loss of basic trust, filtered through the delusion, results in what we call the *specific reaction* of each point, and just as the loss of a sense of holding results in the loss of basic trust, the *specific reaction* is an attempt to deal with the *specific difficulty*. Here, it is the reaction of self-blame, which, as we have seen, is based upon the sense of duality and opposition, and which ultimately blossoms into the attempt to get revenge that is characteristic of ennea-type Eight.

The Holy Truth includes everything—including the guilt and self-blame. It is all-inclusive and all-encompassing; otherwise it would not be holy. The belief that some manifestations are holy and others are not, or that some people are chosen by God and others are not, is not the Holy Truth. The Holy Truth chooses all people—they are its life. This is why it is said that, "The sought becomes the seeker." The Holy Truth itself manifests as the seeker looking for the Holy Truth. So the journey is a matter of the seeker finding out that he or she is what is sought. When we know this, we realize that there is no need for seeking.

CHAPTER TWELVE

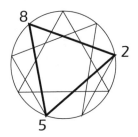

Point Five
HOLY OMNISCIENCE,
HOLY TRANSPARENCY

The awareness that because every individual is intimately connected with the entire cosmos by the operation of objective laws
within their own bodies, there is no separateness or alienation
except as a mental hallucination. Because the cosmic laws govern
every aspect of ourselves, there is no possibility of hiding from the
Cosmos, or avoiding the results of natural processes. When we
understand this, we are completely at peace with our past.
— Ichazo, 1972

In the preceding chapter on Holy Truth, we explored one of the
three Holy Ideas that elucidate the fundamental nature of the universe
when it is seen objectively, that is, with no subjective filters. We have
seen that the cosmos is a living universe in which all levels and dimensions form a unity, and that this one living unity is the ultimate truth
of existence. The way this universal view of reality is reflected in human
experience is described by the next Holy Idea that we will discuss, Holy
Omniscience, which is also sometimes called Holy Transparency.

Our understanding of this Holy Idea expands on Ichazo's definition above. Holy Omniscience is the Universal Mind, which is the multiplicity of existence within the unity described by Holy Truth. Universal Mind includes all that exists in its various manifestations, with all the various colors, the richness, and the continuous transformations of reality. It could also be called God's Knowledge, since what God "knows" is the whole universe in all its multiplicity. You might say that Holy Omniscience is the same perception as Holy Truth, but with a different emphasis. In Holy Truth, the emphasis is on the unity of the universe; it is all "of the same taste," as the Tibetan Buddhists say. With Holy Omniscience, the emphasis is on the differentiations and discriminations *within* that unity. So the focus here is on the various parts, in all their variety and multiplicity, that together comprise the unitive whole. To perceive reality through the facet of Holy Omniscience is like looking at a whole Persian rug, but focusing on the different designs contained within it.

Unity in Multiplicity

So the emphasis in the perception of Holy Omniscience is on the *differentiation* in the unity of all that exists, on the various aspects and dimensions of existence—yet this diversity does not negate the fact of unity. While Holy Truth is analogous to seeing your body as one unit, Holy Omniscience is seeing that your body has arms, legs, a face, internal organs, and so on—none of which are separate from the whole. This perception is a different kind of experience; it is looking at the same reality from a different angle: viewing the wholeness of reality as a multi-colored fabric.

You could say that Holy Truth is the experience of unity, while Holy Omniscience is the experience of oneness—the sense that everything is interconnected and not separate, that everything makes up the one reality of the living universe. Here, we are seeing all the stars, the planets, the mountains, the rivers, the animals, and the people that are part of it, without isolating them from the context of the unity, the Holy Truth.

The difference between these two experiences of the nature of reality is expressed in the Sufi tradition by two different names of God: *Abad*, the inner nature, and *Wahid*, the outer nature of the unity of existence. The experience of the inherent unity of reality is perceiving its inner nature, while the experience of its multiplicity is perceiving its outer nature. In the same tradition, unity is seen as God's nature, and the oneness of appearances as God's face. Holy Omniscience refers to how things appear, the "face" of the universe, and is also what is meant by *Universal Mind* (See chapter 16, *Diamond Heart Book 4*, Almaas, 1997).

The other name of this Holy Idea, Holy Transparency, refers to one-ness seen from the point of view of the individual. Instead of looking at the nature of reality from an "aerial" point of view, which would correspond to that of Holy Truth, we are seeing it from our human vantage point. It is the understanding of our place as human beings within the unity of existence, and from this perspective, we see that we are each an inseparable part of the whole, each a cell in the cosmic body, each a part of the "body" of God, inseparable from objective reality. The human being, then, is seen to be one of the differentiations of the Universal Mind.

In the experience of Holy Transparency, you can see that you are an inseparable part of the whole because your boundaries are transparent. You see that you are an individual and a person, but you are not separate from the unity of the whole universe. You are as inseparable from the universe as the eyes are from the face. And, like the eyes, you see that you don't have an existence separate from the rest of the body of the universe. As a human being, you know yourself to be an inseparable part of God, a particularization of the objective reality, an extension, as it were, of Holy Truth. You experience yourself as an individual, distinct from other things, with a consciousness localized in a certain place, yet you also experience yourself as continuous with everything else.

So the experience of transparency is experiencing yourself as part of the totality, supported by it and not existing apart from it. You see that it is not possible for you to have an existence separate from the unity, and that in some sense the unity also wouldn't exist without you. Not only do you experience yourself as inseparable from the unity, but you experience yourself *as* an extension of the unity. In the experience of Holy Transparency, you are a human being who is continuous with the unity and a particularization, an individualization, a personalization of that unity. So in a sense, you are experiencing yourself as a son or daughter of God. Here, the experience is that you not only come from the unity of God, but that you never leave it. Any feeling that you are not part of the unity of reality is a delusion, a mental hallucination. The protoplasm of the universe is continuous with your protoplasm; you have a cell membrane around you but you are part of one protoplasm, one life force.

The perceptions of reality expressed by Holy Truth and Holy Omniscience are not emphasized or even articulated in many spiritual traditions. Because in the Diamond Approach our path involves transforming ordinary life into a life of spiritual discovery, these Holy Ideas are very important. They help us to understand how it is possible to be a unique individual who is at the same time inseparable from the totality of the universe, making possible the realization of what we call the Personal Essence, or the Pearl. (See *The Pearl Beyond Price*, Almaas, 1988, for an in-depth exploration of the Personal Essence.) This realization is the complete personal embodiment of Being, or Being manifesting through the life of an individual. It is becoming a complete human being, which is an organ through which the universe can experience itself fully.

Eyes of the Universe

Envision the universe as a living being that, through its differentiations and developments, evolves increasingly sophisticated life-forms which are capable of ever-subtler and more inclusive levels of experience. Each form is a manifestation of this being, and as such, each provides it with different experiences of itself. So each life-form is a way that this living being, the universe, experiences itself. An amoeba is a vehicle for a certain experience of itself, as are a bird and a human. But human beings, as distinct from other life forms, also provide the universe with a way to reflect upon itself. And a complete human being is a way the universe experiences itself completely. To know the truth of Holy Omniscience is to know that you are the eyes of the universe. When you understand this, you know that your job (as the Holy Idea of ennea-type Seven, Holy Work, will tell us) is to make that eye completely transparent and completely open so that you can give the universe an experience of itself in all its dimensionality, in all its variety, in all its colors and flavors.

Each spiritual tradition has a different story to explain why we are here. Some say that the unmanifest manifests the universe out of compassion, or out of love, or even out of playfulness. We don't claim to know the purpose of human life. In fact, we admit the possibility that it may not even be possible to know why we are here. All we really know is that the unmanifest manifests the universe—and we know this from our own experience, which provides the perception of the human being as both an individual *and* an organ of experience for the whole universe. Experientially, the sense is that the whole universe is behind you, and you are like a window through which it sees.

This perception clarifies our understanding of what motivates us to do the work of spiritual transformation. From this vantage point, we see that it is not to free ourselves from our suffering, but to become a clear window for the universe. Now, becoming such a window does result in freeing oneself, but if you conceive of it that way, you remain a self-centered and isolated individual who is working at becoming free. Then the whole conceptual framework within which you hold the Work remains shaped by the egoic perspective and entrenched in that subjective position. Thus, your consciousness remains rooted in the ego and you cannot become free of it. Spiritual unfoldment means perceiving and experiencing objectively, and the objective principle that is lacking here is that of Holy Transparency.

Doing the Work for *yourself* blocks your unfoldment. Doing the Work in order to become a clearer and clearer window for the universe is selfless; then you do the Work out of humility, out of love, and out of putting your *self* (your ego) aside. In this case, your unfoldment will happen more easily and spontaneously. It is not a matter of thinking that you, as a separate individual, are going to help God in this way; that is just a subtler way of expressing your sense of separateness. It is a matter of recognizing your true position relative to God, your true function as a human being, your true connection to the universe—which is being a cell in its body. Reorienting your approach to the Work does not mean you should try to control your motivation (which is impossible anyway), or judge yourself when you see that you are being self-centered. Rather, it means that every time you recognize yourself operating from selfish motivations, you try to identify the barrier that is interfering with seeing things objectively.

Separate Existence

So we have seen that Holy Omniscience or Holy Transparency is the view of the human being that corresponds to, or arises out of, the view of reality described by Holy Truth. From the vantage point of Holy Omniscience, we see that as human beings we are inseparable manifestations of the Holy Truth. When this objective way of experiencing oneself and reality is lost, the *specific delusion* particular to this point on the Enneagram arises: the conviction that you are a separate entity, existing in your own right, separate from others and from the universe, separate from God, separate from everything.

We have seen that objectively there is no such thing as a separate self; so when we experience ourselves as separate, we are deluded. The actual reality is that we are not separate, but the contrary conviction is so powerful that we constantly experience ourselves as separate. The belief completely determines your experience. The sense of being like a fortress, with impenetrable walls around you that separate you from everything else, is your actual experience.

The delusion here is not that you are an individual, but that you are an *isolated* individual, with boundaries that separate you from everything else. This delusion is at the heart of the Five ennea-type, and the exact key that unlocks it is Holy Omniscience and Holy Transparency.

If you believe that you are a separate individual, your vision is clouded by subjectivity since you are holding yourself separate from God, which cannot be. There is only one existence, and that is God, the Holy Truth, objective reality, the living cosmos, the universe—whatever you want to call it—so holding on to the conviction that you are separate is like creating two universes, yours and the rest of the cosmos. Then you have a relationship with the rest of the universe, thereby creating the mental construct of this fundamental object relation. By "object relation," here, we mean the construction in the mind of a concept of one's self in relation to the concept of other or of the world. From the perspective of Holy Truth, we see that there are no discrete objects; from the perspective of Holy Omniscience we see that there is no separate self. So with these two perspectives we can see that both ends of any object relation—self and other—cease to be experienced as real.

A question may arise here about whether there really is such a thing as independence, when we see that this is the way things are. There are such things as independence, autonomy, and uniqueness, but not for the separate self. As we experience more objectively, we see that true independence is being independent from the mind that separates us from the universe. True independence, then, is independence from falsehood. When we think being independent means not depending on others or not needing this or that, it is evidence that we are seeing through the subjective lens of the ego. In reality, we are all dependent upon each other and on the world around us. Everyone affects everyone else because our lives interpenetrate. But actually, our interdependence is much deeper and far more profound. We are not only dependent on each other, but we are actually inseparable from each other, since we are all made out of the same substance.

Since the decisions we make about how to live our lives are based upon what we believe about the nature of reality, the more objective our understanding, the more appropriate our choices. In the same way, our understanding of spiritual practice is determined by how objectively we understand that our boundaries are permeable and that we are in direct contact with everything all the time. Without an experiential understanding of Holy Transparency, we will work on ourselves as though we are truly separate individuals, and this will block our progress. The truth of our interconnectedness is basic to the methodology of the Diamond Approach, but it is not restricted to our work—it is an acknowledged principle in most spiritual traditions.

The loss of Holy Omniscience, then, is the loss of the perception of our interconnectedness, and what arises out of this loss is the conviction that we are separate entities. This conviction is based on assuming that the boundaries of our bodies define the boundaries of our consciousness, or our souls. This is one of the most fundamental principles of the ego. The ego is first and foremost a body-ego, in the sense that the self-demarcations that form in our consciousness during infancy are based on our sensory experience of our bodies as distinct from other objects. (For more detail on this point, see Mahler, 1975, p. 46.) The delusion is taking these body-boundaries to define and limit our sense of who and what we are. On the physical level, it is true that each of us has physical boundaries and that this body is separate from that body, but on the level of consciousness these boundaries are permeable. The edges of our bodies do not define where we end and others begin, although if we have this conviction it will feel that way. When we recognize that this experience is a delusion, we see that the ego boundaries we have used to define ourselves are only mental constructs. We realize that we have been holding onto an image of our bodies in order to define ourselves as entities.

Although these ego boundaries form the basis of our sense of separateness, the belief that we are separate entities goes deeper than this. The soul, when it is structured by the ego, has the shape of the body in our consciousness, whether or not we are aware of it. When it is not structured by the ego, you might experience the soul as having a jelly-like, plasmatic form, yet still experience it as a separate entity which, in fact, it is not. It is more accurate to talk about a *soul current* or *soul flow* than to call it a *soul*, since that makes it sound like a separate entity. It is more like a wave being formed by the constant movement of the currents, inseparable from the ocean out of which it arises.

The wave is part of the ocean, but it is distinguishable from the ocean. When you are a wave, it is true that you are not the whole ocean, but you are also not separate from the ocean. Without the ocean, waves would not exist. You could say that an ego is someone who believes that she or he can be a wave without an ocean—imagine the trouble you'd have sustaining that! The dominant feeling would be that there is no support. You would always be trying to hold yourself up! This is exactly our situation without the perspective of Holy Omniscience.

Ordinarily, we do not experience the true nature of our souls because we have defined ourselves vis-à-vis the boundaries of our bodies. We have taken these boundaries to define our identity, believing that these physical boundaries are a fundamental and intrinsic aspect of who we are when, in fact, they are the most superficial aspect of who we are. This conviction that the body boundary defines us actually solidifies the sense of separateness by creating a layer of surface tension in the skin. When we actually experience the body boundary, we feel it as tension on the periphery of the body.

It is not that physical boundaries don't exist—if that were the case, there would be no differentiation, no color, no action. They do exist, but not as partitioning walls; seen through the facet of Holy Omniscience, they exist as differentiating outlines, articulating many different tastes, textures, and colors, without obscuring the underlying nature of everything as One. It is as though you have dropped different colors of dye into a fluid; many colors are swirling around, but it is still all the same fluid. One way of putting it is that the boundaries define a difference, but not a separateness. So I am different from you, but I am not separate from you; people are different from each other, but they are not separate from each other. The existence of boundaries, then, does not negate the underlying unity. Boundaries are characteristic of the objective concepts or noetic forms, relevant on the level of creation and existence. Boundaries and the forms they define are characteristics of the thoughts of God, as it were. This is why we call the universe a mind.

To the ego, separateness means impermeable boundaries, or isolation, but real separation is something quite different. Real separation means particularization out of the unity or, for human beings, individuation. It means recognizing that your true nature is not determined by external influences. At a deep unconscious level, it involves separating from your mother—separating in the sense that who you take yourself to be is not determined by her. This is not isolating yourself, but rather recognizing your uniqueness and individuating.

This mountain is not the same as *that* mountain. They are separate in the sense that each is unique, but they are connected in that they are both part of the earth. There is no such thing as a mountain existing on its own. The ego wants to believe that it is a mountain that is detached from the earth, because it does not experience itself as connected to the earth. To have true separation means that if you are a mountain, you realize that you are a particular mountain and not that other mountain over there, and although you have unique qualities that the other mountain doesn't have, you are not completely separate and isolated from it.

From the point of view of ego, it is difficult to comprehend that boundaries are ideas or concepts. This insight arises when you experience space on the nonconceptual level. It is a different understanding than seeing that concepts are boundaries, which is a more accessible perception. From the perspective of Holy Omniscience, we see that compassion and steadfastness, for example, are different qualities of Being, but both are nonetheless Being—one thing. You could say they are God's concepts, thoughts in God's mind that appear different but that arise out of one source. This is why we consider all differentiations arising out of the Absolute to be universal concepts, thoughts in God's Mind. (For a more extensive discussion of universal concepts, or noetic forms, see *Diamond Heart Book 4*, Almaas, 1997.)

Without differentiations, there would be no experience, no knowledge, no action, no life, no universe—nothing but the unmanifest Absolute. This is why understanding the nature of boundaries is significant in terms of understanding reality. Someone who experiences only Holy Truth, only unity with no differentiations—without even the concepts of experience, unity, or differentiations—for all practical purposes is not alive. Such a person would be in a kind of coma, a *divine coma*.

When you reach the true essence of the truth, this ultimate reality is in a coma in the sense that it doesn't know itself. It is unconscious because it has no boundaries, no distinctions. Differentiation is completely gone, so there are no differences. Therefore, there is nothing to see, nothing to experience. This is what makes it the unmanifest Absolute.

If you experience yourself exclusively as the Absolute with no concepts, you cannot function in the world. If you are in deep meditation, you can sink into it, but you can't walk around that way since you wouldn't be able to discriminate a truck heading your way, for instance. A truck is nothing but differentiating outlines and boundaries—the Universal Mind heading toward you with a certain density and at a certain speed! So it is important to perceive the Holy Truth because that is the ultimate nature of reality, but it is also important to know Holy Omniscience because without it, there would be no life, nor anyone to know the Holy Truth.

Abiding in Holy Omniscience is a very beautiful condition in which you retain your humanity without losing your divinity. The totality of the living universe is present as your support, your ground, and your inner nature, but you are still a person, functioning and living the life of a human being. There is no sense of separation, so it isn't as though you, as a human being, and the unity are two things that are put together. It is more like a kind of *dual unity** in the sense that you are not coexisting with the unity, but you are part of it, an extension of it, without losing your sense of being a human being. There is a sense of loving and enjoying the living universe and the unity, and in loving it, you are also loving yourself since you are an inseparable part of it.

---

* Dual unity is a psychological term used to describe the state an infant is thought to experience during the symbiotic phase of its development (from approximately two months of age through the sixth month). There appears to be the sense that mother and infant are part of one enclosed system, two entities that are part of each other and share a common boundary, in the same way that one's head is related to one's legs. "From the second month on, dim awareness of the need-satisfying object marks the beginning of the phase of normal symbiosis, in which the infant behaves and functions as though he and his mother were an omnipotent system— a dual unity within one common boundary." (Mahler, 1975, p. 44)

Isolation and Withdrawal

As we have seen, when this sense of omniscience and transparency is absent, there is a distorted perception, the delusion of being a separate entity. This delusion of separateness is the seed of the ennea-type, giving rise to its experiential core. For those of this ennea-type, the *specific difficulty* resulting from the loss of the sense of holding is experiencing oneself as small, isolated, cut-off, empty, and impoverished—it is a state of deficient isolation. This sense of feeling isolated, alone, and abandoned as a result of the loss of holding results from the belief in separateness, the *specific delusion* of ennea-type Five.

The *specific reaction* in response to this painful sense of deficient isolation is to withdraw in an attempt to hide from reality. If you feel small, deficient, and isolated, it means that you feel inadequate to deal with reality, so the reaction of this ennea-type is to want to avoid dealing with reality, to hide from it, to try to separate, withdraw, run away from it, to break off contact—basically to not stay in touch with whatever reality is presenting. This reaction again implies the delusion of separateness, since you have to believe you are a separate individual to believe that you can hide or withdraw from reality. What you most want to get away from is the state of deficiency itself. But when you withdraw and you don't let yourself experience it, this behavior becomes generalized, and you end up avoiding everything in your attempt to avoid seeing or experiencing any difficulty, pain, or hurt. This reaction escalates into the personality complex of ennea-type Five, with its characteristic emotional withdrawal and deadness, and the dissociation of mind from body. So the core of this ennea-type is a state of impoverishment and the schizoid defense of withdrawal and avoidance.

This constellation is one of the principles of ego, part of its internal structure and logic; you don't have to be an ennea-type Five to experience it. As we have said, we each have all the ennea-types within us since they are the nine differentiated manifestations of ego, although one type will be more pronounced in each of us.

As we discussed in Part One, the quality of Living Daylight functions like a solvent, melting all boundaries. For this reason, in our work, it is the specific energy required for working on the Holy Ideas. The aspect of space erases boundaries, while Living Daylight dissolves them into itself. In the presence of Living Daylight, boundaries lose their opacity, their rigidity, their partitioning quality, and they become merely outlines. The sense of separateness is dissolved through love, and everyone and everything is seen as love, a manifestation of an ocean of love. When we have this experience, we understand what Holy Omniscience means.

Then we also can understand objectively what it is to be a human being: It is to be an extension of the objective truth. We recognize that, as human beings, we are organs of perception for the universe, and that this Holy Idea explicates the place of the human in relation to the living universe. Through us, the universe experiences or knows itself fully, not only physically, not only emotionally, not only mentally, but on all the spiritual dimensions as well.

The Extension Issue

Recognizing yourself as an organ of perception and an extension of the living universe often brings up a specific issue—more pronounced in some people than in others—having to do with feelings about being an extension of something. Experiencing yourself as an extension of the universe might not appeal to your ego, especially if you characteristically have a need to be the center of attention. Your reaction might be something like, "Wait a minute! I'm not an extension of *anybody*. I am myself, I exist as myself, so don't give me this bullshit about being an extension! Just because we're talking about God doesn't make it any different. If anyone is going to be an extension of anyone else, *I'm* the one who has the extension!" If you have always been the boss, the thought of not being in control and not giving the orders might be abhorrent.

If, on the other hand, your personality has been based on being an extension of your mother or father, and you have not fully worked through that identity, it will surely arise as you face this question of transparency. You might realize that you have been operating as an extension, and that this has been central to who you have taken yourself to be. You might see that you became whatever your mother wanted you to be—that you function as an extension of her hopes, her ideas, and her character. She might have unconsciously wanted you to be her heart, her sense of self, or even her phallus, and you have behaved as though you were this extension. Your whole sense of identity is based on this relation. This is what being an extension means: Your existence is dependent on that other and so, in this case, you don't have an existence separate from mother. You are only a reflection of the object, so separating from your internal image of her would mean losing your identity.

You may have various reactions to this. When you see that you have acted like an extension, you might react to the experience of transparency as a very undesirable state: "I'm my own person and I don't want to be *anyone's* extension any longer—enough is enough!" Of course, this reaction will block the operation of Holy Omniscience. On the other hand, you might see that without the identity of being someone's extension, you feel like you don't know who you are. You might, therefore, remain attached to being an extension, so that when you hear about transparency, your unconscious response is, "Oh good. I don't have to change anything. I can stay just as I am; I'll just project my mother's image onto the whole universe and be God's extension." This, of course, is not Holy Omniscience. It is continuing to be identified with an object relation that originated with your mother, in which you are an image or a mental construct that is the extension of another image—your mother's. This is quite different from the actual experiential sense of yourself as an inseparable and integral part of the whole, whose nature is the same as yours. The similarity, and what gives rise to the issue, is the sense of dependency inherent in both the object relation and the experience of Holy Transparency. Your existence does depend on the whole—that is the reality—and the personality may not like this state of affairs.

You can be identified with either side of this object relation, which is called the *extension object relation*, either as the extension of someone else, or as the central person with one or more extensions of your own.

In either case, you are experiencing yourself as a mental construct in relation to a construct of someone else. This object relation is a narcissistic one (i.e., having to do with one's identity), so losing it feels like a loss of support. This is because, regardless of which end of the object relation you are identified with, the identification supports the ego identity. You might feel as if you are losing yourself by experiencing yourself as an extension of the universe, since the boundaries that you have taken to define yourself fall away in that experience. Or if you have been identified as an extension, you might feel that you are losing yourself by experiencing yourself as central and yet interconnected.

Like other narcissistic projections, the extension objection relation is a form of merged transference in which, although we are not the same thing, you are part of me, or I am part of you. We are slightly differentiated, but not completely separate. This becomes apparent if you are used to being the central figure in this object relation, and your extension doesn't do things the way you want them done. You might feel very hurt and unsupported, as though part of your body hadn't responded the way you wanted it to. This sense of hurt is what is called *narcissistic wounding*, meaning that one's sense of self feels assaulted in some way.

The issue of the extension object relation makes it very difficult to experience and integrate the Holy Idea of Transparency. Because of it, one either resists the experience or becomes attached to being an extension in a way that continues to support the personality. Holy Transparency means experiencing things without your personal mind. Then, as an individual, you are an extension of the universe, an extension of the Holy Truth—and not as a mental construct, not with an image in your mind that you are an extension of the universe. It is only as part of the extension object relation that one has an image of oneself as one side or the other of a merged relationship.

After you work through the need to be the center, being an extension of the universe feels like a great relief. Needing to be the center of the extension object relation is a big job, since you are holding yourself as God. In the pure experience of direct union with the living universe, you know yourself to be completely supported, completely loved, completely held, and completely taken care of as a human being. The living consciousness of the universe is above you, surrounding you, within you, and you know that you are a part of it. This brings a wonderful sense of relaxation and joy. A sense of tremendous preciousness and value arises as you see that not only do you need the living universe to exist and support you, but that without you, that living universe would be blind. You are not expendable.

Holy Omniscience or Transparency is not just a matter of dimly perceiving that you are part of something greater than yourself. That is only the beginning of the experience. The full experience is of the totality of the universe as a living presence of which you are a part; you are a consciousness that is conscious of the totality; you not only feel yourself as part of the whole, but you also experience that whole. You are aware of the whole like a wave is aware of the whole ocean and of the other waves that are also part of it. If you do feel that you are part of something greater, but you are not yet aware of that larger whole, and don't yet experience others as also part of that wholeness, this indicates that there is still some opacity in the experience and that your boundaries are not completely transparent.

You should not expect that once you have experienced Holy Omniscience you will always have it. Also, no two experiences of it will be alike, since each experience depends upon the dimension from which you experience it. For example, you might experience yourself as part of everything and perceive that everything is pure love; or you might experience yourself as part of everything and perceive that everything is pure Being; or you might experience yourself as part of everything and see yourself as a wave arising out of the ocean; or you might experience yourself as a cell, continuous with everything around you. All of these are experiences of Holy Transparency, experienced from different dimensions.

The Holy Ideas are not exactly states of consciousness; they are certain ways of experiencing reality. So you could be experiencing a particular essential state, and at the same time you might experience transparency or not. You cannot, however, experience transparency without experiencing some quality of Being, because if you are not experiencing Being you are experiencing ego, and the Holy Ideas are not accessible in the egoic realm.

As we abide in this Holy Idea and appreciate ourselves as unique and individual waves in the vast ocean, our need for separating boundaries begins to relax. This discriminating wisdom changes our perceptions: Each person, each object, each appearance becomes more real, more palpable, more dimensional. Everything becomes more real and substantial while still being implicitly part of the larger whole. You experience yourself as a definite, individualized person who is at the same time an inextricable part of the fabric of the living universe. The edges between people and objects cease to limit, disconnect, and isolate. Instead, they enhance the reality of existence, revealing the beauty, the richness, and the uniqueness of each person and each existence. Everything stands out in clearer relief. One's sense of oneself is more individuated, but without that sense of definition disconnecting you from the rest of existence. Here, the foreground of differentiated reality is in focus, against a background of Holy Truth.

CHAPTER THIRTEEN

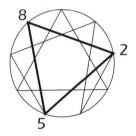

Point Two
HOLY WILL,
HOLY FREEDOM

The awareness that Reality, moving with direction and according to fixed natural laws, flows with a certain force. The easiest way to deal with this force is to move with it. This is true freedom.
— Ichazo, 1972

If reality is a unity of everything that exists, constituting one existential Beingness that is alive and self-existing (Holy Truth), and if we as human beings are inseparable parts and expressions of this Beingness (Holy Omniscience), the question arises: What does this mean in terms of how we live, practice, and work on ourselves? The third point of the triangle that we have been discussing addresses this question. The Holy Idea of ennea-type Two has two names: Holy Will and Holy Freedom. Each name represents the Holy Idea seen from a different vantage point. From the perspective of the universe, this Idea is Holy Will; from the perspective of the human being, it is Holy Freedom.

As we saw in our exploration of Holy Truth, truth has different levels and subtleties of understanding, and the more we unfold, the more our sense of the truth expands. We see that it encompasses more and more, or rather, our understanding encompasses more and more of the truth until finally, we see the totality that Holy Truth describes. Holy Truth is not the realization of a specific truth, as we have said; it is nothing but perceiving reality as it is. If you perceive reality as it is, which is to say, objectively, the perception, the awareness, and the understanding that arises are that everything is truth and that truth is the existence of the universe. From the perspective of Holy Truth, there is only the truth; there is nothing else. When you see that there is only the truth, the perception and experience is not your ordinary one. In this state, you experience unity, oneness, interconnectedness, and a state of harmonious unity of the whole cosmos in which everyone and everything at all levels is one homogenous whole. So when we say that the truth is everything, we are describing the perception from a deep state of consciousness in which everything is seen devoid of the projections of the personality, and is therefore a unity that is imperceptible to the soul informed by the ego.

If the Holy Truth is that the universe exists as a unified Beingness, as an existence that is intrinsically undivided and non-dual, what does it mean to live according to that truth? What are the implications of this understanding in terms of your actions? What is functioning, and what is doing about? These are really questions about change, and they require an understanding of Holy Will.

Cosmic Change

Ichazo's definition of Holy Will is: "The awareness that Reality, moving with direction and according to fixed natural laws, flows with a certain force. The easiest way to deal with this force is to move with it. This is true freedom." By "fixed natural laws," we understand Ichazo to mean that there are patterns to how things happen. For example, if you react to your experience, you get disconnected from your Being. We take this understanding a little further, saying that if you really surrender to the Holy Will, you will realize that you are actually part of this force of the flow of reality. It is not, then, a matter of flowing *with* it, but rather of realizing that there is no separation, that it is all one unfoldment. You also see that the unfoldment is not just the changes in the universe, like the sun rising and setting, rain coming and going, people moving from one place to another. The unfoldment is much deeper than that; the existence of the earth itself is part of the unfoldment, part of the creativity of reality. You see that your existence is part of the creativity. It is not that there are little changes within a static universe, but that the universe itself acts by the whole thing shifting.

Let's say that it is noontime now and the sun is overhead, and in a number of hours it will be dusk and the sky will begin growing dark. Your universe will have changed in the course of time from one state to another, from daytime to nighttime. If you take your hand and scratch your head, the universe you experience has also changed from one state to another, but in this case we say that you have taken an action. If we have understood Holy Transparency, and we know that you are not separate from the stars, why do we call shifts in the relative position of the sun and stars "change," while we call scratching one's head an "action"? We cannot make this distinction unless we believe that the universe is an inanimate object full of other inanimate objects, and that we human beings are living things, having our own will and ability to do this or that.

From the perspective of Holy Truth, the universe is one infinite, multi-level organism. Therefore, what we call "action" is nothing but the changes and transformation that this organism experiences. So, if you perceive and experience the totality of the universe as one living Beingness, then scratching your head and the movement of the earth around the sun are both manifestations of the universe changing its appearance. This means that moving your hand, thinking a thought, talking to someone, touching someone, walking toward someone, and driving your car, are in the same class of events as the explosions of the stars, the galaxies moving farther away from each other, rain falling, and a hurricane destroying a town.

All that happens happens as one unified functioning. We call it "functioning" because we are thinking in terms of doing. When we discuss our actions, for example, we say, "I'm doing this, I'm doing that," indicating our subjective point of view. However, if extra-terrestrials looked at the earth from the vantage-point of their space-ship, their view of us might be very different. Suppose they don't have bodies like ours and don't behave or function as we do. Observing us, they wouldn't necessarily assume that we are doing this or that; they might think, "This spot on that planet is moving this way, and that spot is moving that way." They might think that the earth is one organism that has wiggly things all over it, or that people are hairs on the planet's surface. If these beings were as big as the earth, we would likely seem very small and insignificant to them. But from our subjective point of view, with our belief in our separate sense of self, we think, "I'm doing this and I'm doing that, and the movement of the stars has nothing to do with me." If you understand Holy Truth, it is a necessary corollary that your actions are not separate from the movement of the stars. The only barrier to perceiving this is an emotional and conceptual one: your attachment to the belief in your separate self. If you believe you are ultimately separate, your doing and functioning seem independent of the rest of the universe.

The perception that all changes in the universe are unified as one harmonious, interconnected, interrelated functioning is not yet that of Holy Will, but rather, that of Holy Law, the Holy Idea of ennea-type Three, which we need to understand in order for Holy Will to be intelligible. In the theistic traditions, this Law is called creation, because in a sense, there is a continual creation of the universe. If your view is religious rather than mystical, you believe that everything is run and done by God. But with the actual experience of Holy Truth, the objective view is that everything that happens is interconnected since there are no separate objects, all that happens are changes in the appearance of one medium; therefore, all functioning is simply transformation in the presence of the Holy Truth.

Cosmic Action

Because what happens is the functioning of the organism that is the universe, there is no randomness to the changes that occur within it. Events may appear random to our subjective point of view, but from an objective perspective, an inherent intelligence is seen to be operating, moving things in a particular direction. As Albert Einstein is reputed to have said, "God does not play dice with the universe." This means that the universe does not function mechanically; it is a living, conscious presence, so its functioning is an organic unfoldment. Perceiving that the functioning of the universe has a particular momentum, and moves in a particular direction with a particular intelligence and a particular force, is the meaning of Holy Will. You are seeing, in other words, that there is a unified will in the total functioning of the universe.

Implicit in this perception is seeing all change in the universe as a functioning, a doing. This means that the movement of a star is action and not simply change; it is the action of Holy Truth. There are different ways of experiencing this. If your consciousness is experiencing this from inside Holy Truth, which is to say that you are experiencing who you are as God, the experience is, "I am moving the stars, I am exploding the energy in the sun, I am doing all if it." Your differentiated existence is not what is forefront in the experience of Holy Truth; what is emphasized is the unity, so you are seeing functioning from the perspective of that unity. If there is no sense of identity, no "I" in the experience, then rather than experiencing from the perspective of God, there is just the existence of the universe which is seen to be "doing" all of it, moving everything. The first way of experiencing things is theistic, which is how things are seen in traditions that focus on God-realization. Meher Baba is an example of this perspective when he says, "I am doing everything." The second is non-theistic; the Buddhist tradition emphasizes this experience of there being no central "I" and therefore, no God to do anything. Both are experiences of Holy Will from different vantage points. We can say that God or the universe, depending on your orientation, chooses what happens. The earth rotating around the sun, as well as whatever you are experiencing right now, is the action of the universe.

If everything that happens is a transformation of Holy Truth, then everything that happens is the action of Holy Truth. This means that everything—all change, experience, process—is the action of Holy Truth, arising out of its Holy Will. Therefore, the Holy Will of the universe or God is everything that happens at any moment.

So Holy Will is nothing mysterious, but very few people actually come to know it directly. It is a very subtle and deep perception of the operation of Holy Truth. At the same time, we can experience it as whatever is happening at any moment, whether it is a supernova exploding or your superego attacking you. All of it is Holy Will.

Freedom and Surrender

Holy Freedom, the other aspect of this Holy Idea, is understanding functioning or will from the perspective of Holy Transparency. Holy Transparency, discussed in the previous chapter, is the perception that one exists as a human being who is completely inseparable from the whole. Therefore, your functioning and your actions are inseparable from the functioning of the whole, and are in complete harmony with its functioning. You are, in a sense, a co-creator, a participant in the expression of Holy Will. This is the experience of Holy Will acting through you, and we call that experience Holy Freedom. Holy Freedom, then, means that your action is not separate from the action of the universe, so your will is not separate from the will of the universe. There is, therefore, no conflict between your will and the will of the universe; your will is not opposed to that of the universe or disharmonious with it.

Just as Holy Transparency is grounded in Holy Omniscience, so Holy Freedom is grounded in Holy Will. Holy Freedom is basically experiencing Holy Will from the perspective of being a human being, which specifically means that you don't have a separate will. Just as you see in Holy Transparency that you don't exist as a separate entity, in Holy Freedom, you see that your will does not exist as a separate will. When you recognize that your will is part of the will of the whole, you are free. Being completely in harmony and completely merged with Holy Will is liberating. There is no opposition to what happens but rather, a complete welcoming of it, since your will and that of the universe are one. It is the sense that "My will is Thy will." You are completely in harmony with God's will, completely surrendered to it.

A story is told about the Sufi saint, Rabia, that illustrates this understanding. Before she died, three of her fellow Sufis went to her to discuss some of the finer points of the teaching. The question they were pondering was: What is the best and most objective way of responding to God's chastisement? The first said, "To be patient with it," to which Rabia replied, "I smell ego there." The second one said, "To completely welcome it," and Rabia responded, "That's better, but still not enough." The third Sufi said, "To delight in it," to which Rabia said, "Better, but God wouldn't be satisfied with that." So they asked her how she saw it, and she said, "When there is disharmony, I don't see it because I am seeing God." What Rabia meant is that there is complete forgetfulness of the chastisement because you are seeing the Holy Truth. So whatever you see or experience, even the chastisement, is the Holy Truth. The Holy Truth is everything, including all that happens—what we call good, what we call bad, what is painful or pleasurable to us—all is part of the Holy Truth.

The moment you say that you don't like this or that, you separate yourself from, and set yourself in opposition to, the universe. This is the beginning of the fixation associated with ennea-type Two. However, when there is no opposition to what is, there is surrender to the Holy Will, which is freedom. Buddhism and Taoism have the perspective that freedom is choicelessness, which is the realization that there is no choice. You, the separate individual, have no choice about what happens. Even the choice to surrender indicates that there is still a trace of separateness, because even surrender is the action of Holy Will. It is not your action; it is divine intervention—meaning that whatever happens to you at any moment is not your doing. When you experience yourself as a separate self, you experience your self as doing, as functioning. The moment you transcend this perspective, you realize that all this time you thought you were making things happen, while in reality, things were being done.

When you realize yourself as inseparable from the rest, part of that experience is the perception that action happens spontaneously, arising out of the totality. We don't ordinarily experience this because we're still experiencing ourselves as separate individuals, so we cannot see the Holy Truth and therefore cannot see Holy Will. This makes it difficult even to conceive of action arising in this way. When this is the case, one needs to practice surrendering to what is happening, practice complete *being with*, saying neither yes nor no to what is happening. To really understand what action is, the best place to begin is with your inner experience. You neither accept it nor reject it; you don't push it away, you don't hold onto it. It is what is happening, and that's it. You take no position, nor do you hold any attitude about it. Since you are not making it happen and it is not your choice, the best approach to your inner life is not to try to change it. The ego is always trying to change things, and if you observe your inner experience, you will see that you are in constant turmoil trying to change one thing or another. You try to relax, you try to quiet your mind, you try to make yourself feel better or make yourself feel worse. You are always interfering, trying to make something happen other than what is actually happening. You can only do this if you believe you have your own separate world and you can make things in it happen the way you want, while really, it is not your choice at all. You are alive today not because you want to be, but because the universe wants you to be. If you experience anger today, it's because the universe chooses to. If you experience love today, it's because the universe decides to.

This "choosing" on the part of the universe is not the same as predestination. Predestination implies that there is a plan spelled out somewhere in which everything that is going to happen has already been determined. Here, we are talking about a universe that is intelligent and creative, where what is going to happen in the next moment cannot have been planned because it's going to come out of this moment, rather than out of some plan written at the time of creation. So from this perspective there is no predestination, but there is also no free will.

Everything that happens is totally spontaneous. In non-theistic terms, everything is done through the will of the whole, or in theistic terms, through the will of God. But when most people think of God's will, they conceive of Him as though He were a human being who has ideas about what is going to happen, as if He had a blueprint and was going to make everything conform to it. This is a very limited idea of God. Maybe God is so intelligent that He can create the universe moment to moment without any blueprint!

This is not to say that there is no thread running through everything that happens. The thread is nothing but exactly what is happening now, where you are in this moment, and how this moment unfolds. As you understand what your state is right now, and follow it as it unfolds, you are following your thread. This is Holy Work, the Holy Idea of ennea-type Seven.

So things unfold according to Holy Law in a manner that is not random, but is also not determined. When we understand the intelligence of the universe, we understand how this is possible. This intelligence, which we call the essential aspect of *Brilliancy*, doesn't need to rely on the past in order to act. This intelligence is so bright that it can respond immediately and spontaneously in the most optimal way possible without having to refer to what has happened in the past. If you don't believe God can do that, it indicates that your image of God is based on your own ego, which can only act based upon what has happened to you in the past. This is like saying that God is as conditioned as you are; while in truth, God is what is within and around us that is wholly unconditioned.

If we think of the universe as God, we are thinking of it as not only consciousness but as some kind of pure intelligence. This means that its action is not mechanical and arbitrary, but completely spontaneous and free. The universe manifests at each moment completely spontaneously, and this spontaneous action is the action of intelligence, the action of creativity. So the best way for us to open ourselves to this realization is to go along with it. To become free, we have to learn to surrender, to go along with what happens. This is the most important methodological basis for our work: We stay with what is, and allow it to unfold. The only doing that is necessary is understanding our situation enough to see how we believe we are choosing what happens, when in reality, we are not.

The following passage by Longchenpa describes the Dzogchen view of action and practice—how to live one's life, in other words:

> Let whatever you do or whatever appears
> Just be in its natural state, without premeditation.
> That is true freedom.
> Also,
> The way of living according to me, the creative intelligence,
> Fulfills all aims by letting everything be without striving.
> Because everything is included within this inner reality,
> There is nothing to accept or reject.
> With hope and fear eliminated, anxiety is transcended.
> Whoever recognizes creativity at work
> In the state of sameness where the three times are unborn,
> Is completely beyond verbal understanding or not
>   understanding.
> This is the teaching of no acceptance or rejection.
> (Longchenpa, 1987, p. 46)

Longchenpa calls "creativity" the action that we are calling Holy Will, and "the state of sameness" is the state of Holy Truth. Dzogchen, the highest yana in the Nyingmapa of Vajrayana Buddhism, is the practice of self-liberation, meaning that everything is seen to always be liberating itself. Since everything is a function of the Holy Truth, you don't need to do anything to free it or yourself; you only need to see that everything is already free. So the fundamental stance toward reality in Dzogchen is that of non-interference.

In the Diamond Approach, this attitude of non-interference leads to what we call *nonconceptual freedom*, which is not striving after anything—not even the ultimate state of Holy Truth. One's practice, then, is to cultivate an orientation of not interfering with what arises inwardly and outwardly, of just letting be what is.

To illustrate this, let's say that you are feeling angry. If you reject your anger because you judge it as not being ultimate truth, you are reinforcing the egoic perspective by imposing your separatist will upon what is arising. Preferring one state or feeling over another one, deciding that what is arising in you is not right and should be different, even wanting to be enlightened instead of where you are right now, all indicate identification with the ego which keeps you imprisoned in your ideas about how things should be. If, instead, you recognize that the anger is how the Holy Truth is manifesting in this moment, you will let it be and not try to change it. This is the practice arising out of the understanding of Holy Will, and it will lead you to understanding Holy Freedom. You will see that freedom is not determined by what state you are in; rather, it is complete surrender to whatever state you find yourself in. Only then can you be really free, because then everything that happens is okay. But if you think that freedom means being in a certain state, then the moment you are not in that state, you will think that the universe is manifesting incorrectly because what is arising is not what you think should be happening, and you will have lost your freedom.

Surrendering to the Holy Will is freedom because then you are not placing any constraints, preferences, or conditions upon reality. Everything that happens is fine with you. This degree of surrender must happen at all levels. It cannot be a superficial surrender based on an idea of what is spiritually correct. You can't simply say to yourself, "I surrender to this," while in your heart you wish something else were happening, thereby rejecting your present experience. True surrender means not seeking or efforting. It means totally flowing with the unfolding of reality, "going with the flow," as we used to say in the sixties. It means surrendering to God's will, the flow of the Universal Mind. Whatever He wills is completely welcomed without resistance, without judgment, and without preference.

So the understanding of the Holy Ideas of action, from the perspective of the triangle of Ideas we are working with, is that reality manifests according to its own inherent directionality, its own choice, its own will. Each of us is a part of that will; our very existence is part of this unfoldment. To completely surrender to it means accepting reality unconditionally, including our own states and our own actions. This does not mean resignation; it means acceptance and response out of that acceptance. Responding appropriately to whatever situation you find yourself in, or taking what is called in Buddhism "right action," requires complete acceptance of any situation. So, to use our earlier example, if a truck is barreling toward you on the freeway, enlightened action is neither letting it hit you nor getting angry that the truck driver is endangering you in the first place, but moving out of its way! This moving out of the way, however, does not involve rejecting the situation or having an emotional reaction.

Learning to discriminate between ego reactivity and appropriate response to whatever life presents is a subtle and complex process. The Dzogchen practice is to go with whatever happens, without even trying to understand it. This is appropriate for someone who is abiding in Holy Truth. But the rest of us need to inquire into and understand our responses to determine whether reactivity or selfless surrender is the basis of our actions. If you are acting out, you are not surrendering to Holy Will, you are surrendering to ego's will. Surrendering to Holy Will does not mean buying a car that you cannot afford or eating a piece of chocolate every time you feel like it. So an understanding of your motivations and the level of reality you are grounded in is necessary for appropriate action. If you are feeling inseparably connected with the whole of the universe, your actions will be quite different than when you are taking yourself to be isolated and self-generated.

Because it is difficult initially to discriminate the orientation from which your actions arise, it is important to concentrate on surrendering to whatever arises internally. At the beginning of your work on yourself, your inner experience is not free of judgments and preferences, and your actions will not be either. When you free your inner experience, you will understand Holy Truth, and out of that understanding you will perceive Holy Will and experience Holy Freedom. Then your actions will flow out of that understanding; they will cease being reactions and will become spontaneous responses. But even though your actions are initially reactive, they are still the actions of Holy Will, so while they must not be trusted or indulged, they also must not be rejected. This is a subtle and tricky discrimination.

Understanding Holy Will gives you a foundational basis for spiritual practice. It shows you that to come into alignment with ultimate truth is to first recognize how you are interfering with your reality, how you are in the way, how you believe that you are a separate individual with your own will. Rather than being oriented toward achieving a certain state of consciousness, a practice that makes sense must be oriented toward freedom from *wanting* certain states. True freedom is not the realization of a certain dimension; true liberation is to be free from all dimensions. It is the freedom of completely accepting whatever the universe manifests through you. If it is manifesting through you as love, or as the Absolute, then that's how it is manifesting. If it is manifesting as anger or fear, that is how the universe is manifesting. As an individual, your task is not to choose what happens, but to comply to the extent of recognizing that it is not even *possible* to choose. This is a complete reversal of the position of the ego.

So from the perspective of Holy Freedom, living according to the truth means complete surrender to whatever reality presents. If you are able to do that, you will see in time that it is not a matter of *you* surrendering to what is, but that the universe is doing *that*, too. You have to go through this transition in learning to completely accept whatever is happening. This means having no judgment of your experience or of anything else that happens in the universe, and in time, this means having no preferences. You actually get to a place where you don't prefer the Absolute over your body identity. If there is a preference, there is still a separateness.

So we are seeing that all that happens is the expression of Holy Will, and this means that it is responsible for the transformation of Holy Truth. You will recall that Holy Truth is constantly transforming; it is never in a static condition. The moment you move your hand, you know that the universe is not static; the moment you hear a sound, you know that the universe changes. So the Idea of Holy Truth is seeing the existence of the universe; the Idea of Holy Will is seeing not only the existence of the universe, but that it is in a constant state of unfoldment which we experience as change, movement, and action. From this perspective, we see that freedom is the complete surrender to, and total harmony with, the unfoldment of the universe. This is the Idea of Holy Freedom: Your will and the will of the universe are completely merged and unified, so there is no inner discord. One part is not trying to change another part. There is complete inner unification.

Separate Will

Since Holy Freedom is surrender to whatever you are experiencing, then judging it or trying to change it indicates that there is no surrender to Holy Will. But if you judge your lack of surrender, this indicates a further lack of surrender to Holy Will. Surrender doesn't require certain conditions. At any moment, there is the possibility of completely letting go of trying to control things and letting the universe be, instead of believing that you can and should rearrange it. Egoic pride is the belief that you have your own will and can have your own way, and can change things in the universe. It is the belief that, "I'm going to do it *my* way; I'm going to have things be the way I want them." This pride manifests in the body as a constriction of the fontanel at the top of the head which blocks Living Daylight, and thus, blocks the whole perspective of Holy Will.

The *specific delusion* that arises due to the loss of Holy Will is the conviction that there are such things as separate entities who have their own wills—it is the delusion that there is a separate you who can have things go the way you want them to. We saw that the delusion associated with Holy Transparency is that you have a separate self, and here the delusion is that this separate self has a will and a choice separate from the rest of the universe. We are not saying that you don't have free will, but that you don't have a free will separate from the whole. You want your way instead of seeing that the universe has its way, manifesting through you. We have seen that the best approach is to surrender to the universe, thereby actualizing yourself. Then you become who you really are, because you are whatever the universe happens to be unfolding within your consciousness at any moment.

The following passage addresses what to do when you see that you are taking yourself to be a separate entity, and integrates the whole triangle we are working with:

> Know the state of pure and total presence to be a vast
> expanse without center or border.
> It is everywhere the same without acceptance or rejection.
> [This is the Holy Truth.]
> Blend the nature of mind and its habit patterns into non-
> duality.
> [This is Holy Omniscience.]
> Because entities, whether subjectively conceived or directly
> experienced,
> [when you believe you are a separate entity or are
> experiencing someone or something else as separate]
> Are present as ornaments of one's own state of being.
> [This is Holy Transparency.]
> Do not accept or reject them.
> (Longchenpa, 1987, p. 42)
> [Brackets are author's comments.]

In other words, even when you believe you are a separate self and are experiencing discrete entities, recognize all is still the Holy Truth, so don't accept or reject it. If you accept or reject any part of your experience, even what is delusional, you are identifying with the belief that you are a separate entity. This is a very subtle teaching in which the way one practices affects what one believes, and what one believes affects the way one practices.

Now let's focus more specifically on the delusion that arises due to the loss of Holy Freedom. We have seen that in Holy Freedom, there is complete surrender to your experience with no hesitation, no consideration, without even a concept of surrendering to it. What happens is what happens, period. This includes all of your actions, your feelings, your thoughts, your inner states. Otherwise, the delusion arises that there is a "way that is yours," different from what is happening. This position implies a rejection of what is happening and thus, a rejection of Holy Will.

By pitting yourself against what is, you are acting according to the delusion that you have a separate will and that you can have your own way, different from what is happening. This is one of the principles of ego: that you have a separate will and that you have choice. Even when you believe that you are helpless and can't do things, there is the implicit belief that if it weren't for your helplessness, you could have your own way. From this egoic perspective, it seems obvious that you need to tinker with things, both inwardly and outwardly. This manifests externally as manipulating other people to make them conform to how you think they need to be for you, and internally as constantly evaluating your experience to see whether it is "right" or not, and trying to change it if it doesn't match your ideas of how you think it should be. "What state am I in? Oh, no! I'm being reactive—that's no good—I should be just being. Now I'm being. Good, good. I should stabilize that," and so on, as if it were up to you to make your state become this or that. If you contemplate your experience, you will see this constant activity. The moment you are identified with your ego, you are involved in this activity of trying to make yourself feel better, and not scared or unhappy or empty. All ego defenses are based on this principle of changing your experience to make it conform to how you think it should be.

So there is a constant inner manipulation going on, expressing the delusion that you have a separate will and that you can have things your way, which is separating from Holy Will. You have lost your freedom, since true freedom means freedom from the content of what you are experiencing. Whether you are experiencing yourself as a separate entity, or as the Holy Truth, or as transparency, or as a frustrated mother, or as a stressed-out businessman, or whatever, that is what the universe is creating right now. It's pure magic, so who are you to say to God, "I don't like what I'm experiencing. Why don't you change it?" To really surrender your will means to have basic trust in the universe, God, or reality, and so we see how the lack of basic trust creates the delusion of this ennea-type.

If you are identified with your ego, you are constantly struggling with your experience. Even when you are asleep and dreaming, you are struggling. Holy Freedom means the end of struggling.

The issue of getting one's own way is a big one for the personality, and the thought of surrendering to God's will may seem to involve giving up your own will. However, if you are sincere and truthful with yourself, and you stay with your experience without trying to change it in any way, you find out that having your own way is really a matter of surrendering to your inner truth. Your way is following the thread of your own experience. It is not a matter of choosing or not choosing it; your way is something that is given to you. It is the road you are walking on, the landscape you are traveling through. You discover that it is a huge relief not to feel that the territory you are crossing should be different than exactly how it is for you.

We unconsciously confuse surrendering to God's will—which is really just accepting what is—with capitulating to our parents. "Listen to me. Do what I tell you to do," they demand. When we think of surrendering to God's will, we tend to think of it as a capitulation to some greater force, rather than just completely surrendering to what is happening. Thus, all the loss of autonomy and wounded pride that we experienced as children gets reactivated. This is the only way that the ego can understand what surrender is: "God tells me to do such and such, so I'll do it." This comes from an identification with the belief—usually unconscious and deep within our souls—that we are children who are being ordered about by our parents.

As the ego encounters reality, its process is first of all to decide whether what is happening is right or wrong. The belief that such a judgment can be made indicates the absence of Holy Perfection. If the ego decides that something is wrong with reality, what follows is the idea that you can do something about it, which indicates the absence of Holy Will. The movement of ego is a ceaseless attempt to get its own way, to try to feel better, to try to experience this or that. But you can't change what is, so this ego activity simply brings you suffering and makes you feel entangled and full of frustration. Frustration happens when you want something and are not getting it, when you are trying to impose your will upon reality by pitting yourself against the unfolding current of the universe.

Surrender is not resignation. It is very important to distinguish between them. Resignation means that you are admitting that you cannot get your own way. You are taking yourself to be a separate self with a separate will that is being thwarted by reality. This is very different from true surrender, which is neither acceptance nor rejection, but ceasing to separate one's own will from reality. To learn to surrender means to expose your willfulness—the belief that you have a will separate from reality's, and that you can have it your way.

True Will

One's understanding of what will is changes as one's work progresses. Initially, what we take to be will is the pushing and efforting of the ego in its attempt to make ourselves, others, and reality itself, conform to how we think it should be. We call this *false will* in our work, and when we inquire fully into it and begin to disidentify from it, a sense of deficiency is exposed that carries with it a feeling of castration. We feel that something is missing, that we are inadequate, that we have no inner support or capacity to persevere. This painful sense of deficiency often manifests as the actual sensation of an emptiness where we know our genitals to be, and they may feel devoid of feeling as we are working through this "hole" or sense of absence.* These are all indications that we have lost contact with the essential quality of *Will*, of which

---

* Whenever we are experientially cut off from an essential aspect, the sense of a hole will manifest both physically and psychologically. Physically, there will be the actual sensation of an emptiness or a void in the particular part of the body associated with that aspect. Psychologically, the sense of a hole will manifest as a sense of deficiency, as though a part of our soul is missing. For this reason, we speak in the Diamond Approach of *holes* of the various essential aspects.

fake will is a facsimile, an attempt on the part of the personality to recreate that which it believes it has lost.

As you stay with this hole, essential Will begins to arise in your consciousness, and is experienced at first as a sense of determination—"I will do that"—and a sense of confidence. As you experience this, you see that what you had previously called "will" on the level of the personality is very different from essential Will. On the essential level, it feels like a sense of inner support that imparts the capacity to persevere effortlessly because one is confident in one's capacity to do so. Effort, the hallmark of fake will, becomes meaningless on this level because we see that real will means "going with the flow" of one's Being. If efforting is still present, it means that you are still identified to some extent with the personality. So essential Will is an effortless steadfastness in carrying out the task at hand, resulting from a sense of inner support and confidence.

When we first experience real personal Will, as opposed to the willfulness of the personality, we see that it has this sense of effortlessness about it. It does involve action, but not trying. When you experience this, you begin to get the intimation that essential Will doesn't mean choosing or controlling whatever situation you are in. Because you feel supported by the universe when you are in contact with Being, you don't need to try to make things happen in a premeditated kind of way, and so your action becomes effortless and spontaneous.

Experiencing this sense of effortlessness indicates that true surrender is taking place and that essential Will is present. As we have said, actualizing the Will requires practice in being present with whatever is arising without rejection, without acceptance, without attachment, and without preference. This practice constitutes the foundation of the Diamond Approach. The Diamond Approach is basically a matter of going along with the unfoldment of the whole universe as it is manifesting in your experience in the present moment. Just as the universe is unfolding in the sense that the weather changes, earthquakes occur, the sun sets, and the moon rises over the horizon, the universe is also unfolding inside of you. If you stay with, and surrender to, your inner process, it will unfold in the same way.

However, when shaped by the ego, our inner process flows in a very limited way that is constrained and made to conform to our conditioned beliefs about what is acceptable to experience. Our inner life then follows the rigid and predictable pathways of the ennea-types, and we are trapped in our own virtual realities. Only through being present with what is manifesting within us without judgments and the resulting inner manipulations, can we talk about true unfoldment. Then our experience ceases to be a predictable revisiting of familiar territory, and becomes truly an exploration and an adventure taking us into depths and dimensions of reality that reveal more and more of the richness and profundity of what is here.

The acceptance we are discussing is not a matter of saying, "Okay, I can allow this to be going on." It is not the stance of being someone who takes a positive position relative to something else. Perhaps calling it non-rejection is more accurate, although it is the lack of *any* reaction to what one is experiencing—positive or negative. It is just letting things be exactly as they are, with no inner sense of self that is feeling one way or another about them. It's not meddling in God's work, to use religious terminology. Putting it another way, it is surrendering to the flow of existence, with its own inexorable movement, direction, and force. When you say no to it and try to fight it, you just create frustration for yourself.

A good analogy to the effortlessness of the surrender we are discussing is spending years practicing how to swing a golf club, and then reaching a point one day when you swing the club and it is completely effortless. Likewise, initially, you have to exert great effort to be present with yourself: You have to remind yourself continually to feel your body and remember yourself. The more you work at it, the easier it becomes, until you reach a point when the remembering happens by itself. So there is a place for effort, and the deeper your practice becomes, the less effort there will be.

Castration and Willfulness

We have discussed the delusion of having a separate personal will that arises from the loss of the Ideas of Holy Will and Holy Freedom. Now let's explore how the fixation arises out of that *specific delusion*, creating the core of ennea-type Two. Reviewing the process, at first, the sense of holding and the resulting basic trust are present in consciousness, and this is equivalent to the presence of the Holy Idea. The loss of the holding is also the loss of the trust and the loss of the Idea, as we have seen, and leads to a *specific difficulty*, while the loss of trust leads to a *specific reaction* to the difficulty.

The *specific difficulty* and the *specific reaction* for each point of the Enneagram are determined by the delusion arising from the loss of its Holy Idea. The loss of holding is interpreted experientially through the filter of the delusion, so for ennea-type Two, not getting what you need from the environment (the loss of holding) is experienced as not getting your own way. The implicit belief that there is a separate you who can have your own way creates this sense, and the emotional state that accompanies it is one of humiliated castration. This state is the *specific difficulty* for ennea-type Two. Because of the belief that you can make things go the way you want them to, the loss of holding is experienced as an enormous blow to your pride, a deflating and humiliating slap in the face. This belief that it is possible to have a will separate from the rest of the universe is the pride of ego, and when it is deflated it feels like a castration, like your vitality and force are taken away, like what you are isn't effective, powerful, or good enough.

In the face of the loss of the sense of holding, your basic trust in the universe disappears. You come to feel that the universe is against you, or at least not with you, and so the *specific reaction* arises of willfully pitting yourself against what is. The *specific reaction*, then, for this ennea-type is that of willful action. This stance, which characterizes ennea-type Two, is one filled with pride and stubbornness in which you assert, "I am going to get my own way." People of this ennea-type have a strong willfulness; it is important to them that things go their way and that what they make happen is important because otherwise, they feel castrated and humiliated. The fake will is very crystallized, and there is a stubborn resistance to feeling that they can't have their way since that would make them feel castrated. So instead of feeling that whatever is happening is just what's going on, you feel that your will is ineffective and hasn't worked if things aren't happening the way you want them to or think they should. This reaction of willfulness against the sense of humiliating castration implicitly contains not only the belief that you have a separate will and can choose and determine what happens, but also that you know how things should go.

This whole constellation of the sense of deficiency (the *specific difficulty* of humiliated castration) and the reaction to it (the *specific reaction* of willful action) forms the core of this ennea-type. Out of this core, all of the characteristic manifestations of manipulation, seductiveness, and physical, emotional, and mental influence arise.

Through understanding this ennea-type, we can see how the ego is an imitation of the universe. The ego, here, is basically saying, "I am the truth, I exist as myself independent of everyone else, and I can do what I want." Only God can say that, but the egoic self is implicitly asserting this all the time. The ego, then, takes the place of God, and this is the egoic vanity that we will explore when we discuss ennea-type Three.

When we let it be, everything is beautiful. We see that everything is just right, just the way it is. This is what is meant by Holy Perfection, the Idea of ennea-type One. In fact, that is how it is all the time, but we don't see it because the operation of our willfulness distorts our perception. What we see is of our own making; it is reality seen through the filter of our distortions. When that filter isn't there, you see the same things as before—you see the same people, the same places, the same situations; but your perception shifts so you see the beauty of their existence. This reflects what we discussed in Part One: how the fixations of the ennea-types are not ego structures, but rather, are nine different twists in the soul, distortions in the perceptual system of one's consciousness.

We have explored the delusion of having a separate will that can make choices, and the *specific difficulty* of humiliating castration, and the *specific reaction* of willfulness. We have seen that this constellation forms the core of this ennea-type, and one important manifestation of it—

resulting directly from the lack of basic trust—is the conviction that the universe and/or other people are against, or are standing in the way of, one's freedom. Out of this conviction comes the belief that you need to be willful and try to have things your way in order to gain or protect your freedom. This is the basic tendency of ego, whatever one's ennea-type, and it remains deeply entrenched despite the fact that you can see from outside of this perceptual twist that you obviously can't gain your freedom by willfully pitting yourself against what is; you just get entrenched in the struggle to free yourself, which is not freedom at all.

Spiritual Practice

The impact of this basic tendency of ego on spiritual practice is the often-unconscious belief that working on yourself means making some-thing happen—bringing about a certain state or a particular change in yourself—rather than seeing spiritual practice as a matter of sur-render, of getting out of the way. This also means that a true spiritual practice that will ultimately bring about transformation is one that entails a surrender of your own will, prejudices, preferences, choices, and rejections. We have seen that the pride of ego is the belief that you can choose what arises in your consciousness, and that this is essen-tially an expression of the lack of trust that Holy Truth does and will function as Holy Will. In religious terms, it is a lack of faith in the action of grace.

To the ego, freedom means being able to do whatever you want whenever you want to do it. Because this isn't often possible, you come to see the universe as constraining you and limiting your freedom. But from the perspective of Holy Freedom, freedom is wanting whatever the universe wants. When you are aligned with the universe, what you want and what is happening are the same thing. This is true freedom. This is why the Idea of Holy Freedom is fundamental to the method-ology of the Diamond Approach, in which a basic part of the practice is to be present with whatever happens to be your state. If you react to it, interfere with it, or try to change it, then you can't see it objectively but only through the screen of your projections. If you don't see your condition or the situation in its natural state, you will continue believing your projections about it and won't be able to penetrate its true nature. If you don't see its true nature, it won't unfold and expose itself as the Holy Truth that everything is. Fundamental to our understanding is that while you might have projections upon whatever you are experiencing initially, if you don't interfere with it, the tendency of the universe is to reveal its own nature through your experience. This, of course, requires basic trust.

The Diamond Approach is not the only spiritual approach based on Holy Freedom. Another is the Vajrayana Buddhist practice of Dzogchen, self-liberation, discussed earlier. There, the understanding is that if you are present with an object of perception without interference, it will naturally liberate itself, meaning that it will spontaneously reveal its true nature; or, using the language of the Enneagram, it will reveal itself as nothing but Holy Truth. The difference between Dzogchen and the Diamond Approach is that we see that this revelation of true nature does not usually happen spontaneously and instantaneously. Rather, there is a process of unfoldment involving various states and dimensions before one arrives at the ultimate one of Holy Truth. So another conceptual basis of the Diamond Approach is Holy Work, the Holy Idea of ennea-type Seven, which is the fact that a natural process of unfoldment occurs and that there are many dimensions to that unfoldment. Dzogchen is, in some sense, a purer practice, but a more difficult one because it assumes that there is only one true state, that of Holy Truth. Basically, Dzogchen is a practice for buddhas. If you are a beginning buddha, you can practice Dzogchen; otherwise, it will be very difficult to do, as it is for most people.

The Diamond Approach, then, is not as direct or as pure a practice, but it takes into consideration the fact of unfoldment, beginning with the perception that most people are very far from experiencing themselves as the Holy Truth. So for example, Dzogchen would say that if you are angry, and you stay with that, it will spontaneously reveal itself as the Holy Truth. In our work, we see that if you stay with the anger, it spontaneously will reveal the hurt underneath it; and if you stay with the hurt, it will reveal the emptiness underlying that; and if you stay with the emptiness, an aspect of Being will arise; and if you stay with that, it will take you through deeper and deeper dimensions of reality. If you stay with this process and understand everything that arises, you will, in time, realize that everything is the Holy Truth.

So while many spiritual approaches are the same in terms of final outcome, there are differences in terms of methodology, as we are seeing about Dzogchen in contrast with our work. Other approaches utilize special practices, such as breathing techniques and visualizations, which are designed to take you to certain states of consciousness. While such practices are not as subtle or refined as Dzogchen or the Diamond Approach, their advantage is that they are easy to do and so almost everyone can participate. Our work, in contrast, is not easy to do initially, and it is very difficult to do on your own, since it is usually difficult to learn to allow spontaneous understanding and unfoldment, or difficult to allow at the beginning.

Using the understanding of Holy Will, our method in the Diamond Approach is to welcome whatever happens and whatever it is that you are experiencing. You stay present with it and you become curious about it, wanting to understand it in an experiential way, out of love for truth. The orientation is not toward a certain state, because the moment that you orient your practice toward a certain state, you have left Holy Freedom. Even if the state that you are trying to cultivate is Holy Freedom or Holy Truth, if that is not what is unfolding in your experience, you are imposing your egoic will onto your process to direct it toward the Holy Idea.

Our orientation, then, is toward freedom: complete and total independence from any state or dimension. We see that any state is fine if it is completely surrendered to. What the state depends on is Holy Will, and not on your desires. That is always the case, since that is the objective fact of Holy Will. So the more that you approach your process in this way, the more you will naturally move into the boundless dimensions and, ultimately, into Holy Truth. This will happen on its own because it is the nature of reality to progressively reveal itself, taking you closer and closer to its ultimate nature, so there is no need to direct your process toward it. If you try to push your process in any direction, you are really just standing in your own way.

So to practice using the Diamond Approach means to be present with what is happening without judging it as good or bad, without holding onto it or pushing it away. You stay with it, open and curious about what it is, loving the truth of it as it reveals itself. This is really an expression of love for Holy Truth as it unfolds in its various manifestations. This is real freedom, and is the basis of nonconceptual freedom in the Diamond Approach.

If you do not understand what Holy Freedom is, you will try to live your life by manipulating your outer experience in order to get your own way; or, if you are a spiritual seeker, you will try to manipulate your inner experience one way or another, rather than surrender to the universe. Either way, you end up in the specific suffering of ego: being locked in inner combat with one part of yourself pitted against another. Only after chasing one state and then another over and over, to the point of realizing you truly cannot will what happens, only then does the deep longing for the end of suffering bring true surrender to what is.

CHAPTER FOURTEEN

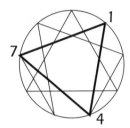

Point One
HOLY PERFECTION

> The awareness that Reality is a process, moving with direction and purpose. Within this movement each moment is connected by the process with the one goal, and thus is perfect.
>
> — Ichazo, 1972

As we have seen, each Holy Idea is a view of reality from an egoless perspective. From the point of view of Holy Perfection, if we experience reality just the way it is, we perceive its intrinsic perfection. We cannot add or delete anything to make that reality more perfect; nothing needs to be done with it. From Holy Truth, we learned that reality is nondual, that everything that exists is one indivisible truth. Holy Perfection teaches us that this reality is not only one indivisible nowness, but that it is absolutely perfect. Holy Perfection is another way of seeing Holy Truth, as is Holy Love. So Holy Truth, Holy Love, and Holy Perfection are three ways of seeing the totality of existence. They are all true at the same time.

140

Holy Perfection is related to the concept of "mirror-like wisdom" in the system of the Dhyani Buddhas in the Vajrayana branch of Buddhism. The perfection of reality can be seen only if our consciousness is like a clear mirror which reflects everything as it is, without projection or distortion. When we perceive with this clarity, we recognize that reality has a sense of purity, neatness, immaculateness, and beauty inherent in it. The experience is both outwardly and inwardly perfect and luminous. We are not seeing reality through the filter of our own ideas, and so its perfection is not based on an opinion, a point of view, a preference, or an evaluation.

The Rightness of What Is

When our perception is like a clear mirror, without subjective judgment, we find reality to be just right. If our mirror creates any distortion, if our perception of reality contains any subjective preferences or ideas, then we are seeing reality from a deluded point of view and we will miss its inherent perfection. This makes our work very obvious: to find out what is in the way of perceiving reality as it is—to find out what our obscurations are, where our perception is deluded.

The way we ordinarily see the world is not the way it really is because we see it from the perspective of our judgments and preferences, our likes and dislikes, our fears and our ideas of how things should be. So to see things as they really are, which is to see things objectively, we have to put these aside—in other words, we have to let go of our minds. Seeing things objectively means that it doesn't matter whether we think what we're looking at is good or bad—it means just seeing it as it is. If a scientist is conducting an experiment, he doesn't say, "I don't like this so I'll ignore it." He may not personally care for the results because they don't confirm his theory, but pure science means seeing things the way they really are. If he says he is not going to pay attention to the experiment because he doesn't like it, that is not science. Yet, this is the way most of us deal with reality, inwardly and outwardly.

To see reality from the perspective of Holy Perfection means to see that reality is just right as it is; it does not need changes or corrections.

This is a very radical notion. If you really took it seriously, you would stop doing many of the things that you do. The moment you see that everything, at every moment, is perfect, you see that your effort to make things better is pointless. You see that what really needs to be done is to observe your mind, your consciousness, in order to see why it is obscured, why it does not see things clearly, and what is making your mirror so cloudy.

Understanding this Holy Idea, then, can profoundly reorient our ideas about the purpose of spiritual work. If reality is inherently perfect, and we are part of that reality, the purpose of working on ourselves cannot be to try to become better or to make our lives better. Holy Perfection, which elucidates the objective condition of reality, tells us that reality is already and always perfect, so if we think that our perfection is something to be achieved, that means that we believe that perfection exists somewhere in the future, and not now. We are then taking perfection to be a goal to be actualized, rather than how things already are, and this can only be the perspective of ego.

Perfection, as the ego understands it, is determined by measuring reality, inner and outer, against some ideal or standard of how things are supposed to be. The criteria for this judgment may vary from person to person, but for everyone, this quest for perfection is the cause of much of our internal striving. This is not perfection at all but rather, perfectionism. The perfection we are talking about here is independent of these ideas; it is true for everything that exists by the mere fact of its existence.

Holy Perfection is difficult to define exactly, because like all the Holy Ideas, it is a universal concept, a Platonic Form. As such, the perfection we are discussing cannot be analyzed or reduced to simpler elements; it is a pure form of manifestation. From the perspective of Holy Perfection, everything looks just right, everything feels perfect and complete, every action is correct and graceful. We see that whatever happens is the perfection of Holy Truth, which is everything. We know this with certainty, without necessarily knowing what makes everything perfect.

This sense of the intrinsic rightness of the reality that is inside and outside everyone is a feeling, a recognition, an action, of intelligence. It involves no conceptualizing about perfection. Holy Perfection reflects the intactness, the completeness, and the glory, of what is. It is the perception of the perfection of all phenomena from every angle, on all levels, all the way through. This is what makes Holy Perfection holy, objective, and egoless. If something were seen as perfect and another thing not, or if it were perceived as perfect now and at another point no longer perfect, this would not be Holy Perfection, but rather, the ego's sense of perfection based on subjective judgment.

If you experience things in the moment, without thinking in terms of the past and the future, just right here in the now, and see the isness of what is here, you will recognize the perfection we're talking about. You won't be looking at what is here through the filter of your ideas, which are the result of what you heard or saw in the past or what you think is going to happen in the future. Holy Perfection is the perfection of what is, and reality exists only now, only in this moment—without the concept of time, without your ideas about what's going to happen tomorrow or what's not going to happen tomorrow, without your ideas about what should or shouldn't happen, without judgments of good and bad—just the experience of the isness of the now. If we see reality the way it is right now, we see that everything we perceive is coemergent with Being, everything is made up of Essence. Everything—your body, your mind, your feelings, your thoughts, physical objects—everything is made out of that complete pure beingness of presence. This is the experience of Holy Perfection.

When you experience an essential state fully, you can recognize that it has a quality of perfection. You can't say that it needs something or that it is lacking anything. If you are experiencing love or compassion, for instance, you perceive it as pure and complete just the way it is. Holy Perfection tells us that everything has that quality of rightness, and not only certain essential states. We saw that from the perspective of Holy Truth, everything is one, an undivided wholeness. Your body, your essence, the world, God, are not separate things; they are all one thing, and that one thing, which is not a thing, is the presence of Essence. Because everything is ultimately essential, it follows that everything is inherently perfect.

We don't normally see reality this way because we are busy looking at it from the perspective of our own delusion. Holy Perfection cannot be perceived from the point of view of ego, because ego wants to change reality to fit how it thinks it is supposed to be. Holy Perfection is a transcendence of that point of view. Realizing Holy Perfection is not a matter of intellectually asserting that everything is perfect so that you can go on being lazy and irresponsible. To experience Holy Perfection is to actually exist in an egoless state and to see the inner nature of everything objectively. What changes is one's way of perceiving, so that reality is seen without distortion.

Holy Perfection reveals that the way things are, and the way they move, are perfect. Seeing the perfection of the way things are, is seeing the perfection of Holy Truth. Seeing the perfection of the way things move is seeing the perfection of Holy Will which, as we have seen, has to do with change and transformation. Holy Truth and Holy Will are relatively acceptable to people, but Holy Perfection is one of the Holy Ideas that many have difficulty with. If we really accept what Holy Perfection tells us about the objective state of things, we can't complain about how anything is, or about anything that happens.

The Fundamental Nature of Things

If there is an earthquake somewhere, for instance, that is the action of Holy Will. It's difficult for many of us to see perfection in it if hundreds of people die. But perfection does not exist on that level of discourse; it does not exist on the level of someone being killed by a falling rock during the earthquake. Holy Perfection recognizes that there is no separate rock and no person being hit by it. What we are calling "rock" and "person" are nothing but manifestations of the essence of God. So, from the perspective of Holy Perfection, an inseparable piece of the essence of God falls on another inseparable piece of the essence of God, and it is very graceful, because it is all the movement of the essence of God.

The egoic point of view is that there are rocks falling on people's heads, and that is terrible. And it *is* terrible from that vantage point. But Holy Perfection is not a matter of seeing what happens from the egoic point of view and then trying to change it to make it conform to what we think is right. If we did that, we would have to control nature, and we would have to reform the whole of humanity until everyone behaved correctly and perfectly according to what we believe is right.

Perceiving Holy Perfection means seeing beyond that level. It means seeing reality from a transcendent point of view, which implies seeing it from an egoless, enlightened condition. From this perspective there is no such thing as an imperfect action; Holy Perfection is seen as inherent in everything that happens. The moment you say that what happened is not right, you are saying that it is not part of Holy Will, or that Holy Will is acting in an imperfect way, which cannot be the case.

This does not mean that you have the license to do whatever you want, justifying it with "all action is perfect." Only one who is established in Holy Perfection, who continuously perceives it, can act totally spontaneously. This action will naturally be an expression of fundamental goodness and love. Such action is spontaneously responsible, because Holy Perfection includes the intrinsic intelligence of Holy Will.

You might object to this perspective by asserting that death is terrible, so everything that happens can't be perfect. From the perspective of ego, yes, it is terrible. But from the perspective of the enlightened state, you don't see people dying and buildings falling. You see the fundamental nature of these things. Whether the form of H_2O is water or ice at a particular moment, for instance, doesn't change its fundamental nature. Death is just one form changing into another form.

Holy Perfection implies, then, that one doesn't perceive just the surface of things, but rather, one perceives this fundamental level. When we remain on the level of differentiation, details, and discrimination, we are involved with preferences and judgments, and this gives us a position. When we look from that position, we don't see the full dimensionality of reality.

Holy Truth, as we have seen, tells us that reality exists in the now, as the now. By "now," I'm not referring to part of a sequence in time. If you stay in the present, and your consciousness is really present in this moment, not wandering to the past or the future, you recognize that the now is not time; it is not a point between the past and the future. The now is this book, is the chair you're sitting in, is you. These are made out of now, they are the now, they are the present. They are presence, and they are Being. When you see the beingness, the thereness of everything, you recognize the intrinsic perfection and rightness of it all. The moment your mind wanders to the past or the future, your focus is not on the intrinsic reality of things. Your mind is focusing on the changing of the forms, and the implications you believe these changes have. Then you lose the perception of what truly exists right at this moment.

So Holy Perfection is seeing Holy Truth in a certain way. It is seeing that Holy Truth means that everything everywhere is just right at any point in time or space. When we recognize this, this becomes an important foundational basis for our work. We can then see that working on ourselves is really not a matter of trying to get ourselves to some place where we feel perfect; it is instead a matter of discovering the perfection that is already here, that is intrinsic to us and to everything. It is a matter of seeing through our obscurations with awareness and understanding, rather than a matter of making anything happen.

Just being with whatever we are experiencing is sufficient to experience its inherent perfection. This acceptance of what is, is not the ego's version of acceptance, which is the opposite of rejection. If you say, "I'm accepting this now," you are making a judgment that now this thing is okay and you've decided to accept it. But do you decide that you're going to accept the sun? The sun's existence is a fact. So the acceptance that leads to Holy Perfection is a not-saying-no and a not-saying-yes.

If you really let yourself be here in this moment, you will find that everything begins to glow. Everything is radiant, luminous, clear, and transparent. That glowing luminous awareness has within it all kinds of wonderful qualities: love, harmony, beauty, and grace. And you will see that there is a sense of perfectness, a rightness about how things are. That is the actual condition of everything, but our lens of perception is not usually focused, so we don't see things as they are. Since our lens has been out of focus most of our lives, we have come to believe that our distorted perception is how things are.

To see the world from the perspective of Holy Perfection, then, we have to be in the moment, in contact with our presence, our beingness. Our awareness must be with what exists right now—what we are experiencing in our bodies, what sounds we are hearing, what the temperature is in the environment. The more we are present in the now, the more we recognize that the now has nothing to do with time and that the now is everything. When we see that, there is a certainty, an innate knowingness, that this is how things are. When your lens of perception is finally corrected in this way, you innately know that you are seeing really clearly, and it is obvious to you how unfocused your lens has been. You know, then, that you are not interfering with reality; you are just seeing things the way they are.

Comparative Judgment

We have discussed what Holy Perfection means. Now we want to explore what happens when the intrinsic perfection of existence is not perceived. As we have seen, a *specific delusion* arises as a direct result of the perceptual absence of each Holy Idea. That delusion underlies a particular way of experiencing and approaching reality, and it forms the center of the core of each fixation. The delusion arises concurrently with the loss of the Idea and with the loss of the sense of being "held" in early childhood. Holy Perfection, as we have seen, means that everything is perfect and just right. If that perception is not there, then there is the conviction that some things are less perfect than others, or that some things are perfect and others are not. There is a sense that something is wrong somewhere. The belief arises that there is really and absolutely such a thing as good and bad, or right and wrong, that some things are intrinsically better than others, and that you can make comparative judgments about what exists. There must be at least two things to be able to make a comparison, and this is the delusion of duality of Point Eight. Here, not only are you comparing things and saying that this one is small and that one is big, but also that big is better. So not only is there comparison of at least two discrete entities, but there is also a value judgment.

The delusion of Point One, then, is the conviction that comparative judgments are ultimate and final. Things can, of course, be compared on the surface, but to believe that such comparisons reflect their fundamental nature is ego's delusion. Comparative judgment on the relative level is useful sometimes, but when we are talking about the Holy Ideas, we are talking about a way of experiencing things that is transcendent to the relative level. So we're not saying that because everything is perfect, you should eat food even if it is rotten. We're also not saying that if you are sick, you shouldn't go to a doctor. Obviously, if you want to be healthy, you take care of yourself, and there is comparative judgment involved in that. Holy Perfection does not negate this level of things, but when we talk about our beingness, our innate existence, we are discussing a level of reality beyond the particulars of whether our bodies are healthy or not, or even whether we are living or not. From this perspective, even the cancer that kills us is part of the perfection of all that is. Ultimately, as we have seen, even our death is simply part of our fundamental nature and part of all that exists, simply changing from one form into another.

We usually adhere to the egoic point of view of reality because we believe that that is the way we will survive. But when we perceive from the objective point of view, we recognize that this point of view will not only help us survive, but that it will help us survive with harmony. The objective point of view does not eliminate the egoic point of view; it underlies and contains it. The body, for example, has a circulatory system and an immune system; these inner features are not apparent on the surface, and if you don't take these into consideration, you are not being objective about the body, and your chances of survival will be lower. So taking into account the objective point of view does not eliminate the surface—yes, there is a face, skin, feet—but adds much more to the situation.

As we have seen, the loss of the Holy Idea of each ennea-type leads to its *specific delusion*. The loss of the holding environment leads to the *specific difficulty*, and the loss of basic trust leads to the *specific reaction*. The delusion is what determines the characteristics of both the difficulty and the reaction.

Wrongness

With ennea-type One, the *specific difficulty* is the feeling or conviction that something is wrong with you, that you are imperfect in an intrinsic way, that you are fundamentally flawed. It is not that you did something wrong and you feel guilty about it, as in Point Eight, but rather that there is something inherently wrong with who and what you are.

From the beginning of the birth of ego, deficiency in the holding environment is experienced through the filter of comparative judgment. You experience something painful about the holding—not being taken care of adequately or not feeling held—and you experience it as a wrongness, a flaw. Because you don't understand or perceive the Holy Idea of Perfection, you interpret the absence of holding as meaning that something is wrong with you. Later, you try to find out what is flawed. Usually you pick on your body or mind, finding one thing or another about you that is wrong, and you believe that that's why your parents didn't love you or take care of you as adequately as you needed. But underlying this is the deeper conviction that something much more intrinsic is wrong with you, that something is wrong with your being itself.

The conviction that there is something fundamentally wrong with you is not restricted to those whose ennea-type is Point One. All egos have it. Just as all children grow up with the conviction of Point Eight that they have done something wrong, so all children grow up feeling that something is inherently wrong with them. This is universal to the nature of ego, and we are all usually busy trying to find out what is wrong with us so that we can correct it.

As with any other point on the Enneagram, this conviction cannot be remedied by the experience of an essential state, because it is not due to the loss of an essential aspect or quality of Being, like love or joy. It is not a hole. When the Holy Idea of Perfection is not present, it does not matter which differentiated aspect of Being you are experiencing; the delusion that some things are perfect and others are not, and the feeling or conviction that you are inherently flawed, remains. It is a conviction in the soul determined by the delusion of comparison. It is a crystallized belief or idea about oneself that twists the soul in a particular way. Only understanding and embodying the Holy Idea will change this.

The Holy Idea is that everything is perfect. If everything is perfect, there can't be anything fundamentally wrong with you, because you are part of everything. The loss of this perspective means that you perceive that something is wrong somewhere, and as we have seen, you usually turn on yourself and feel flawed in comparison to something or someone else. This comparing of yourself to an idea of how you could be began in childhood as the discrimination between how you felt when the holding was there and how you felt when it was not, between what was experienced as perfect and what was experienced as imperfect. So ultimately, the comparison is between your own experiences at different times, and not between yours and someone else's. You feel bad, flawed, imperfect, or not perfect enough in relation to a picture of perfection. Just the fact that you believe that there is something wrong with you indicates the belief that there is such a thing as perfection, which you are not and which you do not have.

This judgment about what is not right about yourself is based on comparisons according to a subjective standard. This standard becomes elaborated later by your superego, your social environment, or your spiritual values. It changes, depending on what you are involved in and what is influencing you most deeply, and there is a righteousness about clinging to it.

Self-Improvement

As we have seen, each point has a *specific reaction*—an activity one engages in, in response to the *specific difficulty*—which results from the loss of basic trust as filtered through the delusion. For ennea-type

One, the loss of basic trust is seen through the lens of comparative judgment, and the result is the reaction of trying to make yourself better. You believe that something is wrong with you, and so you try to fix yourself. There is a resentful attitude of comparing, judging, and criticizing yourself, and an obsessive and compulsive activity to change or modify yourself or your experience.

The presence of the *specific difficulty* always puts you on the lookout for flaws. You observe yourself, scanning for any imperfection or wrongness so that you can correct it. If you are involved in spiritual work, the self-observation that is usually part of it is latched onto by the ego so that you can figure out what your problem is and change it. You check out your level of understanding and development, and compare it to others in the Work. You compare your current state to what it was when you thought you were more enlightened. You measure yourself against your standard of how a truly evolved person is supposed to be, and where in your spiritual development you should be now. There is incessant mental activity. You cannot leave yourself alone. You are always picking on yourself, believing that if you were different, then you could rest. But rest will never come this way, because there is really nothing at all fundamentally wrong with you.

Have you noticed that even when you are having fun, you don't leave yourself alone? Even when things actually feel fine, you still check to see whether this is what is supposed to be happening. "Is this okay to feel? If I were enlightened, would feeling pleasure be all right? Maybe I should be feeling something different." You always find a way to disturb it.

This ego activity is by its very nature resentful, in the sense that you are aggressively and judgmentally saying no to your experience. In resentment, there is aversion, which is made up of anger and rejection toward your experience. You are essentially saying, "I don't want this," to your experience. The resentment is not always felt, but it is implicit in the ego activity. When you try to improve yourself and it doesn't work, you might become aware of feeling resentful, but you are really just feeling the resentment that was already there. This resentment is pervasive in

most people's minute-to-minute experience, whether consciously perceived or not, and is a large part of the content of our suffering.

Most of us approach spiritual work with the belief that if we work
on ourselves hard enough, we will finally hit upon the right state, and
then we will be able to leave ourselves alone. We believe that something will happen to us—we will be hit by a bolt of lightning and be
transformed—and then we won't have to improve ourselves anymore.
Trying to find the right state or the right trick to get into the enlightened state does not work because from the enlightened state we see that
everything, including ourselves, is already perfect and needs no changes.
Enlightenment is our innate nature; we don't need to be hit by anything and we can leave ourselves alone right now.

What we really need to do is to see through the *specific reaction* to
identify the *specific difficulty* within ourselves, then the *specific delusion*, and then the Holy Idea. Only this can stop the obsessive tendency to better ourselves. Then we would be able to see that our
perfection does not depend on what state we are in. It is objective truth
about all states at all times.

This activity of trying to make ourselves better is a reflection of the
distrust that reality is fundamentally perfect the way it is, and that it
will unfold in a perfect way. This distrust is experienced through the
filter of the delusion, so that the judgment of good and bad is seen as
ultimate and intrinsic.

Another way that the activity of the *specific reaction* can manifest is as
an obsessive tendency to prove to oneself and to others that there is nothing wrong with us, that we do live up to the right standards, and that
we are right. Some people, for instance, always need to be right, regardless of what the situation is. This attitude of always proving to ourselves
or to other people that we are perfect and right is a way to cover up the
belief or feeling that there is something wrong with us. It's a reaction formation, doing just the opposite of what we consciously or unconsciously
believe about ourselves. If we really feel we are okay, why do we have to
prove it? Why do we need to compulsively prove that we are right? If we
really felt okay about ourselves, we wouldn't need to confirm it.

The activity of the *specific reaction*, then, can vary between always trying to make yourself better, and always trying to prove that you are good and right. People are divided in terms of which of these behaviors predominates, but underlying both of these styles of behavior is the conviction that there is something wrong with oneself. In other words, it is a *specific reaction* to the belief or feeling that there is something wrong with you.

So now we see the whole constellation: You are always busy watching yourself, comparing yourself, and judging yourself. You don't just see the state you are experiencing as it is. You have to compare it to something else: another state, or a similar state you experienced at another time, or with some idea in your mind. You are not just with your experience. It is always viewed from another perspective, from another place, in a comparative way, instead of just seeing it for what it is, just as it is. And if you look at your experience or someone else or anything in the world in that way, and compare whether it is good or better or less than something else, you do that because you want to make it better. This means that you believe that there is something wrong, which means that you don't see Holy Perfection.

It is very important that you understand that if you think you need to look at yourself and your experiences in a judgmentally comparative way, your motivation is not that of understanding, and your activity will not be that of Being. It will be the activity of ego. Real activity is not a matter of comparing and judging; it is a matter of experiencing things as they are and responding from the dynamic intelligence of Being. The underlying motivation in it is that you are curious to know about what you are observing because you love experiencing reality. This is a very different attitude from that of looking at things with the underlying belief that they need to be improved.

For someone who is operating objectively, whatever comes up is fine. He or she doesn't even say, "Oh, this is what should be happening." Whatever arises is the way it is, and it has a sense of perfection to it. There's no activity of looking for some sublime state to arise. If what arises feels sublime, or if it doesn't, these are just the specifics; its perfection is something much deeper than that. If you are not operating from the perspective of objectivity, you are bound to be operating from the perspective of ego, and your experience will invariably include resentment, judgment, and comparison. There is no alternative. The more you understand Holy Perfection, the more these ego activities will slow down, but it is important to understand that they will still be present until the perspective of Holy Perfection is fully realized.

Being operates without the guidance of the mind. We can directly know this to be true when we see from the perspective of the Holy Ideas. When you are living in the view of Holy Perfection, you don't experience yourself comparing or acting. You simply perceive the world and the whole universe changing. There is no discrimination of who is doing what. The whole universe is acting as one body, flowing this way or that according to its own natural laws, without even the discrimination that that is what is happening. But because we usually operate from the position of believing that we are separate and that there are discrete entities, it appears as if we are making things happen and that comparisons are real. So if you are operating according to comparative judgment, it means that you believe you are a separate entity with your own separate world, and that duality is real. But these are delusions.

When you stop operating under the delusion of ennea-type One, which is to say when you are not engaging in comparative judgment, you realize that you are not a separate individual and you do not have a separate world (the delusion of ennea-type Five) and that there is no duality in the universe (the delusion of ennea-type Eight). So the moment you become free from one delusion, you are free from all of them because each one implies the other. The Holy Ideas are all connected, and the delusions are all connected. They are facets of the same ego, and all the Holy Ideas are facets of the same reality. So it is not possible to have Holy Perfection and at the same time believe you are a separate entity because Holy Perfection means that everything is perfect, and that perfection includes Holy Truth, that everything is one.

We have seen that the Idea of Holy Perfection is, like all the Holy Ideas, not easy to understand or apprehend. This is true because the

Holy Ideas are the opposite of what we usually believe, and what we usually believe is based on the delusions which are the direct expressions of the absence of these perceptions. This makes it very difficult to truly understand and appreciate what the Holy Ideas are referring to. In particular, the Holy Ideas of ennea-types Eight, Nine, and One are the elucidations of reality in general, so they are really attempts at expressing the mystery of Being itself. To understand these Ideas is to have a strong sense—whether through experience or intuition—of what we mean by "intrinsic nature." Really understanding the Holy Ideas, then, means letting go of our familiar point of view, letting go of it and seeing through it in a fundamental and basic way. This is not a little change; it is a great upheaval.

Relative Perfection

To more deeply appreciate the Idea of Holy Perfection, we can further explore the difference between its absolute and fundamental perfection, and the relative perfection of our usual point of view. To do this, we will use the metaphor of gold. From pure twenty-four-carat gold, you can make all sorts of things, such as jewelry or scientific instruments. Imagine that you don't know that gold is precious and that you cannot tell the difference between something made out of brass or out of gold. A ring made out of the gold might be perfectly or imperfectly made, it might fit you or it might not. If it fit you and you liked the way it was made, you would think that it was perfect. If it didn't fit or if it was sloppily made, you would think that it was imperfect. This is an example of looking at its relative perfection.

But from the perspective of Holy Perfection, whatever you make out of the gold is still gold. The fact that it is gold doesn't change depending upon whether the jewelry is well-made or not, or whether it fits anyone or not, or whether you perceive its preciousness or not. Whatever form it takes is incidental to the fact that it is still fundamentally gold. So seeing the gold of it and seeing that that gold is perfect and pure and luminous is analogous to seeing the perfection of reality.

Everything that exists is gold. The gold is Being, and all of reality is Being. The forms that reality takes, such as having the form of a ring or that of a bracelet are incidental. But the ego identifies itself with the shape the gold has taken and says, "That's me—I'm a ring." Then it decides whether the ring is good or bad, beautiful or ugly, and so on. By saying that you are the ring, you forget the fact that you are gold. When you forget the fact that you are gold, you lose the sense of your absolute perfection, and you feel that something is wrong. Obviously, something feels wrong, because you are not seeing the true perfection of what you are.

When you feel that something is wrong, you try to see what is wrong with the ring. Is it too big or too small? Maybe it should have been made in a more modern style, or maybe in a more classical one. You start trying to improve it a bit. But whatever you do to it, something always feels a little off about it. It will never feel right until you realize that the ring is really gold. As long as you don't see the goldness and preciousness of it, you will always feel that something is wrong with it, and you will always try to tinker with it to make it better.

Seeing the gold does not mean that you do not see the ring. It does not eliminate the level of form, the relative level. Just because you realize that it is gold and it is precious and perfect does not mean that if the ring is too small for you, it will feel comfortable. It won't. The relative judgments don't just disappear. They are there for practical reasons. But underlying them is something much more fundamental, which is that this ring is precious regardless of whether it fits or not. What is precious about it is not how it fits, but that it is gold.

This is the perception we are trying to penetrate: to see the goldhood of things rather than the ringhood of things, which the ego is focused on. The ego is always seeing rings, and deciding whether they are perfect or not, and this has become a habit. You have become so focused on the shape of the ring that you cannot see what it is made out of any more. You see its form rather than its nature. And you define yourself by that form. Then, regardless of how wonderful that form is, you always feel that there is something wrong, something is missing, because you are not experiencing the actual quality of your true nature.

As long as you are not in touch with your intrinsic nature, which is the nature of everything, there will be the nagging sense that something is not right. That nagging feeling is the seed of the fixation of ennea-type One. You feel that something is imperfect about you because you are looking at something else and not seeing your perfection. Then follows the activity of comparison, judgment, and trying to make yourself and your situation better so that they will feel perfect. But they will never feel right, you see, until you just relax and discover what your situation really is.

The perspective of the Holy Ideas is that the totality of the universe and of all that exists is gold. Maybe the gold is covered over here and there with different kinds of obscurations, but nonetheless, everything is really made out of gold. This is why there is Holy Perfection everywhere.

So basically, the state of objective existence—Nirvana, enlightenment, or unity—is seeing the goldhood of all of existence. It is seeing that everything is gold all the time; it never changes. We are usually looking at the incidental forms and the changes of those forms, which are not fundamental to their reality. Therefore, if you believe you are a ring, obviously, losing your shape is cataclysmic. Becoming a puddle of gold would be a terrible thing. It is what we call death. But if you know that you are gold, what is death? You know that you will be made into something else next time.

We have discussed the experience of Holy Perfection, and we have explored within ourselves what arises in its absence: comparative judgment and resentful ego activity, and the resulting attempt to make oneself better or more perfect. Now we want to explore more deeply the remaining element: the *specific difficulty*, the feeling or conviction that there is something wrong with us. As we discussed earlier, this is how we experience the lack of holding and the lack of Holy Perfection. This deep belief that there is something wrong with us very often gets projected outside, so we see something wrong somewhere and try to change it for the better.

Working with the Fixation Core

As we have seen, our usual response to the belief that there is something wrong with us is to try to find out what is wrong so that we can correct it. You might think that your hair is what's wrong, so you go to a hairdresser to have it changed. That doesn't do it, so you decide that you are too fat and need to go on a diet. Then you think your features are wrong, so you think you need plastic surgery. Then what's wrong seems to be that you need more money. What's wrong changes all the time, and whatever changes you make never take away the feeling that something is wrong. You need to see that you are always trying to deal with the feeling that there is something wrong with you. There is actually nothing wrong with you, there is just the feeling that there is something wrong with you. What you need to do here is to get in touch with the belief or the feeling that there is something wrong, and see what it feels like. You want to identify and explore this deficient state of the soul that constantly impels you to better yourself.

For different points of the Enneagram, the experience of deficiency will vary slightly, but as long as you have an ego, you have this sense that something is wrong with you. As long as you have the conviction that your soul itself is flawed, it doesn't matter how perfect your body or your mind or your life is. It doesn't do it. You always have the feeling that something is wrong. The point here is not that you are a flawed ring; it is that you are not fundamentally a ring at all. You believe that your real nature is flawed because you do not see that it is gold. You probably think that it is tin. If you saw that it was gold, you would see that it is not flawed and that in an intrinsic way, it is perfect. As you penetrate the feeling of wrongness and recognize that it is just a feeling and has nothing to do with reality, then that can become a channel to reveal your actual perfection.

As long as you believe that you can find something wrong with yourself, you can hate yourself for it. If you investigate the ego activity of judging and comparing yourself, you will recognize the hatred in it. But if you explore the actual feeling of wrongness, you will see that you cannot really find anything that you can put your finger on that is wrong. What's wrong keeps changing. It is a belief that is arising because you do not have a certain perception of yourself. If you really see that it is just a belief, and the feeling of wrongness and of badness accompanies this belief, then you recognize that it is based on a mental perspective, a delusion, and it becomes possible to let go of it. The activity of trying to find out what is wrong with you and make it better becomes superfluous when you recognize this delusion for what it is. You recognize that this activity is a waste since it won't do anything, because there's nothing wrong to correct anyway. So you lose the motivation behind that resentful activity of the ego.

As long as you believe that there is something wrong with you, you feel motivated to continue that activity, that searching. But when you recognize that you have a belief that makes you ignorant about the true nature of things, you see that this is just ignorance, not wrongness. This is what a delusion is: You believe something about reality that is not true. It is a hallucination.

The felt conviction that there is something wrong with you indicates the delusion, the comparative judgement. We need to experience fully the *specific difficulty* of feeling wrong, or of feeling bad, if we are going to discern the delusion implicit in it.

When you really experience the feeling of wrongness and recognize that it is based on the delusion that there is something wrong someplace, it becomes possible to see Holy Perfection. When reality is seen in its objectivity, there is not only the luminous sense of perfection and completeness, but there is also the cessation or lessening of the activity of mental checking and comparison and trying to change your state. You begin to leave yourself alone more, and at some point, you don't even think about whether what you experience is good or bad. There is a sense of settledness, lightness, or softness. A sense of holding and trust manifests that things are right and will be right in an intrinsic way, that the universe is all right and functions in an intelligent way.

So perceiving Holy Perfection allows basic trust to arise. If everything is perfect, then we can trust it. We can trust its functioning and its changes because we realize in an intrinsic way that it is all right. Basic trust means trust about the fundamentals, about the intrinsic nature of things, about ultimate reality.

As we have seen, the wisdom of each Holy Idea helps us clarify our orientation toward the work of spiritual development. From the perspective of Holy Perfection, doing the Work becomes a matter of not doing it from the perspective of judgment, but from an attitude of surrendering to reality the way it is and the way it unfolds. It is a matter of trusting that letting go into reality is the Work, and that understanding means both seeing the delusions that stop you from surrendering, and the process of unfoldment itself. Our practice, then, becomes one of simply letting everything be, of just being present with whatever happens, without judgment or comparison, of being interested, curious, and open to the perfect unfoldment of the truth within you.

Being present with whatever your experience is, means that you are not comparing your experience with someone else's. You are not comparing your experience now with your experience yesterday. You are not comparing your experience against some kind of standard. You are present with it because you are curious about it and want to find out what it is about. If you are judgmental about your experience, deciding whether it is good or bad, or good enough or not good enough, then you are not open to it in a way that allows you to see it and understand it objectively.

The attitude of comparative judgment and trying to change things interferes with the experience, so you can't see it as it is. If you cannot see it as it is, you are interfering with how reality is revealing itself, and you block it from revealing the truth contained within it. You stop it from showing you that you are being deluded, that you are stuck here and there, and you block it from revealing its nature, which you realize, when it reveals itself, is perfect. Comparative judgment keeps you from seeing the the perfection inherent in reality, and your interference blocks it from revealing more and more of this perfection. A judgmental and comparative attitude blocks the flow of reality, and the energy and consciousness become stagnant. What is needed is a surrender to the unfoldment of your reality, and this means not going along with your comparisons and judgments. The surrender, then, is to let understanding do its job instead of trying to make things go a certain way so that you can make yourself into a better person.

If you have a noncomparative and mirror-like attitude toward your experience, in time, understanding becomes the process of unfoldment itself as reality is unfolding within your consciousness. So understanding becomes a spontaneous insight into what your situation is at this moment, regardless of whether you are experiencing a delusion or the actual presence of Essence; you will see it and understand it. Then understanding becomes nothing but the revelation of the perfection of reality in its isness and in its unfoldment.

CHAPTER FIFTEEN

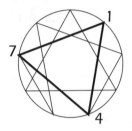

Point Seven
HOLY WISDOM,
HOLY WORK, HOLY PLAN

The awareness that Reality exists as a succession of moments, each experienced as 'the present,' and that it is only by existing in the present that the constant unfolding of the Cosmos [can] be experienced. Only by working in the present can real work be done and real results achieved.

— Ichazo, 1972

The Holy Idea of Point Seven is Holy Wisdom, Holy Work, or Holy Plan. Holy Wisdom is, like other Holy Ideas, a certain way of experiencing oneself and reality as a whole. If you have basic trust and you are being present, you realize that there is an evolution, a transformation that happens, and that there is a specific design to this evolution and transformation.

The Unfolding Design

This evolution happens according to a certain design—a design that is true for all human beings. This design is called the Holy Plan or the

Holy Work. It's a Holy Plan in the sense that there is a specific universal design—which is the same thing as the process of the cosmos or the macrocosm replicating itself in the microcosm. Holy Work is the actual evolution itself, the actual transformation, so it is seeing that there is an actual transformation progressing from one step to another, from one stage to another, and going in a certain direction.

Perceiving this design and this process of transformation is Holy Wisdom, which is perceiving the Holy Work or the Holy Plan. So, again, it has to do with functioning—functioning from the perspective of a design. If you have this perspective, obviously you will have basic trust. Knowing that things are unfolding according to a certain design, you do not need to have your own plans. You don't need to fantasize about how things should be. So we can see how the loss or the absence of this Idea leads you to fantasize about how things should be, how you are going to be, to make plans, to plan for the future.

It is obvious that the fixation has to do with a blind spot of not seeing that there is a universal plan, that there is an evolution that has its own momentum, its own direction, its own plan; we don't need to meddle with it. If we can see that, then just letting ourselves trust and be in the present, *whatever* we do, is the Holy Work. Whatever work we do is the Holy Work because it is the spontaneous evolution and unfoldment of our resources as part of the evolution and unfoldment of the universe. This is the Holy Work which happens according to the Holy Plan. It is not that you necessarily see the whole plan, just that you see that it is unfolding and working according to a design. Once in a while you have that insight when you work on yourself; you realize that the universal process has its own intelligence, it is going its own way. It is when you lack this that you feel the need to make your own plans.

So one definition of Holy Work is work that is done completely in the present. When you are in the present, moment to moment, whatever work you do is Holy Work. This is because if you are truly in the present, you are not in your planning mind, so things are spontaneous; they are going to move according to the Holy Plan, the natural design, rather than haphazardly. That is why doing the Work on ourselves is doing the Holy Work. What are we doing? The Holy Work is nothing but getting into the Plan itself; letting go of our own plans, letting go of our own manipulation, and doing the Work in the process, flowing with it.

Basic trust means that if you are allowing yourself to be present, and there is a continuity of Being, then there is an unfoldment of your natural resources, including all the essential aspects, intelligences, and perceptions, as well as things like understanding what needs to be done. So if you are feeling tired, for example, you might start planning a vacation. This is different from the person who regularly takes a vacation every summer in August. But if you are working hard and realize you are getting burnt out, then you start thinking "When am I going to need a rest?" So you plan your vacation for two or three months ahead. This way, you are sensitive to what is really happening, not just your plan about what is supposed to happen. We're not saying that regular planning is contradictory to the universal plan, but if planning is disconnected from what is actually happening, from the sense of Being, the sense of reality, then it becomes a fixation of ennea-type Seven. The basic thing about this fixation is planning, not just vacations, but planning how you are going to be. It's about planning for your identity, for your life, for the universe, for the whole thing. It is much more basic.

I have been trying to give you a taste or a vision of what reality is like when ego is not the center of it, of what the objective perception of existence is, of what is actually present if we are not looking through the lens of our delusions. So although we are studying the Enneagram of Holy Ideas, this is not really a study of the Enneagram. We are using the Enneagram of Holy Ideas as an organizing map, but what we are connecting with is a reality that the Enneagram only points to.

While I am presenting the objective perception in terms of the nine Holy Ideas, it is the same reality seen through nine lenses, or from nine different directions. Understanding objective reality from each of these directions implicitly reveals the principles inherent in the existence and functioning of the life of the ego, and so the Enneagram is a good map of these delusions.

To elucidate the Holy Idea for Point Seven—Holy Plan, Holy Wisdom, or Holy Work—we will use the language of another teaching, that of the Yaqui shamans, as introduced to us by the enigmatic author, Carlos Castaneda, in his various books. The fundamental nature of reality, which we call the Absolute, is referred to in that tradition as "pure spirit." The Absolute or pure spirit is unmanifest, in the sense that it cannot be experienced or discerned through ordinary perceptions or processes. It is the fundamental nature of everything, and it is ultimately the only thing that exists. But if it is unmanifest, what is it that we are perceiving all the time? From the Yaqui perspective, we perceive what is called "emanations of spirit," of which there are an infinite number. These emanations are nothing but the manifestations of the infinite potential of pure spirit through differentiation and discrimination. So everything that can be seen, experienced, and known is an emanation of pure spirit. This includes not only the physical dimensions, but also what we call the essential aspects and dimensions.

While the emanations of spirit appear in many dimensions, forms, and subtleties, our ordinary consciousness limits those we actually perceive to a restricted band. The band we perceive is determined by our focus of attention, which is called, in the Yaqui tradition according to Castaneda, our "assemblage point." When this point is present in a certain emanation or dimension of reality, it lights up that dimension and you see it. What is spotlighted, then, is what you see and experience, and if a particular set of emanations is continually illuminated in this way, you will take this band to be reality. So the assemblage point is the point of presence which, using a certain cluster of emanations, assembles or creates a particular world view about reality and the self.

Most people have taken on the world view which results from the assemblage point being fixated at the band of emanations of the physical world, with its accompanying egoic mind. The Yaqui term for this band is the "place of reason," which I take to mean the place of thought: It is the reality that is determined by our thoughts, and our thoughts are predominantly conditioned by physical reality. We have the potential to experience the totality of all bands and emanations, but we are stuck at a relatively small, restricted place, and we call this place of thought "reality." This band is real, it is part of the emanations, but it is a very small band; and because it is all we see, our overall perception and our understanding of what we are is limited and distorted. As a result, we end up not accessing the other bands of reality, which contain much greater possibilities for perception, experience, and action.

The objective of the Work is to access the totality of your potential, so that your world will include all the emanations and bands, instead of being focused on, determined by, and restricted to, a very limited segment of reality. The Work, then, is basically to free your assemblage point so that it can move from one band to another, giving you access to the rest of your potential as a human being.

Freeing the Assemblage Point

In the Diamond Approach, there are three stages in the process of freeing the assemblage point. In the first stage, the teacher moves your assemblage point because you don't know how to move it. You can't move it because you haven't got the energy, the consciousness, or the understanding to move it, or because you don't even know that it is possible for it to move. At this beginning stage of the Work, you believe that reality is the way you experience it, which is, for the most part, the way your mother and father told you it is. Every time your teacher works with you, he or she is attempting to move your assemblage point, to open up your realm of experience. So after a while, you begin to experience other realities—you experience Essence in its various aspects and dimensions, and have radically different perceptions of yourself. Each new perception of an aspect or dimension brings with it a whole new perspective, and you start looking at yourself, your life, and the world, differently. When this happens, your assemblage point has changed and shifted to another band. So the work on the aspects and dimensions is very direct work on moving the assemblage point, and in this way you become familiar with the other bands and emanations, and the fixation of your assemblage point is loosened.

In the second stage of the Work, you learn how to move your own assemblage point. This means that through your work, you become able to shift your assemblage point to a different band or emanation, and in this way, more of your potential becomes available to you without relying on someone else to do it for you. For example, you might learn to be open and curious when you feel a particular emotion. You might learn through your practices of self-remembering and inquiry to stay present and not run away externally or internally when you are afraid—instead, you make an effort to sense yourself and understand the fear. This will have the effect of moving your assemblage point from whatever identity and world view was invoking the fear to a state of more spaciousness or of some quality of presence.

The third stage is neither your teacher moving your assemblage point nor you moving it. It is completely freeing the movement of the assemblage point. Freeing your assemblage point requires having the trust to surrender so that spirit will move your assemblage point. In that way, you are not standing in the way of spirit nor directing it, but letting it move your consciousness. When this happens, you don't have to do anything—you just relax, surrender, be, and spirit moves you. This freedom of the assemblage point means that your perception of reality is no longer determined by your fixation in one particular band of reality. It means freedom from fixation in the place of thought, the place of ego. In other traditions, this freedom is called "ego death." Ego death means, in this context, that you are not fixated in any particular band, but that your assemblage point is moved spontaneously by pure spirit.

This work of freeing the assemblage point does not depend on any particular aspect or dimension. If this perspective and understanding is integrated, you will see that you really don't need to do anything except to let go and allow yourself to be moved. Holy Freedom, you will recall, means surrendering to the Holy Will, and the Holy Will is nothing but the will of spirit.

Of course, the process of the Work cannot be neatly divided into one of these three stages. Usually, all the stages of moving and freeing the assemblage point are happening concurrently, with one of them being more dominant. As a beginning student, however, you do need to experience your teacher moving your assemblage point. This is an initiation into other bands of reality and it empowers you to contact those bands. After this, you develop access to your own will, your own strength, you own power, your own autonomy—which means that you are able to move your own assemblage point. But eventually, you need to move beyond yourself as the mover of your process, to bring about the freedom of unfoldment in which whatever happens is a natural and spontaneous arising leading from one experience to another, from one dimension to another, with no person determining it.

As we study the Holy Idea of Point Seven, what we mean by freedom of the assemblage point—which is the freedom that all spiritual traditions attempt to teach us—should become very clear.

Ichazo defines Holy Wisdom as, "The awareness that Reality exists as a succession of moments, each experienced as 'the present,' and that it is only by existing in the present that the constant unfolding of the Cosmos [can] be experienced. Only by working in the present can real work be done and real results achieved."

In my mind, unlike the definitions of some of the other Holy Ideas, this one is very lucid. Holy Wisdom is the wisdom of egoless living. It is the wisdom of how to be, how to live, and how to work; so this wisdom is not exactly knowledge. It is a way of seeing reality in relation to the passage of time, since living includes the concept of time. When we talk about living, we are not referring to just this moment and that moment. The understanding of Holy Wisdom tells us how we can be free within the ongoingness of living. This understanding provides the correct orientation for spiritual practice, which once perfected, will in time become free living. Appreciating this Holy Idea is crucial for understanding spiritual methods in general, but we will focus here on its relevance in the Diamond Approach.

Holy Wisdom arises from perceiving and understanding Holy Plan and Holy Work. Living according to the metabolized understanding of the true meaning of Holy Plan and Holy Work is Holy Wisdom. To understand this, we will begin with a discussion of Holy Work.

The perception of Holy Work is the experience of the cosmos as a constant unfoldment of existence or appearance. There are several insights implied in this statement. The first is that reality is pure existence, pure Being, pure presence. This insight encompasses both Holy Omniscience and Holy Truth: Holy Truth elucidates the truth that reality exists as pure presence, and that it is everything and everywhere; Holy Omniscience refers to the differentiations, specifics, and forms that comprise that Oneness. To know what existence or presence or Being means, you have to experience Essence—there is no other way. You cannot know it through reasoning or discussing it—there is no way of knowing what it is except through experiencing it.

The Unfolding Now

The most central and basic insight is that of Holy Truth: that the totality of the cosmos is pure existence, pure Being. This means recognizing not only that presence is Essence inside of you, but recognizing that everything is presence. This is what is meant by stating that reality is existence, is Being, is presence. Presence is directly experiential; this presence in the present, in the now, is the meaning of Being. This presence in the now is not the juncture between the past and the future; the present moment is the entry into the presence of Being, but it is not time. Presence exists only in the moment and not in the past or the future. Even physical reality is presence, but we do not ordinarily perceive this because we are looking only at its surface without perceiving its other levels. It is like perceiving only the skin of an onion and eliminating the rest of it, so you take an onion to be brittle and stiff and believe that it has no soft and juicy part.

It is interesting that presence or Being is experienced as a nowness, but that this nowness is not a moment of time. The nowness is more of a medium, more of the actual presence, the actual consciousness, the actual substance, of Being. When we realize it is everything that exists, we see that it includes all time. We see, in fact, that it is beyond time, and that time is merely a concept that exists within it.

The second insight contained in the definition of Holy Work is that this presence exists as a succession of moments, each experienced as the now, the eternal presence or the presence of eternity. Eternity here does not mean "everlastingness," since everlastingness is a relationship to time. Eternity is outside of time; it is infinity of presence. It is as though all time is concentrated in the now, not in terms of events, but in terms of feeling. So there is no concept of linear or measured time in the now. Therefore, to talk about unfoldment is to talk about reality experienced as successive moments of now, in which these moments are not disconnected but are always now.

Another way of expressing this is that when you experience Being, it is pure nowness; you aren't thinking about present, future, or past. When you remain in Being, you begin to realize that things change. But these changes do not mean a stopping of Being; they are, rather, a continuum of moments, each experienced as the now.

The third insight contained in our definition of Holy Work is that the continuity of Being, the succession of moments of existence, the flow of the now, is experienced as the unfoldment of presence, which is the unfoldment of the cosmos. Unfoldment, then, is a way of experiencing Being in flow, in change. It is not something static; there is always Being, but it is a flow. The whole universe is like a fountain, always unfolding, always pouring out in different forms—but always remaining water, that is, remaining Being or presence. This is the understanding of unfoldment as the unfoldment of Being. This unfoldment of Being, this flow of presence, is sometimes called "real time," as opposed to linear or clock time.

The fourth insight is that this unfoldment is the Holy Work of God or of Being or spirit. This Work is what is called "creation," or sometimes "new creation," in the sense that the world is created minute-by-minute, like the fountain of water in our metaphor. The water that pours from the fountain in one moment is not the same water that pours from it in the next. The creation is new in the sense that it is renewed every second. This moment is not the product of the last moment, but is completely new and fresh. So there is an emerging, flowing effulgence of Being, an arising manifestation of Being. This flow is nothing less than the very transformation and evolution of the universe, including everything contained within it.

This Holy Work can be perceived and understood only when you are in the present, directly experiencing it. You have to perceive the presence to perceive the Holy Work. It is happening all the time, but we don't normally see it as Holy Work. When we are not perceiving the universe as an unfoldment of presence, we see it as governed by cause and effect, as a matter of physics and chemistry. When we are completely in the now, and know ourselves as part of it, we see the universe as an unfoldment of nowness, of presence, of pure reality. Holy Will, the Holy Idea of Point Two, is the force implicit in this unfoldment, while Holy Work is the action of unfoldment itself.

Cosmic Laws

All of the insights we have just elucidated explain the statement that, "Holy Work is the experience of the cosmos as a constant unfoldment of existence." What, then, is Holy Plan? Holy Plan is the perception that this unfoldment is not chaotic, accidental, or haphazard. It occurs according to its own laws; there is a meaningful pattern to its unfoldment. This pattern of unfoldment is the Holy Plan, although the word *plan* here is not used in the usual sense. It is not as though there were a preordained plan, and the universe unfolds according to it; here, the word *plan* means simply the recognition that there is a pattern to the unfoldment. The pattern is harmonious and inherently meaningful. This pattern, with its meaningfulness and harmony, is always explained by the dominant science of each era. Hence, it has been explained as the work of spirits, as a function of gravity, and as a consequence of random events. But when you see manifestation through the perspective of the Holy Work—that it is Beingness in constant flow—you see it as harmony, as beauty, as an ordered unfoldment. This is one way we recognize the presence of laws in the universe. Laws are simply ways we describe certain patterns that the universe manifests. For example, when clouds become dark in a particular way, and reach a certain temperature, rain falls. This is a pattern. The scientific laws explain this through evaporation, condensation, humidity, and so on. So you can look at the phenomenon of rain as a consequence of a set of laws, or from the perspective of Holy Work, you can see it as simply a patterned or harmonious unfoldment, which we call Holy Plan.

When I say that the unfoldment has a sense of meaningfulness, I don't mean that it has a specific meaning. Rather, there is a sense that the unfoldment is not accidental or chaotic. Things work out, develop, and evolve, as part of this unfoldment. Intelligence evolves, organic life evolves, and we see this evolution as a pattern. We can read specific meanings and purposes into this pattern, but when I use the word *meaning* here, I mean a felt sense that this unfoldment has its own flow, its own movement in a particular direction, that is determined by its own intelligence. The prism through which Being moves as it goes through its transformations is the dimension that we call the Logos. It patterns the movements and gives the unfoldment its differentiations and variations.

We have seen that the pattern of unfoldment that is the Holy Plan is not a predetermined plan, but rather, that the universe unfolds according to inherent natural laws. This absence of premeditation indicates that the universe is intelligent. Its intelligence keeps it from being completely predictable and mechanical; if this were not so, we could discover all of its laws and plot its movement, as science attempts to do. But we cannot do this because Being is intelligence, and thus is responsive, and this responsiveness is completely spontaneous. You can understand this quality of intelligence when you see Being as an organism that is manifesting and expanding. This manifestation and expansion of life has a pattern, a lawfulness, a harmony, that expresses the intelligence of Being. In fact, when you feel the Beingness, it feels like it is teeming with intelligence, and its movements this way or that have a spontaneous intelligence.

To understand this idea of lawfulness, let's look at a few examples. If, for instance, you identify with your image, you will experience yourself as an empty shell. This is a natural law. If you fix your assemblage point, you will only see reality in a particular way. This is a natural law. These laws would be difficult to measure through scientific instruments or procedures, but we know from our experience and understanding of inner experience that they are consistent and true. These laws, then, are a pattern life takes.

The following poem, called "The Hidden Plan," by the Indian mystic, Sri Aurobindo expresses the idea of Holy Plan:

> However long Night's hour, I will not dream
> That the small ego and the person's mask
> Are all that God reveals in our life-scheme,
> The last result of Nature's cosmic task.
> A greater Presence in her bosom works;
> Long it prepares its far epiphany:
> Even in the stone and beast the godhead lurks,
> A bright Persona of eternity.
> It shall burst out from the limit traced by Mind
> And make a witness of the prescient heart;
> It shall reveal even in this inert blind
> Nature, long veiled in each inconscient part,
> Fulfilling the occult magnificent plan,
> The world-wide and immortal spirit in man.
> (Aurobindo, 1952, p. 4)

Here, Aurobindo is basically spelling out what the Plan is, and we see that he is not saying that God has a blueprint for how things are to happen. The universe is so intelligent that it does not need a blueprint; its intelligence is spontaneously self-revealing, expressing pure spirit through its unfoldment. We call this Holy Plan.

You could say that the purpose of the universe is to reveal its hidden spirit, but such a formulation implies a goal toward which reality moves. This is teleological, and that is not how reality functions. Reality functions through manifestation in the moment. It is true that if we look at the unfoldment over time, it appears to be pursuing that purpose, but reality does not have such a purpose in mind. Of its very nature, it reveals itself. Holy Plan is the harmonious pattern of this unfoldment, a pattern that we can only glimpse fragments of once in a while. We will see when we discuss Holy Law that it refers to the harmony in the unfoldment, while the present Idea emphasizes the fact of the pattern itself.

The Soul's Unfolding Design

We have discussed what Holy Work and Holy Plan mean from the perspective of the Holy Ideas, which is the understanding of objective reality in terms of time. In other words, when we conceive of objective reality in terms of change or of transformation or of movement, we are thinking of it from the perspective of Holy Work and Holy Plan. From the perspective of the human individual who, as we saw in Holy Transparency, is an inseparable part of the oneness of Being, we see that he is an inseparable part of this unfoldment. This means that his soul is an expression of Holy Work and Holy Plan. This, in turn, implies the following:

1. The soul is a presence in the now, part of the fabric of the now.

2. One's life is a succession of moments of this presence. It is a continuity of this presence.

3. This continuity of presence is the unfoldment of the soul. Since it is a succession of moments of presence in the present, this unfoldment can only be experienced and understood in the present by being present in the now. This is the "real time" of the individual, the real life. All other time, when one is not present, is a waste in terms of life, for there is no presence in it. Wasted time occurs when there is no unfoldment, when you are fixated and stuck, existing in linear time; basically you are just walking in place, getting nowhere in terms of development of the soul. How much one has been in real time indicates one's true age, since it determines the development and maturity of the soul. Most people have spent a year or two in their entire lives being truly present, so that is how old they really are from the perspective of the soul.

4. This unfoldment of the soul has a pattern, since its unfoldment is part of the Holy Plan. It is a lawful and intelligent unfoldment, which is the growth, development, and maturation of the soul. The Holy Plan for the soul is like the Holy Plan for any living organism, in that it is intrinsic to the soul's nature and potential. This means that there is a specific pattern to the development of the human soul that is different from the pattern that trees, for instance, follow in their development. While there are variations among human beings, there is an overall pattern to the unfoldment of the soul.

5. The Holy Work for the soul is obviously, then, nothing but its lawful unfoldment, becoming what it can be and maturing to its full potential.

6. The method of real Work must be oriented toward the actualization of this unfoldment and maturation. Since this can be done only in real time, the central element must be presence. Holy Work can be done only in the present. It cannot, then, be about trying to actualize something that one envisions in the mind. (We will come back to this point after discussing Holy Wisdom.)

Holy Wisdom, then, is living and working on oneself in a way that is informed by understanding Holy Work and Holy Plan. We can use the analogy of a mandala to describe this understanding: The mandala is the whole universe. Your consciousness, your soul, is the center of this mandala, and the rest of the universe is the environment surrounding it. The totality of the mandala is unfolding according to an intelligent pattern; it is a dynamic mandala. The unfoldment of the center of the mandala is therefore part of the unfoldment of the whole mandala, and we can also say that it is the result of the interaction between the inner nature and potential of the center with the totality of the mandala. In other words, you are not separate from the rest of the world. You are part of the universe, and so you are always influenced by, and influencing, the rest of the environment. This mandala is the totality of your experience and your perception—that is really what "mandala" means. The mandala is a symbol for your experience, in which you are the center. The center of the mandala is a point, and the point is the center of the soul.

Living according to this understanding is wisdom. Practicing according to it is the Work. The central part of this wisdom is the awareness and understanding of Holy Work according to the Holy Plan. So wisdom means living and working with the understanding that all is Being and you are part of this Being; that all is unfolding as the Holy Work and you are part of this unfoldment; and that your maturation is your own unfoldment, which is part of the unfoldment of the totality.

Your unfoldment, then, is the result of your inner nature in interaction with the various influences of the environment. If the environment is holding and supportive, you will tend to unfold more easily. If the environment is inadequate and unsupportive, your unfoldment will tend to be arrested and distorted. Seeing this brings the wisdom to realize that you cannot choose your experience completely, since your experience is the result of the interaction between where you are and what is happening in the universe. There is no such thing as being independent of the universe, since you are part of it. You affect it and it affects you. Taking this perspective into consideration is wisdom.

If the universe is unfolding and you are part of that unfoldment, what to do becomes clear—you just go with it. Ramana Maharshi tells an interesting story about why people don't surrender to their experience: A man who is used to traveling on foot and carrying his suitcase everywhere he goes, is given a ticket and put on a train. On the train, he is still carrying his suitcase, not trusting that if he puts it down, the train will carry it. That's how most people are—they are always carrying their bag, even when you tell them to relax and let it go; they do not trust that the train will take them and their bag wherever they're supposed to go. We usually don't see life from the perspective of Holy Work, which is that things are unfolding on their own and we can relax.

The perception of the Holy Plan in your own experience might take the form of observing yourself all week, and by the end of the week having an insight about how all the things that happened were connected in some way, and then seeing that this insight relates to one you had the week before, and then seeing how this fits into a whole mega-pattern that has been operating throughout your life, and so on. It is the perception of a whole process that is occurring. When you talk about your process, you have to speak in terms of time, but from the perspective of Holy Work, there was no last week—there has only been an unfoldment of your experience. It is a matter of perceiving your whole life as a flow, and recognizing its contours and patterns.

Holy Wisdom, then, is the actual, practical living, being, and work-ing that integrates the understanding of Holy Work and Holy Plan. We have seen that Holy Work is the truth that reality is a presence that is constantly outflowing, constantly unfolding and flowering. We have also seen that Holy Plan is the harmonious pattern of that unfoldment. From the perspective of the human soul, you are part of the larger real-ity and so your unfoldment is part of its unfoldment. Specifically, we have seen how the soul functions as the center of the mandala, and the universe is the environment of the mandala, and how your unfold-ment as the center pertains to your own inner potential in interaction with the total presence of the mandala environment.

To live according to this understanding is Holy Wisdom. The cen-tral implication of this perspective is that real life is presence in the pres-ent, and that this reality is unfolding according to its own inner laws and harmony. We are truly living if we are embodying this presence as it unfolds according to the Holy Plan, knowing ourselves to be an inte-gral part of the universe in its unfoldment. So true life means being in unity with the unfoldment: You are the unfoldment. Holy Work is allowing this unfoldment and cooperating with it.

So our work here is basically a way of seeing the unfoldment, under-standing the unfoldment, facilitating the unfoldment, and surrender-ing to the unfoldment. Facilitating the unfoldment involves the first two stages in freeing the assemblage point—the teacher initially mov-ing it and then you learning to move it yourself. Surrendering to the unfoldment is freedom of movement of the assemblage point, the third stage. Here, you see that freedom is a matter of surrendering to the spirit that is moving you. When this happens, you recognize that when the teacher moves your assemblage point, it is not the teacher doing it—it is spirit; and when you move your assemblage point, it isn't you doing it—it is spirit. It was and always is spirit moving it; the Holy Work does it. This understanding brings the perspective of freedom.

From this perspective, we see that each moment will be the creation of Holy Work, which will manifest according to the Holy Plan through the Holy Will of the Holy Truth. Not only does this imply that you cannot choose what is going to happen, but also that you cannot predict the exact direction it will take. This is what we mean when we say that the unfoldment happens according to its own natural laws and intelligence. This principle is easiest to understand in terms of your inner experience. What's going to happen in the next moment to a table, for instance, is relatively predictable, but not so for your inner experience. We do not know the exact direction it is going to take since it is an instant-to-instant arising.

You cannot, for instance, say that now you are going to experience yourself as the Personal Essence, and in the next moment, as Strength. If you do that, you are superimposing your own idea of what should happen—your own plan—on the unfoldment, and that might not be where it is going. Although it is true that there is a pattern to the development of the human soul, it is very general and cannot be used to accurately predict what will or should happen next. The pattern is analogous to that of the development of a tree, for instance: We know that it is going to develop a trunk with branches that grow above the ground and a root system that grows beneath the ground, but we don't know where each leaf will appear. As with the soul, we can only generally predict the unfoldment; we cannot know what will specifically manifest from one moment to the next.

If we are to allow ourselves to unfold, the only thing we can do is to be completely where we are, to be present in exactly the spot that is manifesting in this moment; and if we are genuinely present, the next movement will unfold and we will find out what it is. So the Holy Plan can only be revealed by going through it—you cannot direct your unfoldment. In other words, to allow your soul to unfold, your orientation must be to be present in the now, and to discover the movement of the unfoldment of presence by *being* it. This is the Holy Work. You can only discover your place in the Holy Plan by living it, in the present, moment by moment.

We ordinarily think that a sense of orientation comes through knowing what to do, which direction to take. This implies that you know where you are going. True orientation, from the perspective of Being, however, is just presence itself. The now is orientation; the only real possible orientation is presence in the nowness. We cannot orient ourselves to the future because we don't know where our experience is going to go. If we are present in the moment, that presence will unfold from instant to instant, thereby creating its own direction.

When you are in the moment, being the presence that is unfolding, that unfoldment determines your actions, and your actions will feel just right, right to the point, because you are not separate from your Being and your action is completely unified with the presence itself. Your actions then are nothing but the unfoldment of Being. Since presence is everything and all of you, it is not as though you are moving your hand from here to there; presence is unfolding in this moment and in this moment and in this moment. The presence has unfolded like successive frames in a film. When this is your state, you feel like you are right on the mark, knowing what you are doing and where you are going. What happens within you and through your actions occurs spontaneously, naturally, effortlessly, because you are not separate from who you are. The moment you say, "I don't want to go that way," or "It would be better this way," you are separating yourself from the presence that is unfolding. When you do that, your action does not have a sense of exactness or of appropriateness; it does not feel "on."

Directing One's Own Experience

The *specific delusion* of Point Seven is the belief that you can direct your unfoldment. This attitude is described very well in the following quotation of don Juan Matias from Carlos Castaneda's *The Power of Silence:*

> He advised me to get used to the idea of recurrent attacks of the same type of anxiety, because my assemblage point was going to keep moving. "Any movement of the assemblage point is like dying," he said. "Everything in us gets disconnected, then reconnected again to a source of much greater power. That amplification of energy is felt as a killing anxiety." "What am I to do when this happens?" I asked. "Nothing," he said. "Just wait. The outburst of energy will pass. What's dangerous is not knowing what is happening to you. Once you know, there is no real danger." Then he talked about ancient man. He said that ancient man knew, in the most direct fashion, what to do and how best to do it. But, because he performed so well, he started to develop a sense of selfness, which gave him the feeling that he could predict and plan the actions he was used to performing. And thus the idea of an individual "self" appeared; an individual self which began to dictate the nature and scope of man's actions. (Castaneda, 1987, p. 149)

When the Idea of Holy Wisdom, which includes Holy Plan and Holy Work, is lost to consciousness, the deluded conviction that you can create your own time-orientation of the flow of your life—that is, that you can plan your life—arises. This implies that you can know what is supposed to happen next in order for you to unfold into your potential. This is different from the delusion of Point Two, which is the delusion of one's own separate will; here, it is the belief that you know the direction in which that will needs to be applied. Specifically, it is the conviction that you can know what direction to take in terms of your inner experience; that you can program the unfoldment of your experience and can direct it in terms of a moment in time.

The Holy Work will happen whether you know it or not. But part of the pattern is that when a person becomes aware of not directing the unfoldment—that the Holy Work is proceeding on its own—the life of that person becomes transformed. Without realizing this, one's life cannot transform; very little change can happen. The assemblage point just makes little shifts here and there around the same spot, even though one may have the illusion that one is moving.

Holy Work is the transformation of everything that exists, the movement, the changes in all of existence—a person walking down the street, another being hit by a car, someone giving birth, someone dying, people being together, people separating—they are all part of the transformation of the unfolding of the universe. It only appears to you that you are making these things happen because you do not see from the deeper perspective of objective reality.

For this ennea-type, the *specific difficulty*, the experience of the absence of holding seen through the filter of the *specific delusion*, is the loss of the capacity to know what to do. The feeling state is one of disorientation and a sense of being lost, the sense that, "I don't know what to do," or "I don't know which way to go." Knowing what to do implies that you know which way to go, which in turn implies that you know what is optimally supposed to happen next. In the absence of the sense of holding, a state of deficiency arises in which you feel that you should be able to know what to do, based on the delusion that you can direct your own process, but that you don't know because something is lacking in you.

The feeling of being lost or disoriented arises when you lose your sense of identity, your sense of who you are. Every time your assemblage point shifts from its customary place, you are letting go of who you have taken yourself to be. As don Juan says, this brings with it a sense of difficulty and anxiety, and there are many ways that this is experienced. For Point Seven, it is experienced as the sense that, "I am lost. I don't know what to do. I don't know which way to go. I don't know which direction to take and I feel disoriented and unoriented." Orientation is being in touch with the flow of presence. In disorientation, what is really lost is this sense of presence, of being who you are; but the way this loss is experienced—since it is filtered through the delusion—is that what is lost is knowing what to do and which direction to take. Without the understanding of Holy Wisdom, the delusion arises and you believe it, and this, in conjunction with the loss of holding of Being, leads to this sense of disorientation.

It can be difficult to apply this understanding to practical action in the world, just as we saw with Holy Freedom, since the level at which this perspective is most readily seen is the level of inner experience. Knowing what is supposed to happen in a concrete situation, such as needing a certain amount of income to cover your monthly expenses and doing what it takes to get it, seems obvious. But when you are dealing with the unfoldment of your soul and your spiritual evolution, you need to remember don Juan's response to the question, "What should I do?" He said, "Nothing." We need to understand the significance of the insight that nothing needs to be done in order to facilitate our unfoldment, which helps us to comprehend the methodology of the Diamond Approach as well.

We have seen that the *specific reaction* of each ennea-type is the expression of the lack of basic trust as it is filtered through that type's *specific delusion*. Here, the resulting distrust is filtered through not perceiving the Holy Plan and the delusion that one can know which direction to take. The reaction is to try to create orientation. This is the *specific reaction* of planning. Planning is nothing but creating direction for your future actions. It implies the absence of trust that there is already an inherent plan that is oriented toward the actualization of your potential. This plan is already present in your inherent nature, and all you need to do for it to unfold is to be yourself in the present. You don't need to, nor in fact can you, plan your enlightenment. You just need to be true to who you are at the moment, and your unfoldment will happen on its own.

But instead of surrendering to the Holy Plan, you create your own plan and engage in ego activity instead of surrendering to the Holy Work. Planning indicates that you have an idea in your mind of how you should be and how you should live and what should happen within yourself and in your life. This means that your orientation is coming from your mind, and that it is determined by a goal that you are attempting to arrive at in the future. It's coming from your lower intellectual center, instead of your higher intellectual center, the source of the Holy Ideas. Your plan is bound to be based on your past experience and therefore, it cannot have the freshness that arises from the organic intelligence of Being, which, as we have seen, is a continuously new creation. A plan cannot be creative in an essential way. It is bound to be based on comparative judgment of your experience, and hence, cannot have the perfection that is inherent in the reality of Being.

You planning your development is analogous to a child planning its development into adulthood. Just as a child does not know—and does not need to know—what it is like to be an adult, you cannot know what it is like to have a grown-up soul. So how can you plan your unfoldment? Since the child cannot know what it's like to be forty years old, the child cannot plan his or her growth—it will have to just happen on its own. Likewise, if you trust and don't interfere with the process, you will become an adult.

We can say, then, that the *specific reaction* is the result of not understanding Holy Plan, and the *specific difficulty* is the result of not understanding Holy Work. If you don't understand the Holy Plan, you have to have your own plan. This is why this type is often called "Ego Plan." If you don't understand Holy Work, you think that you can know what to do and that you determine your work on yourself, instead of seeing that it is a spontaneous unfoldment. Understanding the principles of Holy Plan and Holy Work exposes the delusion of ennea-type Seven, which is one of the principles common to all ego structures. The moment you try to direct your inner process—"I should not feel that way, I should feel this way; I want to feel this instead of that"—you are acting on your belief that you know what you are supposed to experience in the next moment. All ego activity involves this principle.

You might, for instance, sense into your inner experience and realize that you are feeling irritated. The moment you say to yourself, "I must let go of it so that I can feel peaceful," you are acting on a plan based on the belief that you should be feeling peaceful. Whenever you attempt to change what you are experiencing, you are assuming that you know what ought to be happening, which indicates that you have a plan in mind. This plan is not necessarily conscious, but it is an implicit part of your inner activity whenever you manipulate, judge, or criticize what you are experiencing. Even when you tell yourself to relax, you have a plan. For most people, this inner planning is incessant, compulsive, and obsessive. When we recognize this planning component of our inner activity, the delusion that we know what should happen is exposed. If, instead of trying to manipulate our experience, we stay present with it and try to understand it in an experiential way, then our process unfolds. Using our example, if you said to yourself, "Oh, I'm irritated, that's interesting. What is irritating me right now? Oh, I see. The irritation has to do with this"—and so on, this is not planning where your process will go; you are just observing it and experiencing it, and the unfoldment happens by itself.

Holy Wisdom means understanding that you do not know what's going to happen next, and so the only thing that you can do is relax. You realize that if you relax, you are. You become the presence, and when you are the presence, you are in the present. When you are in the present, real work can happen, and that real work is the unfoldment. This is not work in the way it is ordinarily understood, which is that of ego activity; real work is the unfoldment of the soul which, as we are seeing, requires no such activity. If we can allow this unfoldment to happen, the result is freedom, since your assemblage point moves according to the unfoldment. The unfoldment is nothing but the spirit moving your assemblage point from one band to another, revealing all of your potential.

CHAPTER SIXTEEN

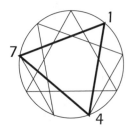

Point Four
HOLY ORIGIN

The awareness that all individuals are born as the result of natural, objective laws; that these laws continue to operate within them throughout their lives. Because all the laws are interconnected, each individual always has an intimate physical connection with the Totality of Reality—the Cosmos. From this springs true originality.   — Ichazo, 1972

The Holy Idea for Point Four is Holy Origin. As well as the above definition, Ichazo also gives a shorter definition: "Everything starts in Him Himself, in God, and everything is going to return again to Him Himself." Both of these definitions say the same thing, one from the perspective of natural laws in relationship to the body, and the other in a more mystical way of seeing the Idea.

What does this mean? Each Holy Idea, as we have seen, presents a particular implicit truth about reality, a certain facet of how reality is and how it appears. If we perceive reality as it is without any filters, we will see these nine Ideas as different manifestations of it. They are inseparable, since they are nine different aspects, expressions, or elements of the same experience. The facet of reality that is highlighted by Holy Origin is the perception and understanding that all appearance (meaning whatever can be experienced and perceived—inner or outer) is nothing but the manifestation of Being, the Holy Truth.

Inseparability from the Source

Everything is the unfoldment of Being, and hence, everything is always intimately connected to Being. In fact, the various phenomena we perceive are the unfoldment of Being. This is a deep and radical perception, although it is subtle: We see that everything we experience is nothing but Being itself appearing to us in various forms. We explored in the preceding chapter the Idea of Holy Work, in which we saw that reality is always unfolding, Being is always transforming from one form into another. Like a movie, reality keeps rolling, and with the perception of Holy Origin, we see that what appears in that unfoldment is never disconnected from Being, since it is Being. The fact that reality is appearing right now as your body or your thoughts or your environment does not mean that these things are disconnected from Being. Everything, then, is intimately and inextricably connected to Being. Being is the Holy Origin, and everything is connected to, and completely inseparable from, that Origin.

So Holy Work emphasizes the fact that there is always an unfoldment taking place, and Holy Origin emphasizes that this unfoldment is always the unfoldment of Being. So as appearance manifests, it never leaves Being, which means that *you* never leave Being. The interconnection of everything, including ourselves, then, is by virtue of the fact that everything has as its inner nature the reality of Being. You are connected by virtue of the fact that Being is your true reality. Just as the body is inseparable from its atoms, so appearance is inseparable from Being. There is no such thing as a body separate from its atoms; likewise, there is no world, no existence, no manifestation, no appearance separate from Being.

This inseparability of appearance from its Source is the perception elucidated by Holy Origin. This is a very deep understanding which is not easy to apprehend. Without it, we can have experiences of our essential nature which actually feel separate from who we are. For instance, we might have a profound experience of the presence of boundless compassion or of indestructible strength, but actually feel that we are having an experience of something other than who and what we are. Essence can feel like something that comes and goes, rather than seeing that our *perception* of our inner nature is what comes and goes because that perception is not clear. Holy Origin is the knowledge that you and your essence are not two distinct things. Essence is the nature of the soul. We might believe that the Divine, or God, is something outside ourselves, residing somewhere else, which we are either connected to or not. Believing that you can be connected or disconnected from God means that you don't understand the Idea of Holy Origin.

The Idea of Holy Origin can be formulated in many ways, depending upon the level or subtlety of realization. We have discussed what it means in a general way, and will now describe some of the different levels of its realization. The first level is perceiving it from the physical perspective, recognizing that we are connected to reality because the natural laws which operate in and through our bodies always connect us to it.

The next level deeper is the perception that everything, including oneself, originates in Being and returns to Being, that Being is the ground in which and from which everything manifests. This is the experience of seeing that there is a Source from which you come and to which you return, and that all of reality comes from and returns to this same Source. It is like perceiving that the waves arise out of the ocean and return back into it.

This is how reality is, whether you perceive it or not. When you are not perceiving this truth, you are asleep. When we say that the Holy Ideas are views of objective reality, we mean that this reality is not dependent upon your mind or your experience of it. It is how reality is, independent of your perceptions of it. So even though you might not perceive it this way does not mean that it isn't this way, any more than the objective truth that your heart is pumping blood through your body is in any way dependent upon your perception of that fact.

At this level, the perception is that reality is in a constant process of creation and dissolution, arising out of, and returning back to, the Source. We perceive the unfoldment of manifestation as an emergence, a fountain of forms rising out of that Source. While Being is seen here as the ground in which and from which everything manifests, there is not yet the sense of coemergence. There is the appearance and there is the Source of it, so there is a slight sense of separateness. The *Logos*, the boundless dimension of manifestation, is seen here to arise out of Being rather than being it.

The third level of perception of Holy Origin is seeing that everything is nothing but Being itself differentiating, discriminating, and articulating itself into the particular phenomena of experience. So there is no separation between appearance and Source, nor is there connection between them since there are not two things that can be disconnected. This third level, that of coemergence, in which one recognizes that everything is always the Source that is appearing in various ways, is the deepest possible way of seeing Holy Origin.

Levels of Source

What we perceive to be the Source, from which everything emanates in the second level of understanding Holy Origin, and with which everything is coemergent in the third level, goes through successive refinements. In other words, our sense of what this Source is deepens. This understanding—that Being can be perceived in subtler and subtler depths—is very specific to the Diamond Approach. We call the progressively deeper experiences of Being the *boundless dimensions*. We see that, as our experience of it deepens, Being is perceived as having fewer and fewer qualities, until in time, it becomes completely quality-less. Many spiritual teachings do not talk about the succession of qualities or structures of Being nor of the progression of experience of Being to its ultimate depth. Buddhism, for instance, considers Being as emptiness or as the union of emptiness and awareness (depending on the particular school), and that that is the ultimate reality to which you are either connected or not. In our work, we say that this is one perception of Being, but there are other levels at which it can be experienced.

The Idea of Holy Origin, then, does not describe a particular level of Being, but rather, a relationship of appearance to Being. So your perception of Holy Origin will vary depending upon which level of Being you are experiencing. On the second and third levels of understanding the Idea, for instance, you might experience the whole universe as love and everything that appears as forms of that love. Or you might experience everything as pure presence without any qualities, seeing that everything is just differentiations of that pure presence. The deepest perception is seeing the Absolute as the Source, and everything as emanations that are indistinguishable from It. Only at the third level of understanding Holy Origin can one perceive that everything *is* the Absolute—this is what I call the *quintessential dimension*. Everything here is seen to be coemergent with the ultimate Source.

To understand this Idea more easily, we can relate it to Holy Truth and Holy Omniscience. Holy Truth, as we have seen, is the perception that there is only one indivisible reality, so there is no duality. Holy Omniscience is this same truth, but seen in terms of the oneness of appearance, perceiving multiplicity as a characteristic of the unity. So from the perspective of Holy Truth, there is only one thing; and from the perspective of Holy Omniscience, that one thing is made up of a multiplicity of objects. We usually believe that everything and everyone is separate and discrete, meaning not part of something larger, which is like believing that the whole universe could disappear and the Earth would remain. So Holy Omniscience describes the same truth as Holy Truth, but seen from the point of view of the differentiations. Holy Origin also describes the same truth, but rather than describing it in terms of the absence of ultimate boundaries between the various phenomena, this Idea describes it in terms of the absence of separating boundaries between those appearances and Being. Holy Omniscience refers to the horizontal oneness, and Holy Origin refers to the vertical oneness. Holy Omniscience eliminates the sense of boundaries or separateness between things, and Holy Origin eliminates the sense of separateness between things and their source, which is Being.

In terms of your own experience, Holy Omniscience means that you are not separate from others or from the environment, while Holy Origin means that you are not separate from Being, your source and essence. So Holy Omniscience is the absence of disconnection on the same level, while Holy Origin is the absence of disconnection between levels. The former looks at the surface, and the latter looks at the depths. Holy Omniscience tells us that all the waves on the surface of the ocean are connected, while Holy Origin tells us that the waves are part of the ocean. And the whole ocean, waves and all, is the Holy Truth. The same reality is being described, with different emphases.

Another way of putting it is that Holy Omniscience refers to the connection of all souls to each other, while Holy Origin refers to the connection of the soul to its source. Our sense of this source or center changes, as we have said, according to the dimension we are experiencing. On the individual dimension, this center is the Point, the Essential Self. Then it becomes Universal Love, then the Supreme, which is pure Being, then the Nameless, which is nonconceptual Being, and finally the Absolute, which is absolute Being. In the language we used in discussing Holy Wisdom, you could say that the center of your mandala which begins as the ego identity, a mental construct, becomes replaced with a progressively deeper center that is real.

Sometimes your sense of that center will be Essence, which is the true nature of the soul; sometimes it will be other dimensions of Being, deeper perceptions of the true nature of reality of which the soul is a part. Each of these perceptions is an understanding of Holy Origin, in which the surface and the center are seen to be one, just as every circle or sphere has a center. The ego does not understand this, believing that Essence or Being or God exists somewhere else and we have to search for it. This belief is due to the lack of understanding of Holy Origin. In reality, the center of everything is always the Absolute, but we take it to be whatever the Absolute is manifesting Itself as in that moment. You might take your center to be your body, which is how the Absolute is manifesting at the time, or you might take your center to be pure Being, for instance. What you perceive the center as is dependent upon your level of perception.

So when you say, "I," it is always the Absolute saying it. No one ever says, "I" without it being the Absolute saying it. The "I" is always uttered by the Origin. No one can say, "I" except for the Origin because of the mere fact that there is only one thing. If you really understand Holy Truth, you understand that there are not two, that duality is an illusion of the egoic mind. You might not be aware that you are the Origin when you utter the word, "I," but nonetheless, it can only be the Origin that is saying "I." We have a case of mistaken identity when we take the "I" to be something that our mind defines as us. When the mind defines what is "I," we have a fake center, a superficial center, a fabricated center, which we refer to as the *pea*. That is the normal identity, the identity of the personality, which functions as the center of our lives, of our actions, of our experience.

We may feel that we are at the center of our experience, but for most people, that center is the ego identity. When we see through this, we initially realize our center to be the Point, the Essential Self. (See Almaas, 1996.) Then we see that the Point is nothing but the reflection of Being in the mandala of appearance. To put it another way, the Essential Self is nothing but the appearance of Being when you see it in everyday life. When we see this, we become more awakened to the nature of Being, and progressively let go of our subtle concepts until we realize Being's absolute nature. Then we know that we are not *connected* to the Origin; we *are* the Origin.

Ultimately, the Origin is the Absolute, but each of us is in a different place in terms of what we are able to perceive and experience, so I am discussing Holy Origin from these other levels as well. We saw in the last chapter that to do the Holy Work means to let yourself be where you are. It means allowing yourself to be wherever the unfoldment is taking you and to perceive and be in touch with whatever the unfoldment is causing to appear—or manifesting in you—as who you are. Ultimately, that is the Absolute, but your perception might not be that deep yet. Many spiritual teachings refer to one dimension of reality as the only true one, and if you don't experience that dimension, the tendency is to invalidate your experience and to try to go to the level that the teaching is postulating. This disconnects you from where you are and blocks the unfoldment. If you see that there are many levels of truth, you take into consideration that there is an unfoldment that goes progressively deeper, and then you can allow yourself to be where you are and allow the momentum of unfoldment to take you deeper. So while Holy Origin means that we are the Absolute, we can experience it from wherever we are; and by being where we are, we allow the spirit to move us to that Origin.

Functioning as Self-Arising

Holy Origin is in the functioning corner of the Enneagram formed by Points Two, Three, and Four, because it elucidates a truth about functioning. The upper corner formed by Points Eight, Nine, and One talks about the truth of the cosmos, while the corner formed by Points Five, Six, and Seven discusses the human being in relationship to the cosmos. The functioning corner discusses doing, or the functioning of transformation. We have seen that the Holy Will creates the Holy Work, which is the unfoldment of the universe. Holy Origin shows that this functioning is a manifestation and an articulation of Being into the various forms. So we see functioning here as nothing but an articulated presencing of Being. In other words, Being presents itself in a differentiated and discriminated way without ceasing to be Being in its purity.

A good way of expressing this is "self-arising," a term used in spiritual literature, which means that everything is an arising that is intimately connected to the source of this arising. The Absolute in its absoluteness is called the "truth of non-arising," since it does not originate from anywhere and is constant and unchanging. So manifestation is an arising of the Absolute which appears as everything without ever ceasing to be the Absolute. In reality, then, the truth of Holy Origin is that there is simultaneous arising and non-arising. When we focus on the arising quality of the transformation, we say that there is functioning and that is the appearance; when we see the fact that there is an unchangeability in it, that the Absolute is always present, we call that non-arising. To talk about an arising out of the Absolute is a contradiction, since It is unchanging and never arises—this is the mystery.

We say that God, or the Truth, never changes and is always the same, while in fact, God is changing all the time since God is everything that we see. So which perception is the truth? Both are true, and this is something that we can't really understand. When we face this mystery, the mind has reached its limit and has to give up. Conceptual elucidation can only go so far, and ultimately, we end up facing paradoxes. While the threads no longer conceptually fit here, experientially, it makes total sense. Just as the atoms in the body are always atoms and always stay the same while the body is constantly changing, the Absolute is always unchanging, while there is always the arising of manifestation out of it. Seeing that these two phenomena happen simultaneously is seeing Holy Origin. You are looking at two faces of the same thing. If you see two separate processes, you are seeing a disconnection which is the absence of Holy Origin.

As I have said, Holy Origin can be experienced in many ways. The conventional way is feeling in touch with oneself. The sense that I'm connected with myself—I feel myself, I'm intimately in touch with myself, I know I am here—is one way of seeing Holy Origin. What changes is our experience of what that self is; as we have seen, what we know ourselves as becomes progressively deeper. At the beginning, you might be in touch with your body, then you are in touch with your emotions, then you are in touch with your essence, then you are in touch with the Essential Self, then you are in touch with the boundless dimensions; until at some point, you realize that to be in touch with yourself, you have to be in touch with the Absolute because you have recognized yourself as that. As your sense of identity goes deeper, when your sense of yourself is located at levels above what you have realized yourself to be, you feel disconnected. Once you have recognized yourself as Essence, for instance, being in touch with your emotions feels like you are not completely in touch with yourself. At the beginning, however, if you are someone who has been out of touch with your emotions, feeling them feels like a big revelation and that you are really in touch with yourself. This is the beginning of experiencing Holy Origin.

For most people, being in touch with themselves feels like a radical departure from their ordinary experience, and a profound sense of connection with something deeper. While this is how Holy Origin manifests on the surface, the deeper you go, the more expanded your sense of that connection becomes. You also see that the moment you use an image to be your center, that becomes the ego identity which disconnects you from what your sense of origin is at that moment. The deepening of your experience of what your origin is, is the same thing as your images and concepts thinning or becoming more transparent or progressively being let go of.

While we speak of a progression of realization of the Origin, in reality we never leave it, as we have seen. However, actually perceiving this is a very deep realization. It is far easier to see that you are an extension of the Source, as opposed to realizing that you are not only an extension of it but that you never leave it. When most people experience the Absolute, they still see it as a source that they come from and return to. To see that it is everything—that even physical matter is the Absolute—is a much more radical experience and a further integration of reality. While this is objectively the truth because the Absolute and appearance are one, for a long time we see everything as arising out of Being or the Absolute, or that the Absolute is the ground underlying everything. To recognize that even the forms themselves and even our images are made out of it is difficult to perceive and to experience because of not having yet fully realized the Idea of Holy Origin.

When you reach this level of experience, even the concept of an origin no longer makes sense. Spatial metaphors altogether cease being relevant when you experience coemergence at this third level of realization of Holy Origin. At this level, you perceive that there is no place that *is* the Origin while another place is separate from it. You can't even speak of connection here, since there is only One—appearance and Being are inseparable.

At this level, it is not as though the forms disappear; rather, our understanding of them changes. We ordinarily think of physical reality as solid matter, of objects existing on their own. In terms of objective reality, there is no such thing, but this does not mean that there is nothing there. The forms exist, but in a different way than we had thought. They exist as articulations that are expressions of the creativity of Being. That creativity is what we see as the world. So there is no question of whether physical reality ultimately exists or not; the question is: What is the nature of what we are perceiving?

If you consider your hand and the atoms that constitute it, you cannot ask which one is ultimately real, since they are two elements of the same thing. If you look at your hand under a microscope, you will only see the atoms, but does this mean that the hand has ceased existing? This is analogous to the idea of ego death: It is not that your personality dies, but that you are experiencing yourself at a deeper level. All that has ceased is the idea that your ego identity is all that you are. Nothing dies; you are just seeing things at a different level. The Idea of Holy Origin means that you are seeing both levels at the same time—you're looking at your hand with two lenses: One sees the hand and one sees the atoms, both at the same time.

Separate Identity

We have explored freedom from the perspective of Holy Origin. Now we will turn to the patterns of ego stuckness that derive from the lack of this perspective. It is summarized well in the following quote from don Juan, in which we can take "silent knowledge" to mean Origin, as we have been defining it:

> As the feeling of the individual self became stronger, man lost his natural connection to silent knowledge. Modern man, being heir to that development, therefore finds himself so hopelessly removed form the source of everything that all he can do is express his despair in violent and cynical

acts of self-destruction. Don Juan asserted that the reason for man's cynicism and despair is the bit of silent knowledge left in him, which does two things: one, it gives man an inkling of his ancient connection to the source of every-thing; and two, it makes man feel that without this connec-tion, he has no hope of peace, of satisfaction, of attainment. (Castaneda, 1987, p. 149–150)

This quote expresses well what happens when the Idea of Holy Origin is lost to our consciousness, which is the same thing as the aris-ing of the *specific delusion* of Point Four. (The loss of the Holy Idea and the arising of the delusion are simultaneous and not causal, as we have seen.) To conceptually elucidate the delusion of Point Four, I will compare it to that of Point Five. Because Holy Transparency is the per-ception that there are no ultimate separating boundaries in reality, such that it is not possible to exist as a separate entity, the loss of it leads to the conviction in the concept of ego boundaries that separate the indi-vidual self from others. From the understanding of developmental psy-chology and object relations theory, this sense of separating ego boundaries that is based on the body's boundaries is one of two pri-mary defining structures of the individual self. The other structure is that which arises as a result of the loss of Holy Origin. Holy Origin, as we have seen, has to do with the connection to our depths, to the Source, which is the center of our consciousness, so its loss gives rise to the delusion of a separate identity. This ego identity, what we call the pea, separates us not from each other (as in Point Five), but from our center.

In other words, the *specific delusion* of Point Four is the conviction in the concept of separate identity—that your "I" is ultimately sepa-rate, independent, different, and unique. This is the element of the ego that has to do with the feeling of identity, the sense of self, as opposed to the demarcating boundaries that are the province of Point Five. It is the sense that your identity exists on its own, separately and independently from all other people and all other things. Ennea-type Fours, in fact, typically take great pride in having an original, unique, and independent self. Holy Origin tells us that this is a delusion, since our true identity is the Absolute itself, which is the center of everything. If you believe that you have an independent and separate source, then everyone must have their own Absolute, which, of course, is impossible.

Holy Origin shows me that I am connected to the Holy Origin and so is everyone and everything else. While everyone and everything is an expression of the same Source, each is a unique expression of that Source. No wave is exactly like any other wave; no cloud is exactly like any other cloud. When you understand uniqueness from this perspective, you realize that uniqueness is not specialness, nor is it based on separateness. This means that whenever you believe you are original, you are merely expressing the ego identity. What most people call originality is this expression, and most people believe that they are expressing themselves and being unique and original when, in fact, they are expressing their ego identity.

So a characteristic of the delusion of Point Four is an obsession about originality and uniqueness, which will color even one's understanding of the experience of self-realization—the Essential Self, the Point. In reality, the Point is a reflection of the Origin, the ultimate Source. So if you still have the delusion of the separate self, even experiencing the Point will not alter your conviction that you have a separate, independent, and ultimately abiding identity. It is as though you were out on a full-moon night holding a cup of water and staring at the moon's reflection in your cup, and believing you have your own moon—everyone goes around believing they have a separate identity from everyone else. You will fall under the delusion that the Point indicates separateness from other identities, instead of seeing it as the expression of the Holy Truth—that it is, in fact, the transition from the mandala of one's life to its ground and source, that it is what connects the soul to the Source of everything, what don Juan calls "silent knowledge."

In a rose bush, are the roses ultimately unique and separate from each other? From the egoic perspective, we tend to focus on the separate roses, rather than on how they are part of the same bush. So when a person experiences the Point, and he thinks he has an independent identity, it's really the ego identity—the pea—believing it has an independent identity. Despite this deep experience of realization, if one has not integrated Holy Origin, one's ego identity will just perpetuate itself through believing in its separate identity. The Point is really nothing but what connects the soul to the Absolute. This is one reason we call it the Point—it is a point of connection between the soul and its Origin.

This is similar to how the lack of integration of Holy Transparency affects one's experience of the Personal Essence, the Pearl. If one's perception is clouded by the delusion of a separate self, the presence of the ego identity will make you think that not only are you a personal expression of Essence, but also that you have a separate essence. You will experience the Personal Essence, then, through the filter of ego boundaries. So, the delusion of Point Five gives the experience of the Pearl boundaries, and the delusion of Point Four gives the experience of the Point separateness. Despite repeated and profound experiences of these essential aspects, these subtle differentiations may persist for a long time, until you see through the delusions obscuring your perception.

So just as ego boundaries give the delusion that the autonomy of the Pearl means separateness from others, ego identity gives the delusion that the uniqueness of the Point means not only being different from others but also, and more importantly, being separate from the ground of Being. While it is true that ennea-type Fours are prone to this delusion, we must not forget that the delusions are ego principles that are true for all ego types. Everyone, then, has the delusion that one's inner nature, one's sense of self or sense of identity, is distinct and separate, discrete and independent.

It is the conviction that I have an independent, separate self and separate identity. The delusion of Point Five is like believing that you are a balloon and that its boundaries define you, and the delusion of Point Four is like believing that the air inside your balloon is independent, separate, and different from the air inside other people's balloons. My air smells and feels different. This conviction separates you in this moment from a sense of presence, which is your true center. Believing that one is a separate self with a separate identity makes the soul experience itself as disconnected, cut off from its Source.

The lack of the Idea of Holy Origin manifests as a *specific delusion*, and this delusion goes along with the loss of holding in the environment and the loss of basic trust. Experiencing the delusion as part of the experience of the holding environment will be seen as what I call the *specific difficulty* of that point on the Enneagram. Experiencing the delusion from the perspective of the loss of basic trust will be experienced as the *specific reaction* of that point.

So from the perspective of Point Four, the loss of holding will be experienced from the point of view of the delusion that there is a separate identity and center. The *specific difficulty*, then, is the experiential state of feeling disconnected, estranged, alienated, cast out, and abandoned. This feeling state is different from the sense of isolation, which is the *specific difficulty* of Point Five. The feeling here is a disconnection from oneself, from reality, from the Source. This is what gives people of this ennea-type the sense of melancholy, despair, and sadness, since the disconnection is ultimately from the Beloved, from the ultimate Source. So the state of disconnection is a painful condition in which you feel not held, but also *estranged* from the source of holding. It is the narcissistic difficulty, but experienced specifically as being cut off, being unreachable, or feeling that the source of holding is unreachable. So we are seeing here the particular way that the loss of holding is experienced when reflected through the facet of this particular delusion, in contrast to the sense of connection in which one feels at home, at peace with oneself, and intimate with the Beloved.

This sense of disconnection resulting from the loss of holding makes the Idea of Holy Origin inaccessible. It goes along with the belief that you have a separate identity, because without that sense of separateness, how could you be disconnected? So inherent in the feeling state of disconnection and estrangement is the delusion that you are a separate self with a separate identity. This feeling of disconnection can be experienced on any level, beginning with feeling out of touch with oneself or somehow disconnected, alienated, or estranged. It can become deeper and more specific, manifesting as the sense that you have been cast out of Heaven, that what is lovable is inaccessible or unreachable, that you are alone and abandoned, lost, with no way to come into contact with what is real, or as the feeling of disconnection from your true nature, disconnected from what is real in you.

The Effort to Control

The absence of the Holy Idea also manifests as the absence of trust because the holding is lost, which leads to the absence of basic trust. So the *specific reaction* that results is the expression here of distrust filtered through the belief in a separate identity. It is the ego activity of control—the attempt to control one's experience so as not to experience the feeling of disconnection. This activity of controlling basically supports the identification with the ego, which creates a fake center, to avoid experiencing the absence of a real center.

Here we find that we cannot separate the pea from the activity of control, or to phrase it differently, we cannot separate the ego identity from the actual activity of control. So the loss of control would amount to the loss of self, revealing the underlying absence of the real self which, as we have seen, is the true connection to the Source of everything. Control of one's inner and outer experience is an attempt, in a sense, to feel connected. Physically, the activity of control is characterized by a contraction in the region of the perineum. Through toilet training, we learn early on to control ourselves through contracting the anus, and every time we control anything as adults, we also contract that region of the body. This contraction creates a sense of center within oneself, which, as we have seen, is missing if we are identified with the ego. In this way, the activity of control gives us a false sense of center, masking the absence of connection with our real center. This reaction of controlling becomes generalized to all stressful situations or experiences, and does not remain limited to the experience of disconnection. Whenever there is any difficulty in life, one's tendency is to try to control oneself and one's environment.

So rather than connecting us, the attempt at control ends up only supporting our sense of being an ego, someone who is cut off from what is real. This controlling of experience is in sharp contrast with the sense of complete freedom of the Source. This freedom is complete openness and flow, since at the very center of who you are, there is not a hint of control.

Here we are again, looking at ego activity, as we did in exploring the *specific reaction* of Point Seven, but we are considering it from a different perspective. There we saw how inherent in the ego activity is planning, while here, we are seeing it as an attempt at control.

So the *specific difficulty* of disconnection and the *specific reaction* of control become the core of this ennea-type, formed around the seed of the delusion. Dealing with this core is usually a painful or scary process, but if we are to see through it so that this core can dissolve and we can reconnect to the Holy Idea involved, we have to go through it. Control is an expression of distrust, so if you allow yourself to lose the control, the distrust will be exposed. This distrust then needs to be explored, because its absence makes you feel frightened and therefore, having to control. As you feel and explore it, you might get in touch with the *specific difficulty*, and ultimately with the delusion that forms the kernel of both. So as we are seeing, every time we explore the core of an ennea-type, we are dealing with a whole constellation, a whole complex.

Control is only one of nine mechanisms that perpetuate the existence of the ego—the nine *specific reactions* of each point on the Enneagram. In time, we see that all the reactions are actually part of the same ego activity. Sometimes one of them is more prominent in our awareness, but they are all present in egoic activity, just as each of the Holy Ideas are all present when we see reality objectively. When we see all of these activities that are the expressions of distrust, we see the nine pillars that uphold egoic existence and constitute the structure of your stuckness. We are studying the nuances of the ego in a very minute way, and as we progress through the nine points of the Enneagram, we are considering one side after another. The more we let ourselves explore and question the nine threads holding the ego together in this way, the more it begins to unravel.

In exploring the question of Holy Origin and the consequences of its absence, we are dealing with one of the dilemmas of being a human being. Human beings have two options: being in contact with the Source, or being in a state of disconnection from it. Being disconnected from the Source is not the loss of a luxury, of something extra—this loss lies at the very heart of human suffering because this Source constitutes your most real nature, the true center of who you are. Without it, life is deadened in all its aspects and becomes meaningless. We don't simply lose a sense of peace or contentment, or the intimacy of feeling at home with ourselves, but we also lose the source of all of our real capacities that we need to deal with and live our lives fully and correctly. So this is not a small loss or simply a philosophical one—it is a very practical and immediate one. Working on regaining the Holy Origin—realizing our unity with our Source—is not supplemental, something to do when everything else is taken care of. It is basic and fundamental. Not to do it is like trying to live your life without your insides, your bodily organs—what kind of life can you live? Without the connection with your Source, in which your life is lived as a continuity of Being, life becomes a prolongation of hollowness.

Disconnection from the Source

So the loss and the sense of feeling disconnected that is the *specific difficulty* for this point is a very wrenching kind of estrangement. To really get a sense of it, imagine a two- or three-year-old child who has been more or less continuously with its mother, and then is taken away from her suddenly and completely. How would this child feel? What condition would the child be in? Even if the child survives, life loses its flavor and becomes dull. There is not only emptiness but also grief and depression. So the sense of disconnection that we are discussing here is a profoundly unhappy state, in which it feels like the one you love the most is unreachable and inaccessible.

All human endeavors are ultimately attempts to regain that connection, attempts to return home, to go back to where we feel contented and without worry, where we feel things are just the way they should be. Everyone is working on the same task of returning home, whatever their projects and enterprises. But trying to return home is a very tricky and subtle thing, because we are estranged by the very way that we see ourselves. It is not as though you were thrown out of paradise as a punishment for something you did wrong; nor is it a matter of doing some exercise or going through some difficulty to regain contact with the Origin. To regain the Origin is, in a sense, the process of annihilating oneself, because the very way that we think and the way that we perceive ourselves is what disconnects us. As we have seen, what disconnects us is the delusion that we are a self with a separate identity, so it doesn't matter what we learn, what we attain, what we gain, how far we go—these things will not reconnect us. Even talking about connecting is a linguistic formulation that is not accurate, since the disconnection itself is a delusion.

Although the disconnection that we sense is not ultimately real, we experience it as real psychologically because reality is such that our beliefs determine our experience. If we believe that we are independent entities, we will experience ourselves as independent entities, and hence, as disconnected. So the return home to our Source is a matter of education; it is a matter of seeing through certain beliefs. But in letting them go, you are letting go of the very fabric of who you believe you are, so the process is very difficult, very subtle, and very radical.

We can fight or complain or kick and scream in protest about our predicament, but all of these are simply the expressions of the belief in a separate identity and do nothing to change the situation. Even if we have an experience of grace or blessing, it is temporary and does not dissolve the belief that you are someone who is disconnected, because you are busy defending the belief that you are someone who is separate. Since God is merciful, He lets you believe whatever you want to believe—He's not going to take away from you something you cherish.

So as you can see, it is quite a dilemma. We have to turn ourselves inside out, in a sense, so that we can see reality in a way that is completely different from the way we usually see it. It is not as easy as changing the lens through which you are looking at reality; it's more like you have to completely strip yourself of everything you are wearing, which means stripping yourself of your very sense of yourself. So how do we do that?

We are trying to understand the subtlety of the situation—how we believe in our separate identity, how this belief is a constant, crystallized, entrenched, and deep conviction that we have taken to be objective reality, and how this very conviction is really equivalent to the disconnection from our Source. As we have seen, this disconnection is not real; Holy Origin reveals that all of appearance is always part and parcel of the Source, at all times and in all situations, universally. So the disconnection is itself not an objective experience but a subjective one that is determined by having particular images and beliefs in your mind upon which your attention is riveted. By perceiving the delusion and by working through the painful emotions connected with the delusion, you allow the possibility for your attention to be less focused through that delusion. In that way, your perception becomes free to see things as they really are.

You may have experiences of connecting with, moving closer to or farther away from the Source, as though there is the Beloved and there is you and a rapprochement occurs. Many people have these experiences, but they are part of the delusion because although they bring us closer to ourselves and our hearts may open some, they are still based on a lack of perception of the objective situation. The objective situation is that the Beloved is not an object that you can move toward or away from. The Source is not something that is an other. The Source is not an object of perception, nor is it a conceptualized percept. The Source or the Origin is the very nature of what we are and of everything that is. It is not only pervasive and omnipresent, it is completely, one hundred percent coemergent with, and indistinguishable from, everything and anything. This perception is both difficult to attain and also difficult to maintain because of our continuous belief, supported by all kinds of things in our lives, that we are independent entities and that reality or true nature is something we can gain or lose.

Complete resolution of this dilemma cannot really happen unless one truly, genuinely, authentically, and sincerely investigates for oneself the situation in its complexity, in its subtlety, in its profundity, and finds out for oneself what the objective truth is. This is not something that will happen through an experience, because as we have seen, experiencing Holy Origin is not enough. The delusion needs to be seen as a delusion, and this requires a great deal of deep investigation and study of the content of your consciousness and of the content of your belief system.

The Idea of Holy Origin is implicit in the attitude of the Diamond Approach toward truth. In the Diamond Approach, the method is a matter of seeing, understanding, and realizing the truth. The truth is ultimately the Holy Truth, and its essence is the Holy Origin. By doing the Holy Work, which is being present where one is, one's assemblage point is moved from one aspect to another, and then from one dimension to another, until one realizes the Point, followed by Being in its increasing subtleties. Loving the truth is finally loving the Origin, one's source and center. Living understanding reveals the truth that we are never disconnected from the Origin.

CHAPTER SEVENTEEN

Point Nine
HOLY LOVE

The awareness that though the laws which govern reality are objective, they are not cold, because these cosmic laws inevitably lead to the creation of organic life, and Life itself, like all natural phenomena, fulfills a cosmic purpose. As soon as the mind's word mechanism is destroyed, love, the natural condition of the mind, appears. Love begins the moment man contemplates the Creation and says "Thank you, God." All men feel this somewhat, no animal can feel this at all. Man alone can know that all comes from God.
— Ichazo, 1972

Each Holy Idea is a certain mode in which objective reality presents itself to our experience. We are using the term *objective reality* in contrast to *subjective reality*, which is reality seen through our inner mental filters that are shaped by our past conditioning. Objective reality is how things really are. Although it is possible to perceive objectively, we cannot take in the totality of reality and say anything about it; we can only point to some of its characteristics. So whenever we explore reality in any specific manner, we have to leave out something. For example, when you describe an orange, you cannot say anything about its totality. You have to talk about its color or its taste or its shape. If you want your description to encompass the whole thing—its color, shape, and taste all together—you can only say, "orange." It is the same with objective reality. If you want to say anything about it, you have to focus on its specific characteristics. One way to do this, using the system of the Enneagram, is to talk about the Holy Ideas. Using our analogy, the color of the orange would be one of the Holy Ideas, its shape would be another, and its taste would be another. The Holy Ideas, then, are not really separate, but are all facets of the same perception. They are specific presentations of reality as it really is. So the objective qualities of reality in the system we are using are the Holy Ideas. We are exploring the totality of objective reality by looking at nine specific characteristics of it.

In contrast, the essential aspects and dimensions can be experienced separately. They are particular manifestations of Being, rather than characteristics of Being itself, so they are more like the oranges and apples that make it up. The perspective of the system of the Enneagram arises from a different world view than that out of which the aspects and dimensions arise. We are making the connection between these two channels of teaching, but it is important to remember that they are different ways of looking at reality. Since the Holy Ideas are characteristics of one thing, you cannot have one without the others, but of course we need to discuss them one at a time. The Enneagram is an objective map in the sense that reality can actually be seen as comprised of the nine Ideas, and the loss of each one of them leads to a specific ego type, and so we see that objectively the ego has nine types.

The Heart of Truth

The Idea of Holy Love is in some sense the most fundamental of the Ideas. The other Ideas cannot be established without establishing Holy Love. Likewise, the core of each ennea-type cannot be resolved without resolving the core of Point Nine. So Point Nine forms the center out of which all the other points on the Enneagram, representing both the Holy Ideas and the ennea-types, emanate or differentiate.

Holy Love is at the center of the three Ideas at the top corner of the Enneagram. These three ideas pertain to the intrinsic characteristics of the cosmic truth, the living Cosmos, or Universal Being. Points Eight, Nine, and One are, as we have seen, elaborations on what this cosmic reality is, what its characteristics are, and how we perceive it in terms of its existence, its truth, and its experience.

We began our study of the Holy Ideas with Point Eight, Holy Truth: the fact that reality is one undifferentiated cosmic presence from which nothing is separate, revealing that there are no discrete objects. Truth is presence that is everywhere and everything. This is the understanding of nonduality or unity, both horizontally and vertically, the unity of all dimensions and all objects. Then we explored reality from the perspective of Point One, Holy Perfection, which tells us that reality is just the way that it is supposed to be, that everything is inherently perfect. This Idea refers to the intrinsic rightness, completeness, meaningfulness, and organic intelligence implicit in this universal existence.

Holy Truth is like the existence of truth as one body. Holy Perfection shows that this body has an intelligence that makes it arise in such a way that its functioning is always perfect and right. Holy Love would then be like the heart of truth. When we use the word *truth* here, we mean the most all-encompassing truth, the truth of the totality of the wholeness of all of existence as one. This level of truth, Holy Truth, is of course, the ultimate truth sought in any spiritual search and in any spiritual tradition.

Ichazo describes Holy Love as: "The awareness that though the laws which govern reality are objective, they are not cold, because these cosmic laws inevitably lead to the creation of organic life, and Life itself, like all natural phenomena, fulfills a cosmic purpose. As soon as the mind's word mechanism is destroyed, love, the natural condition of the mind, appears. . . ." His definition implies that reality has heart, that there is some warmth in the way reality functions. This sense of heart is not actually something that reality *has*, like a physical heart or a specific attribute. This heartfulness is rather, a quality inherent and implicit in the very existence of truth. So when we refer here to the heart of truth, or the heart of the universe, we are referring to a certain way in which the universe can be experienced as heart.

This sense of the heart of truth cannot be separated from the mind of truth or from the body of truth, since all of the Holy Ideas are perceptions of the same existence. While all of the Holy Ideas are inseparable, one or the other may be more dominant in one's experience, due to one's particular attunement. This doesn't mean that the others aren't there; they are just in the background.

The body of truth is reality's very existence—the fact of this existence, its presence, its thereness, its factness. The mind of truth is the intrinsic intelligence implicit in its perfection of both presence and unfoldment. The heart of truth, then, is the aesthetic or appreciative mode that is always an intrinsic and inseparable quality of the perception and knowing of truth.

Nonconceptual Positivity

Holy Love is not the feeling of love, nor the essential aspect of love. Holy Love is a quality of existence that makes that existence lovable. Its loveliness and lovableness is what generates in our hearts sentiments of love, appreciation, value, enjoyment, pleasure, and so on. So we are talking about the quality of lovableness of reality when it is seen without distortion, rather than through the filter of the ego. In other words, Holy Love is the fact that objective reality has an intrinsic quality of being wonderful and pleasing—it is intrinsically lovable. This is Holy Love— whatever it is that makes it lovely, enjoyable, lovable, whatever it is about it that we can't help but appreciate.

When reality is fully perceived, one cannot help but enjoy and appreciate it. One cannot but respond with awe when the Holy Truth is fully apprehended, and one cannot but be full of wonder when Holy Perfection is realized. One cannot but melt in appreciative sweetness when beholding Holy Love. Holy Love brings you the experience of love, but it is not the love itself; it is something much more comprehensive.

It is a quality of reality as a whole and is very difficult to fully define. We could say that Holy Love is the intrinsic quality of the reality of Being that is nonconceptual positivity. It is pure and unalloyed blissfulness. It is the value-saturated quality of truth. It is pure goodness, the Good of Plato.

When we say that Holy Love is the "nonconceptual positivity" of reality, we don't mean that it is positive because our subjective minds respond to it positively. We mean that is how reality is, regardless of how we feel about it. What we normally describe as positive is something that we like, and what we describe as negative is something that we don't like. However, the point about Holy Love is that when you objectively apprehend reality, when you experience and see the Holy Truth, you cannot help but feel positive toward it. In this experience, there are no positive or negative categories that your mind has divided things into. There is no polarity here; this nonconceptual positivity is beyond all polarities. The nature of reality, then, is such that the more it touches your heart, the more your heart feels happy and full, regardless of your mental judgments of good or bad.

This understanding of nonconceptual positivity is a very unusual idea, since ordinarily, and at the beginning of working on oneself, we think that there are things that are good and things that are bad. As we progress, we realize that this discrimination is only subjective, that dividing things into good and bad is arbitrary. Holy Love refers to the fact that when you really suspend all comparisons, all judgments, and all opinions, you will experience reality as an unalloyed positive value through all the sense modalities. It is pure goodness, and its expression is always goodness.

Because language is inherently conceptual, and thus comparative, dualistic, and judgmental, it is hard to convey this nonconceptual positivity. It is difficult to describe the quality of experience beyond all mental concepts; it is "good" in a way that is not a judgment or an opinion. This positivity is not the result of comparison; it is reality's own intrinsic characteristic that cannot be separated from its very existence.

Judgment and comparison block or distort this nonconceptual mode of presencing reality, and because most people don't believe this, it is very important to understand Holy Love. Most of us think that reality can be divided into good and bad, positive and negative, painful and pleasurable. Holy Love says no; that if we let go of our dichotomizing minds and experience things as they are—without our subjective filters—we will recognize reality's sheer positivity, its pure delightfulness. This characteristic of reality is usually referred to as the blissful and ecstatic quality of Being, or the loving and compassionate.

In Hinduism, the true reality is called *satchitananda*. *Sat* refers to its truth or existence, *chit* is its consciousness or intelligence, and *ananda* its bliss, joy, or love. *Ananda* refers to this intrinsic positivity of reality. It is God's intrinsic beauty, His intoxicating quality. It is goodness or positivity through and through: sheer value, sheer goodness, sheer beauty. This quality is intrinsic in that it is an inseparable part of reality, an inseparable quality of the fact of its existence.

The nonconceptual positivity that is Holy Love is not just a feeling. It is how reality looks, how it feels, how it smells, what touching it feels like. In terms of seeing, it is beauty. In terms of hearing, it is harmony. In terms of tasting, it is sweet. In terms of smelling, it has a quality of perfume. In terms of feeling, it is positive affect. It is what truly turns on all your senses, what stimulates and is pure pleasure to them, making you feel happy and loving. So Holy Love invokes descriptions like positive, blissful, ecstatic, pleasurable, uplifting, wonderful, delicious, enjoyable, warm, delightful, and so on.

To understand what we mean by Holy Love and to not restrict it to one conceptual quality or another, it might be helpful to see how it manifests in some of the essential aspects; or to put it another way, to see what the Holy Love is in them. Holy Love is a clear and distinct quality of the very substance and consciousness of each essential aspect. Holy Love is seen in the positive, uplifting, and blissful affect and effect of each aspect. It is the sweetness and softness in Love. It is the lightness and playfulness in Joy. It is the preciousness and the exquisiteness of Intelligence and Brilliancy. It is the purity and the confidence of Will.

It is the aliveness, excitement, and glamour of the Red or Strength aspect. It is the mysteriousness and silkiness in the Black or Peace aspect. It is the wholeness and integrity in the Pearl or Personal Essence. It is the freshness and the newness of Space. It is the depth, the deep warmth, and the satisfying realness of Truth.

We can see from these examples that when we use the word *positivity*, we don't mean any particular quality, but rather the positive nature that all manifestations of reality—all the aspects and dimensions—share, and which is expressed differently in each. If you experience the clear aspect, for instance, it has a freshness, a transparency, and a clarity; and not only does it make you clear, but there is an intrinsically pleasurable quality to that sense of clarity. This inherent positivity in all the aspects of Being is why it is impossible for any of them not to be good. This goodness, Holy Love tells us, is not only an intrinsic quality in the differentiated manifestations of Being that we call the essential aspects, but is a characteristic of reality as a whole, of all of existence within the whole universe.

Our descriptions of the various positive qualities of some essential aspects in no way exhausts the characteristics of Holy Love in each of them. We could speak for hours about the goodness in each aspect, and still not exhaust it. The kindness of the Green aspect, for instance, is not only warm and soft, but it is also light and scintillating and pure. Holy Love is an inseparable quality of the essential aspects, so when Essence is experienced completely, fully, and purely, it has an uplifting impact on the soul, and there is a sense of value, worth, significance, meaning, positive regard, expansion of the spirit, and an overall appreciative flavor to the experience. It makes you love and enjoy yourself and others, and life in general; it makes you love and enjoy truth and all of existence. To understand Holy Love is to be in touch with the blissful beauty of existence which is its intrinsic goodness. When the Sufis refer to God as love, they mean Holy Love rather than the affect of love, or any of the forms of love on the essential level. So when the great Sufi mystic, Rumi, describes everything in reality as good, with a loving and a lovely quality, he is speaking from Holy Love.

This intrinsic goodness of reality is part and parcel of its Being and its functioning. So to understand Holy Love means to be attuned, to be aware, to be in touch with the fact that reality has an intrinsic goodness, an inherent beauty, a delight, a blissfulness, an ecstasy that is completely inseparable from its existence and from its unfoldment. Holy Love is so inseparably a quality of existence that if you truly experience existence, you are bound to experience its intrinsic goodness. If you experience existence but do not feel the Holy Love of it, this indicates that your experience of existence is filtered through your subjectivity and is therefore incomplete. So whenever our experience of reality lacks this sense of goodness, this beauty, this value, this uplifting quality, this blissfulness, this delight, we know that we are experiencing it through the filter of the ego.

If reality feels painful to us or if we experience it as negative, these perceptions are layered over it, extrinsic to it, incidental to it, and are therefore transitory rather than abiding. They are the veils of reactivity, of the mind distorting what we see and experience. Suffering, then, is nothing but reality experienced through our subjectivity. When a person is not perceiving the Holy Ideas, he or she is experiencing some degree of suffering. From the perspective of someone who is seeing objectively, that suffering is just in the person's mind, but as far as that person is concerned, the suffering is very real. So the one seeing objectively will naturally have compassion and a desire to help, not by alleviating the suffering, but by helping the other see correctly, because when we see correctly, our suffering disappears. Even physical pain becomes less painful if you are perceiving Holy Love, which means being in a state of bliss, because the psychological suffering that contributes so profoundly to the pain is gone. It is possible to realize Holy Love so completely that nothing can make it disappear.

Absolute Goodness

The way you look at reality determines how you experience it. If you look at it from a subjective point of view, a mental construct, it will appear dark, and will for the most part feel painful. If you look at it with a fresh mind and a fresh heart, you see that it is good and feels wonderful. The sense of goodness is more real and fundamental since its existence is not dependent upon your point of view. It is only when you don't have a point of view that you perceive that that's how reality is. This is why the inherent goodness of reality is considered to be abiding and more real than any perspective. The sense of reality as filled with pain and suffering, on the other hand, is dependent upon your beliefs, and while they exist as part of reality, they are incidental to it. So we are differentiating between what is fundamental and what is incidental to the nature of reality. The perspective of Holy Love is that if you don't try to see reality one way or another, you will discover that it is wonderful, and it will actually become wonderful. You don't have to do anything to make it that way; it is like that on its own. All you need to do is relax. If we tighten up and get scared, things look negative and become painful. That's how reality works. Eventually, we learn that it is more skillful to see reality as it is because doing so makes our lives easier.

Reality always has the quality of goodness about it; goodness is its nature. It cannot be taken away from it, just as you can't take the quality of roundness away from an orange. Holy Love, like the other Holy Ideas, is a quality of objective reality, so it can't be there sometimes and not at others, or in one part of reality and not in another.

The sense of goodness that we are describing is not goodness in the moral or ethical sense. It transcends moral concepts. Reality is good in the sense of how it feels and how it affects us, touching us with its blissful and ecstatic nature. This blissfulness is nothing but nonconceptual pleasure, nonconceptual goodness, nonconceptual positivity. While it is easy to see this quality in the essential aspects—the blissfulness of Peace or of Compassion, for instance—which is why we used them as examples earlier, Holy Love says that this blissful quality is inherent in everything.

Of course, we can't really know this until we experience it. When we have the experience of Holy Love, we realize that this is how reality is all the time, and that our *experience* of reality has been incomplete.

We usually have the sense that, "Oh, it is like this all the time and I didn't even realize it!" This is a deep insight into the nature of reality, and is different from an uplifting experience. You might, for instance, experience Essence and feel wonderful, without really seeing that it is your very nature. Essence feels like a passing state, the particular cloud floating through your consciousness at that time, especially in early experiences of it. After a while you realize that you have been experiencing Essence through subjective filters, which made it appear as an emotional state. You see that Essence is not only wonderful, but that it is you, and this insight has transformative power. The perception of Essence is a necessary step, but you need to take the next one—seeing that it is the nature of who you are—for such experiences to transform your identity. Perception without insight does not fundamentally change your sense of reality—inner or outer.

Essence is *your* essence, the nature of your soul. In time, the more your experience and understanding of it deepen, you recognize that it is not just your essence, but the essence of everything. Deeper still, you see that it is not only the essence of everything, but that Essence is the only thing that is actually present; there is nothing but Essence, in other words. Then you recognize that the Holy Ideas are ultimately qualities of Essence or Being.

As we have seen, each Holy Idea is a characteristic of reality at all locations, at all times, and at all levels. Holy Truth explicates this understanding. Here, we are saying that not only is reality just one presence that is boundless and real, but that it is also positive, blissful, and wonderful. So not only is God one, but God is also wonderful and made of love. The truth, then, is loving and lovable, which is why we say in the Diamond Approach that you must love truth for its own sake. If your orientation is that you love truth so that it will change you and make you a happier person, your orientation is out of sync with how things objectively are; if you see reality as it is, you can't help but love it.

It follows, then, that objectively there is no evil. We see evil only when we perceive reality through a filter. A person who behaves in what we consider evil ways is a person acting through a distortion. In spiritual work, concepts of a devil, of dark forces, of some evil that exists on its own outside of the goodness of reality are considered manifestations of ignorance, both in terms of believing in such concepts and in terms of the manifestations attributed to such forces. All spiritual work would be pointless if there were such a thing as ultimate evil.

Localized Love

Understanding reality's quality of intrinsic goodness and positivity is not enough to confront the delusion of Point Nine. We need to confront that positivity in its universality. Holy Love means that not only does this quality exist, but that it is an inseparable quality of all of existence, of everything, everywhere, and at all times. It is the heartful quality of Holy Truth, an innate quality of Being, of both its presence and presencing, its existence and unfoldment. We can call the presence of Being love, and its unfoldment the loving action of Being. The fact that this lovely and lovable quality is characteristic of everything at all points in time and space means it is nonlocalized. The moment you localize it to one place, person, or time, you restrict it, cease to see it as an intrinsic quality of existence, and begin to believe that it is dependent on certain conditions and circumstances. If you can localize it in time or space, you are not seeing it as an inherent quality of reality, so understanding its nonlocatedness is an essential part of understanding Holy Love. The moment you see it present in this person and not in that person, or in this person today but not yesterday, you are not seeing Holy Love. If you do not perceive it everywhere at all times, this indicates that you are disconnected from the perception of it and you are seeing reality through your subjective filter.

Holy Love is the heart of existence, and to really experience the whole of existence as heart necessitates having nothing held back in your own heart. If there is a particular emotion that you don't let yourself feel, whether it is love or hatred or any other emotion, that repression will act as a barrier to perceiving the Holy Love in the universe. It is difficult to perceive or even accept the Idea of Holy Love if there is any splitting, any belief in the dichotomy of good and bad within you. In terms of Holy Love, that dichotomy does not exist. What we call good and bad are surface discriminations; the inner nature of everything is good.

Obviously, then, Holy Love transcends any racial discrimination. Whether a person's skin is black or white, he or she is made out of the same human protoplasm as everyone else. The surface may appear brown or black or whatever, but seeing that in reality everyone is made out of the same colorless protoplasm is Holy Love.

Experiencing the lovingness and the beauty of existence is so central to the soul's capacity to value, that even if they experience the other Holy Ideas without experiencing Holy Love, most people don't care about them. The attitude is, "So what if everything is one if it doesn't feel good?" or, "So what if things are always unfolding on their own if there is no love in it?" This is why understanding Holy Love is necessary in order to integrate the other Ideas. It is a foundation, without which a person cannot really work through his or her *specific difficulty.*

The various spiritual traditions do not necessarily focus on this way of experiencing reality. Some traditions say that what is intrinsic and omnipresent in reality is the fact of Being. Others say that if you really see reality objectively, what is most important and will resolve your suffering is the perception that reality is empty. While the fact of Being or the inherent emptiness of reality are ultimately true, they are looking at reality from different perspectives than when the perception is of the nonconceptual positivity of reality. Nonconceptual positivity means that it affects the soul directly, regardless of what your mind thinks of it, and the heart responds by feeling happy, released, and uplifted. We can call what is perceived from the perspective of Holy Love either loveliness—the sense of a lovable beauty—or lovingness—the sense that the universe has a loving quality.

If we don't perceive this nonconceptual positivity, or if we do, but don't believe it or take it seriously—which is to say that when Holy Love is lost to our perception or not understood—the result is the *specific delusion* of Point Nine. This delusion is not the belief that there is no such lovingness in existence—human beings can't survive without some sense of love—but rather, that this lovingness is a local phenomenon, occurring at particular points of time and space. This delusion results in the belief that love is conditional, which explains to us why we perceive it at one place and time and not at another. On the surface, we sense these wonderful, beautiful feelings sometimes and not others; some people have it, others don't; it is present in some parts of the universe and not others. But the actual core of the delusion is that love is conditional.

The Inferiority Complex

So the belief in the conditionality of love and the sense of it being localized are two sides of the same deluded perception of reality. This delusion forms the seed out of which the ennea-type Nine grows and develops. The core of each ennea-type is a complex, as we have seen, made up of the *specific delusion*, the *specific difficulty*, the *specific reaction*, and the dynamic interaction among all of these. This notion of the core being a complex is particularly relevant to Point Nine because its core is what is called, in psychological terminology, the "inferiority complex." The loss of the Idea of Holy Love and the difficulties in holding are colored here by the delusion of the localizability of love, resulting in the subjective state of feeling inferior. In other words, when the loving holding in the environment is lost or inadequate, a belief arises that love and lovableness are conditional. When you don't feel held, you feel that you are not loved because you don't have what is lovable. Obviously, to feel that you are not lovable involves the delusion that lovableness can be a local phenomenon, that it's not within you, and that it must be located somewhere else.

If you had retained the sense of Holy Love from childhood, you could not believe that you are not lovable, since you would still perceive that the nature of everything is intrinsically good, including you. This is why the understanding of Holy Love is the specific antidote for the belief that you're not lovable. When you feel that you are not lovable you are believing that you don't have inside of you anything that is wonderful, beautiful, lovable, enjoyable, or valuable; the soul feels diminished, minimized, denuded of its good qualities, and ends up feeling like an inferior soul, lacking what makes the soul good. This feeling of deficiency is a sense of being intrinsically lacking in qualities that others have.

Since each delusion is an intrinsic property of the nature of ego, the ego could not be an ego without believing that it is inferior. In a sense, this sense of inferiority is true, because when the soul is formed by the ego, it does not experience all the qualities of Being as part of itself. This sense of deficiency is not a sense of emptiness, the sense that a particular quality of Being is missing. It is more a deficient feeling, tone, or affect, that shapes the whole soul. This deficient tone is the sense of worthlessness, of not being good enough, or of just not being enough, along with the sense that something is not right, and a consequent loss of self-esteem. Most specifically, it is a feeling that you are intrinsically inferior, regardless of what you have, what you do, what you know, what you develop, or what or who you are. One of the associations people frequently have with this feeling is of being a second-class citizen, of being lower class or of a peasant class, and so it is directly related to social discrimination. It is a diminished sense of who you are, as if your very being, your very soul, is less than it should be, that what you are is second-class.

This conviction that you are inferior is much more subtle and comprehensive than the sense that you lack a particular capacity, such as Will or Strength. It cannot be traced to any particular deficiency, and so it cannot be eliminated by recognizing within oneself any essential aspect connected with capacity. Also, experiencing Essence does not necessarily eliminate this sense of inferiority. You can fill all your holes and still feel inferior, because the actual substance of the soul—what is experiencing the holes—feels bereft of its positive quality.

Ego intrinsically feels inferior. No matter what it owns, what it has, what it does, or what it can do, it will continue feeling itself to be inferior. As long as you allow the possibility that intrinsic goodness can be located in one place and not another, you allow the possibility that it can be located somewhere else. If you are identified with the ego and anything goes wrong, you immediately assume that it happened because what is good is not inside you. The slightest criticism, the slightest negativity, and right away you believe what is good is located somewhere other than inside you. This is why all children begin to believe that there is something wrong with them as they come to identify with the ego.

If this difficulty is not understood and worked through, it will remain even if you are experiencing Essence. You cannot fully see or feel the beauty, importance, value, and loveliness of your own nature, which is Essence or Being, of your functioning or creativity, and of your existence or life. The issue here is not disconnection from Being—that is the particular difficulty of Point Four—it is, rather, that you are not in touch with its blissfulness even as you experience it. You can be in touch with Being, but cannot feel or see its loveliness, as though the essential presence were covered by a membrane or a veil shading its ecstatic luster.

This is why when many people experience Essence or Being, their reaction is something along the lines of, "This is nice, but what's it good for? Will it help me at my job? Will I have better sex from now on?" Such responses indicate that one is not perceiving its real beauty. This is because the sense of inferiority is acting as a barrier against seeing that Being is you. Often people have essential experiences, but because they don't see that it is themselves that they are perceiving, they think that their teacher is transmitting the state to them, or that God is visiting them, since they feel their own nature is sinful or not holy. In these cases, they are projecting their true nature outside themselves. Sometimes, even if you do see that the Being you are experiencing is you, the lack of integration of Holy Love prevents you from experiencing this revelation as wonderful, as precious.

As long as you do not understand Holy Love, you cannot know it as the nature of yourself and of everything that exists. Instead of feeling love for yourself and enjoyment of your life, you feel low in spirit, or bored with yourself. You feel that you are not good enough. When you deeply and clearly feel this state, you feel a sense of inferiority that feels as though your very soul is inherently ugly or deformed. Like a creature frequently seen in mythology, you might even feel like a twisted animal living underground—like a troll or like Gollum in J.R.R. Tolkien's series, *Lord of the Rings*—that is utterly without any redeeming qualities. Just as inferiority is always associated with ugliness and deformity, beauty and the sense of being lovable always go hand in hand.

This sense of inferiority is not a feeling that you were once pure and became contaminated, that you are inherently good and something got into you. It is, rather, the sense that you were deformed from the beginning, that God created you with a flaw. Because the ego-identity arises originally from identification with the body as being who we are, and because at the beginning of our work on ourselves, we don't recognize that we are a soul, we usually decide that our body is what's wrong with us. When people feel they are inferior, they think it is because their skin color is wrong, their nose is too big, their body is too fat, and so on. This is especially true during the teenage years when one's sense of inferiority is completely focused on the body and physical image. Later, adults often shift their focus: If it's not your body, it's your mind; if it's not your mind, it's your heart—that's what is wrong with you. But it is none of these things; it has nothing to do with them. We only use these things to explain the feeling of inferiority.

Everyone has this sense of inferiority, but most people keep it to themselves because it is accompanied by a feeling of deep shame. You feel deeply ashamed of yourself because you really believe that there is something fundamentally wrong with you, and you don't want other people to know about it. If they did, they would see that you really don't deserve love. So everyone keeps this secret to themselves and suffers over it privately. Teenagers, again, especially suffer with this sense of inferiority, and are continuously comparing themselves to others, showing themselves exactly how inferior they are, and feeling deeply ashamed of themselves but not saying anything about it.

Point Nine's sense of inferiority is different from Point One's sense that there is something wrong with you. The sense of wrongness in Point One is a judgment about oneself that is not necessarily global; while the sense is that there is something wrong with you, there are also things that are right about you. In Point Nine, the inferiority is overall, as though something has dredged through your soul, removing all the good qualities, and that what's left is devoid of any value, or as though each atom of your protoplasm has had one electron removed. The difficulties of all three points at the top of the Enneagram are different sides of the same thing: the sinfulness of Point Eight, the inferiority of Point Nine, and the wrongness of Point One.

This profound sense of deficiency and inferiority not only affects your feelings about yourself, it also has a big effect on your attitude toward your work and creativity. It disconnects you from seeing your own value, preciousness, and usefulness, and makes you believe that there is something wrong with what you do and what you produce, some imperfection that is subject to judgment and comparison. If you don't believe that you are intrinsically lovable, you won't allow yourself to acknowledge your capacities and your attributes, and this not only disconnects you from your accomplishments, but also disconnects you from Essence, which leads us to the *specific reaction* of Point Nine.

Falling Asleep to Reality

The *specific reaction* here is the expression of distrust filtered through the delusion that lovableness and hence, love, are conditional. The soul goes unconscious or "falls asleep" to its true reality and the reality of existence. This falling asleep to one's true nature is true of all egos—you can feel this quality in everyone whose soul is not awake. It is a particular state of the soul that feels groggy, barely aware of what's happening, heavy, thick, and dull. The falling asleep is basically a giving up, a resignation, forgetting and going unconscious. Even if you had an essential experience yesterday, you don't remember it today—it is as though it made no impression on your soul. It didn't wake you up or change you. So regardless of what experiences you've had, your soul is still asleep, not awake to the objective reality of things.

The soul informed by the ego is asleep. This is why enlightenment is called *awakening*—your soul wakes up to what is really here. Many people believe that this awakening happens automatically the moment you have an experience of Being. Some parts of your soul may wake up, but the soul is very deeply imprinted by the egoic sense of inferiority, and this depth of the soul does not awaken easily or rapidly. When your awakening does approach this level, the first thing you wake up to is this sense of inferiority.

The most evident manifestation of the soul being asleep is one's unshakable conviction in conventional or consensus reality, and in the content of one's overall social conditioning. Regardless of what profound experiences of Being you may have had and how objectively you may have seen reality, when you get up off your meditation cushion or leave a meeting with your teacher, you act, feel, and behave as if reality is the world you learned from your mother. When you do this, you are expressing the asleepness of your soul. Even when they have had the experience that everything is love, most people go on acting as though it's not true. We can talk about Essence and the realm of Being, but for most of us, when we really get down to it, that is not reality. Reality is our experience of the world filtered through our conditioning; our bedrock is consensus reality. This conviction that the egoic perspective is how things really are is what the Sufis are referring to when they say that man is asleep. They mean that you take conventional reality, which is just the superficial layer, to be the ultimate truth. Not seeing what is real or not believing it to be reality, and consequently adhering to the status quo of conventional reality, reveals a laziness in the soul in relation to the truth and to reality.

At advanced stages of the Work, after you have extensive understanding of Being, this reaction of being asleep manifests in not acknowledging oneself as Being itself. You continue to think and believe that you are not realized; you already know who you really are, yet you continue behaving as if you don't know. It is as if you are not the one who is having all these experiences of realization and understanding. Identifying with the *delusion* of Point Nine manifests in not seeing, realizing, or believing that you are really who you are; that you are not really Essence and Being, or even a soul. You continue to believe that reality is what the social consensus says it is: the life, world, and personality of ego.

So the unconscious denial of Being or of its value, which is characteristic of Point Nine, may remain, regardless of your experience and understanding. When you continue to think, feel, and behave as if Being were not present all the time, you are expressing the distrustful belief that love is not your very nature and the nature of everything. If there is no love inside or outside, why stay awake to reality? So the resignation, the apathy, the indifference, the laziness about facing the truth (especially one's inner truth), arise in response to the perception of a lack of love, to the lack of awareness of the beauty, wonder, bliss, and lovableness of reality, both inner and outer. When you do not treasure your existence, your life becomes a matter of merely surviving and subsisting. Life, then, is dead, superficial, mechanical, and boring because the magic of truth is not present.

Ennea-type Nines are described as "lazy about Essence," but this laziness is not that paying attention to Being is too much trouble. It is more a neglect of your Being because you do not believe that it is lovable. If there is anything valuable and good, it will be outside yourself, so why look inside? So, unlike the other ennea-types who may respond to their disconnection from Being with anger or sadness, Nines respond with apathy, resignation, laziness, inertia, and a sense of stuckness. Nines are not necessarily lazy people—they can be very energetic and active in the world of conventional reality— but they neglect what is essential: Being. This negligence is not limited to people of this ennea-type; it is true of all egos and is a characteristic of egoic life. The soul taking itself to be the personality is neglectful and lazy about realizing the truth and about doing what it takes to wake up. Underlying this is the fear that if you wake up and find out who you really are, what you will find is that you are even more ugly than you had imagined, so it is better not to look. In other words, because you believe that you are an inferior soul, your inferiority is all you can hope to find when you seek the truth, so why bother?

However, the moment you recognize that true nature is such a beauty, such a preciousness, you will do anything for it. No sacrifice is too great to realize that beauty, that radiant, lustrous preciousness. It is difficult to convey verbally the sense of this preciousness, this beauty, and the wonder and magic of it. Physical beauty is a very pale reflection of the beauty of Being, which is the nature of your soul. If you really recognized that the truth of who you are is so beautiful, so precious, so full of value, and so magnificent, you would devote the totality of your life to it. Everything in the universe, from beginning to end, is like dust compared to this magnificence, and every action and situation is expendable for this preciousness.

To summarize, we have seen that Holy Love is the recognition of the intrinsic blissful goodness inherent in existence. It is the beauty and wonder that makes reality lovable and lovely, the heartful quality of existence, the experience of existence as heart. This is not what is usually meant by the word *love*, but it is what makes love possible. It is the beautiful, delightful preciousness of Being. When we see reality without our subjectivity, without our ego bias, we recognize that inherent to it is this wonderful, enjoyable, lovely, and lovable quality. This quality is not a part of reality, but is, rather, the nature of it, just as wetness is an inherent quality of water. You cannot separate Holy Love from Being any more than you can separate the wetness from water.

We have seen how the *specific delusion* of this ennea-type appears in the *specific difficulty* of inferiority, and seen how this leads to the *specific reaction* of going to sleep, going unconscious. Another way of describing the reaction is that it is forgetting who you are and forgetting objective reality. This is why the particular practice needed to wake up is that of self-remembering.

The Superficial Life

Now we will explore the *specific difficulty* in more depth. The felt conviction of being not lovable is the opposite, in a sense, of the quality of Holy Love. Holy Love is a quality of beauty, magnificence, preciousness, and complete, intrinsic, radiant, pure, immaculate loveliness, while the state of inferiority is a feeling of ugliness and twistedness, the sense that one is a deficient and impoverished soul. This is not what is called "mystical poverty," which is a state of feeling an emptiness that allows God to descend into you. While this sense of impoverishment in the soul—in contrast to its true richness—is the central issue for ennea-type Nines, it is shared by all egos.

With the ego crystallized around inferiority, believing that your soul doesn't have this richness and preciousness, it naturally follows that you wouldn't see any point in working on yourself, and this creates the deep inertia that confronts us until advanced stages of the path. The surface becomes all of life to egoic consciousness, and you get lost in the particulars and activities of everyday life as if they have intrinsic value in themselves. If the quality of Holy Love is missing in your everyday life, your activities are empty. But for the person who is convinced of his inferiority, the attitude is, "Well, at least I'm surviving." Some comfort, some little bit of excitement, some stimulation or titillation, is available here and there. Basically, these superficial pleasures are distractions from being present with, and sensing yourself, and appear to be a better alternative than feeling as if you are a cursed soul. Therefore, distracting oneself with externals is a central and omnipresent characteristic of the ego.

So the state of inferiority is the lynch-pin; if you don't deal with it, it is difficult to integrate the perception and the understanding of Holy Love and conversely, the inferiority cannot be dispelled and dissolved if you do not truly understand Holy Love. If you really understand Holy Love, if you see it as a fact, you cannot believe that you or anyone else is inferior. The knowledge that the intrinsic quality of who you are is love, wonder, and preciousness, eliminates the inferiority. Even if you perceive the beauty of Holy Love but have not dealt with the inferiority, you remain identified with that inferior sense, and will explain away your perception of Holy Love as not yours, or as being somehow incidental. So if the inferiority is not worked through, your understanding of Holy Love will remain partial and distorted.

Holy Love is not just a perception; it imbues all of one's experience with sweetness, delight, lightness, blissfulness, and ecstasy. This quality of consciousness is something most people are not even aware of as a possibility. Most people's experience of themselves is dull and thick, filled with the insensitivity and darkness of the sleep of unconsciousness, and they are not even aware of this. They don't realize how thick-skinned they are, how primitive, undeveloped, and unrefined their nervous systems are. Because of this, it is not possible to understand how feeling can be so fine, so delicate, so exquisite, so fresh and clean, so wonderfully uplifting, as though there were sunsets and sunrises in one's very atoms.

Most of the time, the feel of ego in the soul is like drab, gray, cold, winter days. It has a depressed quality, because its consciousness of itself is depressed or muted. This depressiveness or thickness is the antithesis of the awake soul, and, as I have said, most of us can't imagine what awakeness would feel like. Even when we have an experience of it, we don't let ourselves realize that this is actually the natural state for a human being and that it is possible to live in it most, if not all, of the time. The exquisiteness, refinement, beauty, warmth, and aliveness of consciousness is the Holy Love quality of our true nature. The moment you really let yourself know that this quality of consciousness is possible for you and is, in fact, your natural state, why would you strive for anything else? What does it mean to have a "good life," if you're not working on allowing that wonderful exquisiteness to inform your consciousness? That is the essence of the spiritual quest: bringing this quality to our consciousness. And the *specific reaction* of sleep, apathy, and laziness is about just this task. With this *reaction*, it becomes more important to watch a football game than to work on oneself. It seems more exciting to watch one person bash into another one—this is a way to make us feel *something* through the thick skin of our consciousness. Or we want to go on a roller-coaster ride in order to feel some aliveness, or get involved in all sorts of activities and entertainments as a way of distracting ourselves from feeling what we believe is our inferiority, and from the deadness of our experience. We really don't need to do anything external to feel alive; all we need to do is turn away from these distractions and be committed to our true nature, and worship it totally.

When we see the Holy Love quality of the nature of Being, we see its preciousness. Its radiant glory feels like a sunrise. Inferiority is the negation of this glory, and the *specific reaction* is an attempt to get away from that diminished sense of self. What is needed is to confront that part of our psyche rather than to run from it, so that we are not afraid to wake up to ourselves.

As we understand it, the sense of inferiority develops not because you are a child, or you happen to have some defect in your body or some social lack in your environment. Its origin stems from the fact of not recognizing the precious quality of your Beingness, and this lack of recognition is universal, with very few exceptions. Even if you felt loved by your parents, for instance, they didn't necessarily love you because they could see the preciousness of your Being; they loved you for what you did, how you behaved, whether you were smart or cute or pretty, and so on. Because the preciousness of your nature itself was not seen and loved, you would still feel inferior.

There are, of course, more traumatic reasons why children grow up with the feeling of inferiority beyond the fact that their preciousness was not seen and held. Some children are mistreated, unloved, neglected, and so on. Any lack of holding—physical, emotional or spiritual—will affect the child in such a way as to engender a sense of inferiority. The child does not see that its soul has that innate, intrinsic, and fundamental quality of being the most precious and wonderful thing in the whole universe. The child loses this sense of herself, and part of the resulting sleep is identifying with the consensus reality in which the parents live. Later, you explain the feelings of inferiority with whatever means you can find, such as physical appearance, behaviors, intelligence, capacities, and so on, with children of different ages emphasizing different things.

As long as we look for causes and solutions on this superficial level, we cannot resolve our inferiority complex. A sense of mastery and accomplishment will not resolve the issue. It may diminish it a little, but it is only a compensation. The issue is not helplessness. The resolution is a sense of preciousness and inner beauty, which, when we contact it, is so powerful and radiant that it makes all else insignificant.

As we mentioned earlier, the phenomenon of social discrimination is closely connected with this *specific difficulty* of inferiority. When you discriminate against someone else, you are compensating for your own sense of inferiority; this is obviously a rejection of another person. Discrimination is based on value judgments of inferiority and superiority, and is rampant in our society. There are many kinds of discrimination, such as racial and cultural, in which one skin color or ethnic group believes itself superior to another. Black people, for example, were and are discriminated against in this country and in many others, as well. Some cultures choose a scapegoat, based on religion, race, or culture; or there is class discrimination, as in India, where the untouchable caste is supposed to be inferior to, and to contaminate, those of higher castes who touch them. Gender discrimination, in which women are typically seen as inferior to men, is pervasive. Children are often discriminated against, in the sense of not being taken seriously because they are not adults. To discriminate against someone is to inflict great suffering, since it touches the wound of inferiority that everyone has. It will bring up a tremendous lack of self-esteem, as well as a deep sense of shame about this painful wound within. Any discrimination of any sort—relating to another as if they are less than you—is a projection of your own sense of inferiority.

Many of us have feelings of inferiority about one thing or another. "My parents were poor and I didn't get as many toys as the other kids, so I always feel inferior. I didn't go to the right schools, so there is something inferior about me. I was never popular, so there must be something wrong with me." There are so many causes that people pin their sense of inferiority on, causes which, from the outside, don't make much sense. This indicates that there is a predisposition toward feeling inferior. To really see the delusion of ennea-type Nine, we have to see through all of these causes that our minds have locked onto, and see the naked sense of inferiority itself—the sense that we lack intrinsic goodness.

Only when we experience this naked sense of diminution does it become possible to see that it is based on the false belief that there are some places in the universe that have intrinsic goodness and some places that don't. Without seeing this, you are operating on the unconscious belief that you are inferior and taking this belief to be reality. In this case, there is no point in becoming more conscious, so distracting oneself is the only sensible thing to do. Only when we experience our sense of inferiority in its rawness can we begin to appreciate our lack of understanding of Holy Love, and begin to move beyond this error.

CHAPTER EIGHTEEN

Point Six
HOLY STRENGTH, HOLY FAITH

The awareness that the Cosmos is a self-regulating mechanism, existing in a state of balance, and as long as the objective laws which govern this balance are respected, an individual can exist in a state of harmony with Reality, moving toward his own personal fulfillment. Faith is a Holy Idea, not a belief. It is the certitude that each of us has an Essence and that this Essence coming from God, belongs to God. — Ichazo, 1972

While Holy Love explicates the objective view of existence in the triangle of Holy Ideas formed by the Nine, Six, and Three enneatypes, Holy Faith or Holy Strength refers to the experience of the soul, or the view of man, in relation to this objective view. We have seen that the Holy Ideas in the upper corner of the Enneagram describe the truth of all of existence, that the Holy Ideas of the Six corner focus on what a human being is, in relationship to that existence, and that the Holy Ideas of the Three corner refer to how functioning and change occur.

231

From the perspective of ennea-type Five, the view of man is that his soul is inseparable from the rest of existence—this is Holy Omniscience or Holy Transparency. So if we are perceiving reality objectively, we see that the human being is inseparable from all the rest of existence and can never be removed from it. The perception of Holy Transparency shows us that the feeling of separateness and isolation, the sense of an ultimate entityhood, is a delusion.

From the perspective of ennea-type Seven, we saw that the view of man is reflected in what we call the Holy Work: The soul's development and unfoldment is inseparable from the unfoldment of the totality of existence. So not only is the human being inseparable from the rest of creation, but his evolution—both personal and collective—is also inseparable from it. The soul's unfoldment, then, is part of the unfoldment of the totality of the universe.

The Essence of the Soul

A similar insight is reflected at ennea-type Six: Holy Faith is the experiential realization that Being is the inner reality and inner truth of every human being. This understanding also underlies that of the Four ennea-type, Holy Origin, with which it is sometimes confused. Holy Origin is the objective view that you are never disconnected from your center, which is Essence, at whatever level it is operating on; that this Origin is the Source of the soul and its final home; and that this Origin is characterized by the Ideas of truth, perfection, and intrinsic goodness, the Holy Ideas at the top of the Enneagram. So these three qualities characterize the Origin from which the soul is never separate. Holy Faith, in contrast, is not a matter of feeling connected to this Source, but rather a matter of realizing that this Origin actually exists and that it is your inner nature. Regardless of whether or not one feels connected to one's essential origin, one knows from experience that it does actually exist. This is Holy Faith. Holy Origin depends upon the realization of Holy Faith, because there can be no question of connection or lack of it if you do not know that there is such a reality to be connected to. So the primary insight of Holy Strength and Holy Faith is that Essence exists and that it is really your true nature. The recognition is that one has an essence.

We can see from this that Holy Origin is an extension of Holy Faith—it is not only a matter of realizing that there is such a perfect truth, but of realizing that one is an expression of it and hence, cannot be disconnected from it. While Holy Origin includes Holy Faith, it is perceiving from a slightly different angle; it is not about the recognition that there is an Origin, but that we are never separate from it, so the recognition of that Origin—the insight of Holy Faith—is implied. In other words, Holy Faith is the experiential recognition that there is truth within your soul that is perfect and intrinsically good and lovable. One can experience Essence but not recognize it as one's fundamental nature. So to recognize Essence as your essence is not the same thing as just experiencing it.

Most simply, Holy Faith is due to the recognition of Essence. By recognition, we mean the direct experience of Essence as one's true existence (Holy Truth), as perfect existence (Holy Perfection), and as intrinsically good and loving existence (Holy Love). To completely recognize Essence means to recognize the three qualities of *satchitananda*—that it is a real presence, that it is intrinsically good, and that it is just the way things are supposed to be. We can refer to this realization of Essence as Holy Strength, meaning that the strength of the soul lies in its nature as Essence. Perceiving this truth is seeing one's nature through this Holy Idea. The fact that Essence is the fundamental nature of the soul is its objective strength, and is what gives the soul its feeling of strength. To perceive this truth is to know one's reality through the lens of Holy Strength. Holy Faith, then, is the effect of this realization or recognition upon the soul.

Another way of stating this insight is that Holy Strength is the perception that the inner nature of the human being is Essence, and that as a result of this perception, the transformation that occurs in the soul is Holy Faith. So we are differentiating between the recognition of Essence as the inner truth of the soul and the effect of this experience on the soul. Holy Faith is a kind of knowledge, then, a conviction, a certainty. This use of the word *faith* is different from the conventional use of the term, which refers to a mental belief that is not based on our direct experience, but rather, on what we've been told by someone. So Holy Faith is not a matter of reading the Bible and subsequently having faith in Christ; Holy Faith means that you have actually had the experience of contacting Christ, so that your faith that there is a Christ stems from your own experience. However, it is possible for someone to have the direct recognition of Essence as one's inner nature without the faith developing. The depth of the faith generated depends on the person and on the depth and completeness of the experience.

This distinction between Holy Strength and Holy Faith is similar to the distinction we made about Holy Love—between the recognition of the intrinsic goodness and beauty of Being, and the soul's response of loving reality. The only difference is that here, we are using two different names for these two sides of the Holy Idea for ennea-type Six. We will find a similar situation when we come to Holy Hope. So all the Holy Ideas of the central triangle of the Enneagram (Points Nine, Six, and Three) are unique in that they refer to both a particular perception of reality and also to the effect of this perception on the soul. The remaining Holy Ideas refer only to perceptions of objective reality.

Essential Faith

The recognition of Essence is not yet faith, but it is a necessary element for faith. Faith is an objective experience rather than a mental belief, as I have explained, and refers to a transformation of the soul. When faith is present, the consciousness is changed in a fundamental way, changed in its very substance. So it is not a mental belief based on an inner experience; it is not a matter of having an experience of Essence, and thereafter knowing in your mind that Essence does indeed exist. It is really a transformation that takes place in the soul, in which Essence as one's nature becomes a certainty, a given, and not something that you need to remember or remind yourself of. This knowing has become integrated and has transformed your consciousness itself. As long as one's faith is only mental, doubt can creep in, and since doubt itself is mental, something that is only a memory is an easy target for it. When real faith is present, a transformation has taken place and there is no going back. Things might arise that weaken or challenge your faith, but it is there, regardless of what happens.

Two important insights are necessary for the realization of Holy Faith. The first is the experience that there is a truth that exists in a fundamental and genuine way, a truth not constructed from beliefs and ideals. This recognition must include the insights of Holy Truth, Holy Love, and Holy Perfection, at least to some rudimentary degree. The second insight is the recognition that this truth of Essence is the inner reality of the soul, including *your* soul, and not merely something that exists somewhere. We are making the distinction here between an experience of Essence that doesn't feel like you, that feels like something alien, or something imposed on you, or induced or transmitted by someone else, and the experience of Essence as your own inner reality. This is an enormous distinction. Many people experience Essence and believe that they are just feeling their spiritual teacher or that they have been hypnotized, and this implies a lack of recognition of Essence as their nature.

Both these insights are needed for the transformation of the soul into the condition of faith. So faith includes the certainty of the existence of Essence and also the effect of recognizing that it is the nature of your own soul. When faith is present, one feels trust, confidence, security, a sense of support, relaxation, and courage. These are the qualities of a soul that has faith. You have the sense that even if you are not in touch with it right now, when you look deeply into yourself, you will find Essence there. This gives you confidence, trust, and courage.

All of these are implicit characteristics of what we call "faith," but they don't actually convey the felt sense of it. It is an actual feeling, a particular state of the soul. It is similar to the feeling you have when you genuinely say to someone, "I have faith in you," or "I believe in you," but here, you are feeling it in terms of your inner reality. When you tell someone that you believe in them, you are not saying that you believe they are *this,* or that you believe *that* about them; you are saying that you have trust and confidence that the person will be able to be or do what is required. To have faith in that person means that you have an implicit certainty that he or she is dependable and will come through. You can have such faith in a person, in a situation, in a teaching or a teacher, but with Holy Faith, we are talking about faith in the inner reality itself. It is the certainty that arises from the direct experience that there is a true existence that is beautiful and loving; the feeling of security and support that arises because of the recognition of it as our inner reality; and the trust in it that arises from the recognition of its qualities.

The realization of Holy Faith is a transformation in the very experience of who you are. It is not based on a belief or a conviction; nor is it a memory. It is *knowing* that there is Essence and that it is one's inner nature, taken for granted as a given. This faith is a tremendous help on the path because when things get difficult and you're scared or unhappy, when you are not experiencing Essence and there is no one around to help you connect with it, what keeps you going besides faith? Without faith, it becomes very difficult to continue. The faith has to be real faith, because when you're terrified, feeling disintegrated, or deeply hurt, a mental belief will not get you through. The true transformation that we call faith gives the soul courage which makes it persevere, because it has the unquestioned certainty that there is true reality and support even though it is not explicitly obvious at that moment. The Spanish Christian mystic, St. John of the Cross, discusses this faith in his writings about the "dark night of the soul." When you don't know what is happening and you don't feel any support, only this faith will keep you going; trying to remember what your teacher said or what you experienced yesterday will not.

This faith is a knowing in the heart rather than mental knowledge. It is one of the developments of the heart represented by the Holy Ideas of the central triangle, which are called the "three theological virtues." This faith makes it possible to persevere and not lose heart when there is a disappointment, and ensures that despair cannot dominate completely. It arises in degrees, depending upon the duration and extent of one's direct experience and recognition of Essence. Our experiences of Essence are different, varying in degree, depth, and extent of completeness. The more one experiences Essence, the more *fully* one experiences it; and the more one recognizes its various qualities and perfections, the more one's faith grows and deepens. Faith, then, is something that can develop, deepen, and expand. When Essence is experienced from the perspective of Holy Truth, that is, from a more universal and cosmic level, then one's resulting faith is also more universal and cosmic.

There are three levels of experiencing faith. The first level results from experiencing Essence as your inner nature; this is the individual level of faith. The second is the boundless level, in which you recognize Essence as the nature of everything. At this level, you have faith in God or reality. The third level is from the perspective of reality, the level of the Holy Ideas. Here, you experience and understand reality directly and objectively, perceiving and understanding its dynamics—what it is and how it works. The faith of this level is the most complete and total, since it arises from experiencing reality in its totality. We can say, then, that the understanding of the various Holy Ideas contributes to the development of faith, but the central and indispensable element in the arising and development of faith is the recognition of Essence as one's own essence.

To talk about faith is to talk about an important development of the path, because it is the expression of a profound transformation in one's soul. At the beginning of the Work, we can talk about the goal being the realization of the truth, understanding what reality really is. The path is the process by which the soul comes into harmony with that reality, and faith is a by-product of that harmonization. When the soul is in complete harmony with reality, the experience is beyond faith; it is then simply the direct experience of the strength of Essence, which we call Holy Strength.

In Holy Faith, the heart is completely convinced and certain of Essence through direct contact with it. This particular opening of the heart is what we mean by faith representing a transformation in the soul. The soul transforms in response to many factors as it realizes its true nature, and part of this transformation is the development of what we call Holy Faith. The very substance of the soul becomes purified, developed, and matured, until its complete fruition, in which the soul is completely transparent to, and in harmony with, objective reality. Faith, then, becomes implicit.

Unlike the faith that we can have in another person, in a situation, in a particular teaching, and so on, Holy Faith is enduring because it is based on the recognition of our self-existing and eternal nature. Our faith in someone might change, for example, if that person begins to behave differently. Essence, on the other hand, always behaves in the same way. So as you recognize it as who you really are, your soul is permanently changed. It is as though the very molecular structure of your soul transforms, taking another shape. So reflecting the immutability of Essence, the faith that develops is no passing state, although it can deepen, develop, and mature.

If you have a conscious or unconscious belief that is opposed to faith, it must be exposed and understood; the experience of Essence itself might not completely dissolve it. If, for example, you have an experience of Essence one day, and the next day you say to yourself, "That wasn't really who I am—I'm really a terrible person," what does this mean? It reveals that you have an underlying conviction about who you are and what you are like that runs counter to the experience of Essence; so for you to develop faith, this belief must be inquired into. On the other hand, just seeing the illusion itself—recognizing that you don't believe in Essence and don't recognize it as your true nature—is not enough. The actual experience of Essence is necessary. We have to have the experience of Essence and we have to work on the barriers to it in order to develop faith.

We can see that Holy Faith is similar to basic trust and to the sense of real holding. When we pursue and deeply explore any of the Holy Ideas, it always leads us to basic trust and a sense of holding, because all three are reflections of the same thing. The absence of the Holy

Idea leads to a *specific delusion;* the loss or inadequacy of the holding environment is reflected in the *specific difficulty;* and the absence of basic trust is reflected in the *specific reaction.* So when the triad of Holy Idea, basic trust, and holding, are lost, they are replaced by the egoic triad that forms the core of each ennea-type.

Cynicism

For ennea-type Six, when Holy Faith is lost, there is no faith, knowledge, or certainty that our inner nature, that of others, and of the universe, is an essence that is a true, perfect, and intrinsically good existence. This lack of faith is not exactly the absence of belief in God, which is what many people think, since you can be an atheist and still believe in the intrinsic goodness of humanity. The absence of Holy Faith is reflected more in the absence of faith in human nature or in the nature of the universe. This means that one does not believe in and trust human nature, including one's own. This manifests in believing that how people are and act is purely electro-chemical in origin, that we are only physical entities, and that there is no intrinsic, intelligent essential nature that can be present and can operate. It also manifests in believing that whatever goodness human beings manifest is only the result of an adaptation to ensure survival. While it may be adaptive, believing that that is the origin of goodness reflects the lack of Holy Faith.

This lack can manifest on three levels: You could believe that there is no such thing as Essence; you might believe that while some goodness might exist, it is definitely not your nature or human nature since man is basically corrupt, and goodness or Essence exists in some god-like entity somewhere else; or you might believe that while Essence is your inner nature, it comes and goes randomly. So just as there are three facets of faith—that Essence exists, that it is your inner nature, and that it is dependable—there are three varieties of the lack of it.

Ultimately, this lack of faith is based upon the belief that human beings do not have an inner reality that is true, good, loving, and perfect, and so are inherently selfish, self-centered, and self-seeking. If you don't have Holy Faith, you have this other kind of faith: the conviction that human beings are entirely made up of ego. Life then becomes a fight for survival, and if any goodness is shown to another, it is purely out of self-interest. This cynicism is the *specific delusion* of ennea-type Six. The dictionary defines a cynic as someone who believes that all people are entirely motivated in all their actions by selfishness, and a cynical attitude reflects a contemptuous disbelief in human goodness and sincerity. So the absence of faith manifests as cynicism, whether it is related to human beings or to the cosmos. It manifests as a doubting and a questioning of oneself, one's nature, human nature, Essence, truth, God, or the universe in general. It is a suspiciousness that reflects the underlying cynical attitude, the absence of Holy Faith, and the consequent hopelessness, despair, and frustration. Doubting one's own or others' motivations may be implicit or explicit: Are they being loving because they are expressing an inner goodness, or is there some ulterior motive? Such constant questioning indicates the lack of faith in human nature. You don't believe that it is possible for someone to do something out of the goodness of her heart, or for the universe to present you with something nice—you don't believe in grace. If something nice happens, the cynic in us wonders, "Is this a test? What's going to happen if I enjoy it? Am I going to be tricked?"

Cynicism is beyond doubt. You might experience doubt or skepticism because you haven't experienced something and so don't know it, and this kind of doubt may be useful and healthy, motivating us to find out what is true about someone or something. Cynicism, on the other hand, is doubt that is based on a foregone conclusion. For example, you doubt another person from the pre-assumption that he lacks goodness and so will not come through for you. Cynicism comes in many degrees and levels. It might take the form of not believing that there is such a thing as Essence, or believing that if it does exist, it is not part of you. Or it might exist as part of you, but it is fickle and unreliable. However it appears, it makes you invalidate your own experience, even of Essence. "Was it really me? Did it really happen, or did I make it up? Was it my experience, or did someone make it seem that way? Was I hypnotized, or the victim of suggestion?" This is not an attitude of exploring one's experience to find out what is true, but an expression of having already made up one's mind about what one is going to find. It is not an open questioning that invites exploration to find out the truth for oneself, but an attitude of debunking, of questioning something to eliminate it, to cut it down and cut it away.

Insecurity and Suspicion

This cynicism, then, is the *specific delusion* that forms the core and then develops into the whole ennea-type. The *specific difficulty* of ennea-type Six is the experience of the inadequacy of the holding environment as reflected through the filter of cynicism. In other words, it is how you experience the lack of holding from the perspective of cynicism. The lack of a sense of holding, or the holding being negative or inadequate in some way, plus the lack of belief that there is real goodness within oneself and in the environment, leads to a lack of trust that reality is supportive. So the sense of not being held adequately, seen from the cynical perspective, makes you feel that it is not possible to be held adequately. No one is going to be there for you out of selfless and caring goodness, and real loving and true support and nurturing are not possible. So not only do you feel that holding is not present, you also come to believe that it is not possible to obtain.

The loss of the Holy Idea, the loss of the holding, and the development of distrust are all components of the same process, and they happen simultaneously over the course of the first five years or so of life. The sense may be that my mother is there for me only because she's my mother and it is her duty and responsibility—not because she loves me. Or the cynicism might be more extreme—that she's not there at all. In either case, the feeling-state that results, the *specific difficulty*, is a fearful kind of insecurity. You feel insecure and scared at the same time. There is an underlying and intrinsic sort of insecurity that is constantly present because you don't feel held, and since you don't feel that you're going to be, you feel constantly edgy and scared. This fearful insecurity reflects the belief and the feeling or sense that the world is a dangerous place inhabited by self-seeking people, and that there is no inner essence to support and guide you in this frightening world. Your soul feels insecure because the world appears as a scary jungle and you don't have inner strength to deal with it.

This is a very sensitive and delicate place in the soul where one feels touchy, scared, paranoid, alone, unsupported, abandoned, and vulnerable. It is quite a difficult emotional state to tolerate, and so you readily resort to defensiveness (inner, outer, or both) to evade it. On the one hand, you feel alone and unsupported externally, and on the other, you feel that you don't have inner strength or support. So there is no faith that if you just relax, what you need will be present. This is what gives rise to the fear that is part of the *specific difficulty*. This painful and difficult state is more than fear, however, since you can feel frightened without necessarily feeling insecure, and you can feel insecure without necessarily being afraid. Here, the fear and insecurity together form one state, and create a very touchy, scared place inside. Because it is such a sensitive place, when you're dealing with it in yourself or in others, you need to be quite attuned, empathic, and responsive.

The *specific reaction* for ennea-type Six is an expression of distrust, as reflected in the mirror of cynicism. One has no basic trust in oneself or in the environment, one believes that human nature is not intrinsically good or supportive or trustworthy, and at the same time one feels afraid and insecure in a dangerous world that has no loving and supportive God or inner nature. This manifests in the *specific reaction* of defensive suspiciousness toward the world.

Like the *specific difficulty*, this *specific reaction* is not just one particular feeling, but a complex that constitutes one's inner state. This defensive suspiciousness has fear and paranoia in it, as well as aggression and hostility. You are suspicious of others, questioning their motives and intentions; you are alert in a paranoid manner; at the same time, you are edgy, reactive, on the defensive, hostile, and ready to strike in self-defense. It is how one might feel alone and frightened in a jungle, since that is how the world seems here. It is a very specific but complex emotional state.

The *specific reaction* of ennea-type Six is characterized by an alert, paranoid kind of suspiciousness, always being on the look-out for danger. If you are around someone having this kind of reaction, they might ask you all sorts of questions, and you can tell that the underlying attitude is one of fear, suspiciousness, anger, and aggression, as though they are wanting to expose some selfish motivation within you that they are sure is there. You can sense the fear and insecurity in the person, as well as their attempt to protect themselves; they don't know whether they can trust you, and already suspect you.

This reaction is a defense against an environment that appears hostile and threatening, but it is also the main defense against the inner sense of fearful insecurity. One is always suspicious and on the defensive, for relaxation and trust would bring an expectation of external danger, as well as the feeling of insecurity and vulnerability in the face of it.

This attitude or style of behavior is different from the counterphobic style of some ennea-type Sixes, which is to deny the *specific difficulty.* That style is a way of saying, "No, I'm not scared—the world is a safe place, and I'll prove it by climbing a mountain. You'll see—nothing will happen to me." Such people take risks and put themselves in dangerous situations to prove that they are not afraid or insecure. So, in spite of the opposite styles, both a phobic and a counterphobic Six have the *specific reaction* of defensive suspiciousness. The former will withdraw and overtly display a suspicious stance, while the latter will charge ahead in order to override the defensive reaction.

The defensive suspiciousness can be directed not only outward, but also toward yourself. This could take the form of being suspicious of your own motives or not letting yourself go deep inside yourself, because you fear what you're going to find there, and you suspect it won't be good.

When you are identified with this defensive and aggressive suspiciousness, you are not usually aware of the vulnerable and fearful insecurity. While anxiety may be present, you are usually feeling angry and hostile, doubting and suspecting others and their motives. The aggressive, attacking quality of this reaction may be expressed overtly to various degrees, or it can be an inner posture only, which you are not expressing, but are feeling inside.

It is important to remember that each ego has all nine inner complexes, and that each of us must deal with our cynicism, our fearful insecurity, and our defensive suspiciousness. We need to experience this constellation that forms the core barrier against Holy Faith, because if it remains unconscious, it will block the development of faith, regardless of your essential experiences. Because this constellation is present in the unconscious, it needs to be exposed and dissolved, and to do that, we need to experience the *specific reaction* and the *specific difficulty*, and then see how both are based upon the *specific delusion* of cynicism. In this way, we can diffuse the core and clear the way for our essential experiences to give rise to faith.

Barriers to Essential Faith

Defensive suspiciousness manifests not only in individuals, but in society as a whole, and the dialogue between cynicism and faith arises in many areas: in our friendships and intimate relationships, and in our relationship to ourselves, our teachers, and social issues in general. An example of the latter is in the ongoing debate about what to do with criminals: Should we punish them or educate them? If you are fundamentally cynical, you believe that they can't be rehabilitated and should just be locked away from society. If you have more faith in human nature, you believe that it is wrong to give up on a person because he may have a spark of humanity that can be rekindled through education.

Our defensive suspiciousness manifests in suspecting the motivations of those we are in relationship with—our friends, lovers, spouses, bosses, co-workers, even teachers. You might suspect the reason your teacher appears to be there for you, or you might question whether he or she even has the capacity to be there. Defensive suspiciousness is based on cynicism, the belief that either there isn't anything essential in a person, or if there is, it isn't available to you. This is not healthy skepticism, in which you don't know something and want to find out what is true. Healthy skepticism is an openness, not the invalidating, angry, and attacking, doubtful quality of this form of reactivity.

What ultimately needs to happen is for each of us to develop faith in ourselves, which means having faith in human nature. When we have that, we can't help but have faith in all human beings. This does not mean blind trust. It means that you know for sure that every human being has an essential nature, even though it might be buried and a person might be acting out of ignorance or cynicism. It means that you give the other person a chance, that you allow the possibility that she can be kind and selfless, even though she doesn't always act that way. It means that you know that such a quality exists in her and in you.

The real battle is not with other people but within yourself. You don't need to trust other people as much as you need to trust yourself. The meaning of faith is the certainty that your innate nature is good and supportive—it does not imply trusting other people or even trusting yourself all the time. It means that you know that there is a quality within yourself that is fundamentally trustworthy. That faith will help you persevere in the Work so as to make that quality more available and more permanent.

Many people believe that they are not worthy of love. This is an expression of cynicism, because they are saying that there is nothing within them deserving of love. When you dig deeply, you see that all the delusions are connected and are just different expressions of the basic disconnection from Being.

Cynicism is a delusion; it is not intrinsic to our consciousness. It is the product of a particular ignorance, and the insight that will resolve it is the perception we call Holy Strength and Holy Faith. Many people adopt cynicism as a philosophy and base their approach to life on it; this becomes especially prevalent during periods of physical, social, or economic catastrophe. If you were born during a war, for example, it might be very easy for you to become cynical because your soul developed in an atmosphere of danger and was surrounded by people motivated predominantly by their survival instincts.

A person who is really cynical has given up on humanness. Having faith means that you have not given up on the possibility of yourself and others having humanity. It is understandable that if you grew up in an inadequate or, worse, an abusive environment, you would tend to be more cynical, since your experience was that human beings are dangerous. The real difficulty that results from cynicism, however, arises not only from believing that your parents or the environment are not human, but from believing that you, yourself, don't have the human qualities of intrinsic goodness, strength, and intelligence.

We are discussing these difficult and painful states at the core of the fixations because they are in all of us, and we need to become aware of them in order to be free from them. As I have said, if you do not deal with this core, faith will not develop even though you have essential experiences, or if it begins to develop, the core will surface and you will have to deal with it then.

The Importance of the View of Reality

An important part of the Work is to understand the view of objective reality. This understanding comes through discussions about it and through your own investigation, your own exploration and experience. This view is, in some sense, not one experience, but what unifies all experiences. It is the over-arching picture that makes all experiences intelligible and meaningful. The more we understand the view of objective reality, the more we know where we are in our journey. The more we understand the view, the more we know how distorted or how objective our experience is. Thus, understanding the view is a valuable guidance and an important orientation. In time, as our realization process progresses and deepens, our experience corresponds more with the view. When experience is exactly harmonious with the view, this is what is called total realization or enlightenment.

The view is an elucidation of how things are, what our nature and the nature of everything is, rather than someone's theory or perspective about it. Perspectives about reality vary because they are informed by the particular path one takes to arrive at that perspective, but objective reality is objective reality. It is not like anyone's ideas about it. Different people may view it from different angles, but this does not mean that they are seeing a different reality. It is as it is; this is what makes it objective reality. We are trying to understand this view by working with the Holy Ideas, which, as I have said, is not the only way of realizing the view of objective reality.

We have explored Holy Strength, which is the direct experiential recognition of Essence and its truth, its lovingness, and its perfection—the recognition that it is *our* essence, *our* innate nature. And we have seen how Holy Faith is the transformation that occurs in the soul consequent to the experience of Holy Strength. When the soul recognizes Essence, we see that this is what gives us strength and courage, and this transforms the soul through the action of what we call Holy Faith—not faith about a person or a particular thing, but faith in reality, in Essence. This faith is a heartfelt certainty, an unquestioned conviction that Essence is one's innate nature. Along with this knowing comes the perception that it is constant and reliable, and you—rather than it—come and go. If you really know that Essence is your nature, to say that it comes and goes doesn't make any more sense than saying that the atoms of your body come and go. Your perception of it might come and go, but that doesn't mean that your inner nature comes and goes, as one often feels early on in the Work.

The presence of Essence with its truth, its intrinsic blissfulness, and its intelligence, is there all the time—it cannot go. If Essence is gone, you are dead. You can't be conscious or aware without Essence. So when we perceive that Essence comes and goes, we are saying that it is limited, indicating that we are projecting a past relationship onto it, relating to it as though it were our mother. It also means that we have not yet fully understood that Essence is *our* essence, as fundamental to us as atoms are to the physical body. It is not something detachable from the soul that can come and go. It is the actual substance of the soul. When we don't know this for certain, it means that our experience is incomplete and that we need to keep inquiring into what is limiting our experience. We need to ask ourselves, "Why do I believe that

Essence is something that comes and goes? Where does that idea come from? What's that experience like?" If the view that we are discussing is accurate, if Holy Truth is the nature of all of reality, what gives rise to the experience that it comes and goes? Where could it come from and where could it go to?

So if we have an understanding of how things really are—if we know the view of objective reality—then every time we experience Essence as coming and going, instead of believing this projected past relation, we can say to ourselves, "Wait a minute! That's not how it really is, but I'm experiencing it that way. What does this mean?" We have some guidance, an orientation toward our experience. We recognize a distortion, even when it feels real; and the more we see our distortions, the more faith in Essence arises.

The Holy Ideas of the central triangle of the Enneagram—love, faith, and hope—are what are called the three primary "theological virtues" in Christianity. These Holy Ideas form a group distinct from the others in that while all the Holy Ideas are perspectives arising from specific direct experiences of objective reality, those of the triangle also describe the transformative effects of such experiences on the soul. In discussing the other Holy Ideas, we explored the view of reality from each of those vantage points without much discussion of how that view affects and transforms the soul. Each of the theological virtues, in contrast, includes a specific and distinct experience of objective reality, as well as an understanding of the transformative effect of this experience on the soul.

As we discussed at the beginning of this book, the Holy Ideas are views of reality that are perceived when the higher intellectual senses are open, when the mind experiences reality without the veil of ego. They are the "ideas" of the *path* center, the head center, and so are "real ideas," or Holy Ideas. Basic trust, as we have seen, is an integration of trust on a nonconceptual and pre-verbal level. It is not an idea or a feeling, but a lived knowing, implicit in how one functions, and so is related to the belly center, the *kath*. The three theological virtues have to do with the heart center, the *oth*. They are attitudes and feelings engendered by the perception of the Holy Ideas.

The Transforming Effect of the Ideas

These three Holy Ideas are also distinguished from the others in that they are qualities that are specifically needed to travel the path, while the other Ideas are more accurately the fruits of the path—the realization itself, since they are facets of the view of objective reality. Love, faith, and hope, then, are the elements that the soul needs to make its journey home. Love of the truth motivates the soul to want to set out on the journey; faith sustains and supports it as it proceeds; and hope gives it the optimism that things will unfold in the right way. Objective love reflects the recognition of the intrinsic goodness of Being; objective faith reflects the recognition that Being is one's inner truth and also one's support, strength, and ground; objective hope reflects the recognition of the optimizing thrust of its dynamics, which will be discussed in the chapter on Holy Hope. Each of these Holy Ideas is a reflection of a certain facet of the view. They are not really separate; they are all one reality. They are like snapshots of reality from three different directions.

Love, faith, and hope can develop and deepen because they are qualities of the transforming soul, and transformation is a dynamic process—not just an experience. Faith helps the soul to go deeper into experience, as the soul learns that it has a true, good, and intelligent nature or Essence, that its interiority is Essence. At the beginning of waking up, the soul can feel supported by the fact that there is true Essence within—that keeps you going. At deeper levels, as the soul develops and experiences deeper dimensions, especially the boundless dimensions of Being, we can no longer accurately speak of Essence as the soul's inner nature. This is because, on the boundless level, we are experiencing the inner nature of everything, and all of reality is experienced as one thing. At this level, Essence, the nature of the soul, is superseded by Being, the nature of all of reality. Being is then experienced as the ground of the soul which makes it feel held and supported. This ground that gives rise to the soul is also seen as the ground of everything, the nature of everything. Faith, then, is the reflection of the certainty that there is a real ground for the soul to stand on and experience its reality and life. Our faith, of course, increases when we recognize Essence in its boundless dimensions, since we see that it is not just the nature of our soul, but the nature of everything, which enables us to have faith in all of nature, all of reality, all of existence.

We have begun to explore the inner core of ennea-type Six, which is the reflection of the *specific delusion* of cynicism due to the absence of Holy Faith. In order to truly understand, and thus move beyond, identification with our ego structure and its perspective on reality, we need to see how this principle is crucial to the structure of ego operating in our consciousness. We say that the delusions are principles of the ego because they support the presence of ego. The more we see through the delusions, the more that sense of the ego dissolves. Without the delusions, the ego cannot maintain itself; the presence of the ego and the delusion are, in some sense, the same thing. As we allow ourselves to see through the *specific reaction* and the *specific difficulty* to the *specific delusion* implicit in them, the *specific delusion* becomes conscious and cannot be maintained. As the *specific delusion* dissolves, the state of Holy Strength arises, which is the recognition of your essential nature and the faith in it.

The possibility of experiencing real holding arises as the *specific difficulty* dissolves, since it is the result of the inadequacies of holding in early childhood. The holding that arises is the natural holding that is always present, and that brings basic trust, which dissolves the ego's distrust. As this happens, Holy Faith arises: the sense of trust and confidence and ease.

We have seen how this delusion of cynicism underlies the *specific reaction* of defensive suspiciousness, and we need to also see clearly how the painful state of fearful insecurity that is the *specific reaction* of ennea-type Six is the reflection of inadequate holding in the mirror of cynicism. This state of fearful insecurity is painful, not in the sense that it hurts, but painful in that it is difficult to tolerate. It is a frightening state of groundlessness that can be very hard to remain present with, but staying with it is necessary if the egoic view is to be dissolved. The more we can experience and inquire into this scared and shaky place within, the more it can be transformed into a pillar of strength and faith inside us. As long as we are identified with ego, we cannot help but feel insecure—the ego is groundless, since it is a mental construct that structures the spaciousness of Essence and divides the one reality into parts. If the ego is who we take ourselves to be, we will inevitably feel shaky because we do not perceive that there is a ground—the ground of Being.

As you let go of the ego structure, you see that its nature is empty, since it is actually conceptual and not ultimately real. This is when you feel the emptiness; the sense of emptiness is really just the revelation of the structure's immateriality. As you stay with the emptiness, it reveals itself as spaciousness. Then the spaciousness brings out the fullness inherent in it, which is all the holding and lovingness and gentleness. It may seem that you have moved from one place to another, but that is not what happens. If you experience yourself as your real presence, you just see one thing dissolving into another in the middle of your presence. If you are identified with the structure, it will feel as if you are disintegrating, and then there is emptiness, and then presence arises. This impression is only because your attention is focused on a certain part of you, and so you are not experiencing your totality. You do not fall apart or disappear, although it feels that way if your ego is the part of you that you are identified with.

People who work on themselves develop their inner vision so that they can perceive their essential nature. This is analogous to looking at matter in a microscope: If you look through the microscope, you will see the molecular structure of the material; if you don't look, you will not see what it is made of. The more people see the essential nature they are made of, the more the actions in their lives are informed by that perception. If you don't perceive your essence, it does not affect you or your life very much. A lot of work is required to refine one's perception to become aware of Essence at all, much less to become aware of it as the essence of one's consciousness itself. Because this is a very subtle perception, most people don't have the sensitivity to see it or to understand its nature. Those who do perceive it usually think of the experience as a bit of grace that God throws you once in awhile, like a blessing that happens to hit you occasionally.

To conceive of Essence in this way is not to see objectively. The objective view that the Holy Ideas explicate is that Essence is actually the nature of our consciousness and the nature of everything. The more we see this, the more faith develops in us. That is the work of self-realization—to become aware of, to become certain of, and to become continuously in touch with, the fact that Essence is one's intrinsic nature. It is difficult work, but that is the Work.

When I say that Essence is the essence of the soul, I am describing the initial experience of it. At the beginning, it feels like there is a soul and there is Essence inside it, like a container with its content. This is not really the situation, but it feels that way initially because of the limitations imposed on our experience by our identifications. If our minds are not identified with anything, we see that Essence is completely coemergent with the soul, just as the molecules are coemergent with your body. Essence is inseparable from the soul; it is part and parcel of it. Any sense of separation is due to a mental delusion, specifically, the one resulting from the absence of Holy Origin.

The quality of Living Daylight that arises as we integrate Holy Strength is one of purity and support. There is a sense of strength and confidence. The feeling of holding is felt as a sense of support and security that is soft, gentle, and loving. Experiencing Holy Strength is experiencing the support, the strength, the confidence, and the relaxation and ease that come through recognizing that Essence is what you are made of—it is what is holding you and supporting you, and it is not outside of you but is fundamental to who you are.

Holy Faith is a specific condition or state, a specific development of this sense of purity and implicit confidence or trust. It is needed to embark on, and to continue traveling the path, because as we journey on our path, we do not have full knowledge of reality. We do not have complete access to this view, and so most of the way along the path, we don't know what's happening. We don't know where we are or where we are going, except for occasional glimpses. Because of this inevitable ignorance, faith is very important; in fact, it is necessary to keep you going when you can't see the road clearly. When we have complete understanding and perception of reality, faith is no longer necessary. But as long as we are passing through what St. John of the Cross calls "the dark night" of not seeing reality clearly, we need faith. At times, the journey is easy, at times it is difficult, and at other times it feels downright impossible; and for the most part, we don't know why, nor do we understand what it is that is happening to us. In the face of this not knowing, our faith keeps us going; and when there is faith, we don't need to know where we are going or how to feel secure. If we knew exactly where we were heading, there would be no discovery, no adventure, no magic. Holy Faith sustains us on our journey into the unknown.

CHAPTER NINETEEN

Point Three
HOLY HARMONY,
HOLY LAW, HOLY HOPE

The awareness that there are no exceptions to the natural laws which govern the Cosmos, and that these laws are completely objective, operating as an inter-connected unity. The highest law is the totality of Reality itself. Certitude in the objectivity and total applicability of those laws is true hope.
— Ichazo, 1972

Understanding what we have been calling the "view of reality" can and usually does make the difference between getting bogged down somewhere on the path, or continuously opening and progressing. This view becomes an important ground for our work, and if we do not have a good grasp of it, we could get stuck in one place or another and not even be aware of it. Because this view is not related to a specific experience, spiritual or otherwise, and is not dependent on experiencing a particular essential aspect or dimension of Being, it transcends all dimensions, and is a formulation of what is objectively true about any experience on any dimension. It is an understanding of how reality is, and how it functions, regardless of which state of consciousness one is experiencing. So the focus in this study is not on the specific content of experience, whether the experience is of the ego self, of emotions, of emptiness, of the essential self, of the body, or even of hearing celestial music, seeing angels, or being healed. The view is unconcerned with these specifics and applies to all of them. When you apprehend the content of your experience from the perspective of this transcendent view, you see that all your experience is part of the greater reality illuminated by this view.

Without this perspective, your experience will be grounded in the egoic view, regardless of how exalted, sublime, or subtle, the state. So if you are ignorant of the objective view of reality, you might very well get trapped in one dimension or another, and never know what it means to be free from the ego. The Holy Idea of ennea-type Three, which we are about to explore, is particularly germane to this issue of stuckness versus continual unfoldment and realization.

The view of reality that we are elucidating, then, clarifies whether one's experience—whatever its content—is perceived from the egoic view or from the objective view. Understanding the objective view means understanding experience when there is no ego informing it. It shows us how any experience or dimension of reality will be perceived when seen objectively, in contrast to how it will be perceived when seen through the egoic filter of the nine delusions. For example, you might have a very profound experience of divine love and perceive it as being particular to one time, place, or person, and not to another— which is the egoic view—or you might perceive it as the nature of everything—which is the objective view.

The objective view of reality facilitates progressive unfoldment by continually opening up our experience, while the egoic view tends to hold and fixate it. Through understanding how reality works, we develop basic trust in the nature of Being. Trusting the reality of Being is of primary importance in facilitating our experience to unfold and mature.

It does not matter whether you like the view of reality or not. It is how things are. If you like it or don't like it, that's your business—it's not the business of reality. If you don't like how things are, the best you can do is to find out why, so that you can begin to harmonize yourself with it. Otherwise, you will suffer. This doesn't mean reality is punishing you. It simply means that if you harmonize yourself with reality, you will experience a sense of peace and freedom, and if you don't, you will experience discord.

There are three ways in which we can understand the Holy Idea of ennea-type Three, and so it has three names: Holy Harmony, Holy Law, and Holy Hope. As we will see, all of these aspects of the Holy Idea are interrelated. Here again is Ichazo's definition: "The awareness that there are no exceptions to the natural laws which govern the Cosmos, and that these laws are completely objective, operating as an interconnected unity. The highest law is the totality of Reality itself. Certitude in the objectivity and total applicability of those laws is true hope."

To understand what this means, we need to see that this Holy Idea is about functioning, meaning that it deals with activity, events, changes, transformations, movements, processes, the passage of time, and so on. In other words, this is the main Idea on the Enneagram that can help us understand how changes and movement actually happen. The other Ideas that deal with the perception of changes and transformation are Holy Will, Holy Origin, and Holy Work; but these are all dependent upon, and elaborations of, the Idea of Holy Law, as we will see.

Holy Hope is one of the three theological virtues of Christianity, which are represented by the Holy Ideas of the Nine, Six, and Three ennea-types. As we have seen, each of these Ideas not only elucidates a particular experience of objective reality, but also describes the transformative effect on the soul of this experience. Holy Hope is the specific transformation in the soul that is the consequence of Holy Law and Holy Harmony. This is similar to what we saw in our study of ennea-type Six in which Holy Faith is the transformation of the soul that happens as a consequence of understanding Holy Strength.

So to understand the theological virtue of Holy Hope, we need to understand what Holy Law and Holy Harmony mean. Holy Law is the completely egoless perception and understanding of functioning and activity, which means the dynamic characteristics of Being. It roughly corresponds to the Fifth Awareness or Buddha in the Vajrayana Buddhist system of the Five Buddhas: the "all-accomplishing wisdom," which is related to the action of compassion.

Dynamic Oneness

Understanding the energetic, dynamic, and creative element of Being is vitally important as we travel the path, because many people become frightened when they experience presence, and realize that it involves non-doing, a state of deep rest. We become concerned about who is going to take care of things and how things will be accomplished if the truth of who we are is this non-doing. How will the rent get paid? Who will do the laundry? Who will get the groceries and how will dinner be prepared? If you don't understand how functioning actually happens objectively, you will believe that if you abide in this presence, nothing will happen. You will have no trust that things will be taken care of. When people first recognize the profound stillness that manifests in being deeply present, and they become afraid about whether things will be taken care of, they try to use their experience to support their egoic view of functioning. They ask, "How is this useful for my daily life?" This is analogous to someone having a vision of Jesus Christ, and then asking his priest, "How can I apply this to my life?" These concerns indicate a lack of understanding about objective functioning.

Holy Law shows the unity of existence when seen in its functioning, dynamic mode. This Idea is a formulation of the dimension that we call the *Logos* in the Diamond Approach, which is the dynamic and creative element inherent in the reality of Being. We have explored the idea of the unity of existence in Holy Truth and Holy Omniscience, seeing that all of reality is a unity, that everything constitutes one infinite and boundless presence. This is the basic spiritual perception: the unity and oneness of existence. This oneness takes the form of a multiplicity of appearance and experience, just as in ordinary perception, but there is no true separateness between one thing and another. In reality, there is no duality, no isolating boundaries or partitions. The separateness of various phenomena is only apparent, and discrimination only differentiates, rather than partitions. When we see this unity in process over the course of time, and understand how it moves and changes, then we understand Holy Law.

From this perspective, what we see is quite different from the ordinary perception of the world of objects which is inhabited by living beings who are centers of action and filled with movements and transformations dictated by physical laws. The ordinary view is that we live in a universe of physical objects made up of physical matter that obey physical laws of various kinds, such as the law of gravity, chemical and biochemical laws, electro-mechanical laws, and so on. Inhabiting this inanimate universe are beings who do things and make things. This perspective completely ignores the fact of oneness and the unity of existence. If reality is one, if there are no separating boundaries between one thing and another, then there are no objects in the usual sense of the word, nor are there separate individuals. Believing that changes occur because one thing acts upon another—like the sun acts on the earth and the earth in turn acts on the moon, or you are doing something that affects someone else—assumes a belief in separateness.

But if separateness is not ultimately real, how do these things happen? Exploring this question can bring about an understanding of Holy Law. From its perspective, we perceive a progressive unfoldment of the unity of existence, all of existence changing and transforming in unity, since everything makes up a boundless oneness. Changes are not seen as separate and isolated from each other, or even as causing each other. All of the universe, even those parts of it that we consider static and unchanging, is continuously transforming from one total and unified condition to another total and unified condition. That is Holy Law: the unity of all change.

So Holy Law means that the whole universe changes and transforms as a unity, like one ocean whose surface is in a constant state of change and transformation, continuously rippling as one. It is not that things are changing in unison, but that one completely unified mass is moving without the possibility of any part going its own way or changing, independent of the rest. If one thing were to change separately, the unity of existence would be broken.

Clearly, this view is a radical departure from our usual way of perceiving things. It challenges all kinds of assumptions. For example, we see that the so-called law of cause and effect does not exist, since causality means that one thing causes something else to happen. According to Holy Law, there are no isolated objects or events, so to experience one thing as causing another is not accurate. From this perspective, for instance, the experience that you are turning the pages of this book is not what is really happening—there is no separate book with a separate you turning the pages. There is actually a wholeness, a whole movement of reality in which the pages turn. You cannot walk from one place to another, since there is no separate you and there are really no distances to be traversed. The whole picture changes from one instant to the next. What we think of as walking from here to there is more like the changing arrangements of dots on a television screen; at one moment, they're arranged so that you are here, the next, you are there, and so on. So there are no actual distances crossed. If you really understand the unity of Being, how else could it be? The moment there is separate functioning in any part of the whole, the unity is broken.

Holy Law is more difficult to perceive than unity. To perceive it, you have to experience the continuity and the unity of Being for some time, and then you might begin recognizing Holy Law. From this perspective, we realize that the universe does not exist in time. It is continuously and instantaneously being created second by second. This is not the same thing as saying that God creates or moves everything, which is the traditional religious point of view that sets God apart from the rest of the universe, an indication that one is not seeing or understanding the unity of existence. Understanding Holy Law renders meaningless the religious belief that the universe was created by God at some moment in the distant past. The entire universe is being created anew in every instant, so it is not true that a creator created the universe at some point and then things began happening within it. The latter is an idea that falls within the view of ego. From the perspective of Holy Law, there is no such thing as time in the way we usually think of it; there isn't a universe made up of discrete objects, nor is there such a thing as a God separate from it.

The perspective of Holy Law, then, illuminates the fact that the unity of Being is not a static existence, but rather, a dynamic presence that is continuously changing and transforming as a unified field. Here, we see the aliveness of Being and the universe, its energy and flow and vigorous transformation. This Holy Idea confronts some of our very basic convictions about reality, but if we don't understand it, we cannot really understand what unfoldment means. This is because the unfoldment of the soul is Holy Law operating in one location, so when we perceive it, we are seeing in microcosm what is happening everywhere all the time. Holy Law is not an easy thing to swallow, since in the process of perceiving it, you—as you have known yourself—get swallowed up.

Perceptions of the Dynamic Flow

This perception of the unity and the inseparability of all change and transformation can take many forms. First, it can be the experience of seeing all of existence as a presence that is patterned. This presence is not static but is, in its unified totality, in constant flow. This unified flow occurs in such a way that its pattern is continuously changing and evolving. It happens in this way because first of all, the unity according to Holy Omniscience, as we have seen, has patterns in it, differentiations and differences, which, while not separating, make a pattern. This pattern is always changing as the flow is unfolding. So, the unfoldment or flow of Being manifests as the changing of the pattern of the unity, continuously changing the patterns of how things appear. It is like seeing the whole universe as one river that is constantly changing as it flows. We not only perceive this change as changes, transformations, movements, and evolutions in the cosmic pattern, but we also see that these changes and movements include what we ordinarily perceive as our actions and the actions of other living beings.

So Being is not only presence, but the flow of presence. It is a flow of nowness in continuous transformation of the universal pattern. This flow is what we usually perceive as the passage of time. In other words, what we call time is a limited way of intuiting the flow of Being. Since we ordinarily don't perceive the unity of existence, and so don't experience change as the flow of Being, we think of change as due to the passage of time.

The flow itself is what I call *real time*. When we perceive all of reality in constant flow, then we are perceiving real time; otherwise, we see the situation in a distorted way, as separate changes happening in time. So the flow, the experience of Holy Law, is in a sense the source of time, since time is a concept arising from a distorted perception of Being or the totality of the universe in a constant state of flow.

Being is very fluid, continuously arranging and rearranging the pattern of appearance. The contemporary Buddhist teacher, Tarthang Tulku, describes this in his book, *Time, Space and Knowledge: A New Vision of Reality*, in which he calls this dynamic flow, "Great Time." "When fully appreciated, Great Time is seen to be a kind of perfectly liquid, lubricious dimension—it is quintessentially 'slippery.'" (Tulku, 1977, p. 161) When you feel the flow, you realize that Being is not static, but constantly moving like quicksilver.

So this is one way of seeing Holy Law, as a continuously changing flow of Being. A second way of perceiving it is as creation. In contrast to the Biblical creation story, this is the idea of continual creation, of the universe being continually created instant by instant, always new. The focus in this perception is not on the fact of the flow and process of change, but on the fact that the flow is not in time, not coming from the past through the present and into the future. The perception of the flow as creation reveals that it is from non-existence to existence, a flow that is continuously being renewed. When we think of water flowing, we usually think of the same water moving, but here, it is more the sense of a fountain of newly-arising water, constantly being created. Seeing that the flow is always in the now, you realize that it is a new creation. Everything is constantly manifesting, as in a magic show when a rabbit is pulled out of an empty hat. So when we talk about creation, we see that it is not a flow from the past to the future, but rather, a flow from non-manifestation to manifestation.

This continual creation is not separate from presence or the Divine Being; it *is* Being manifesting through countless and varied forms. It is difficult to perceive this continual renewal, this constantly new creation, when one is still caught in the delusion of separateness. Being and what is being created are the same thing. It is Being outflowing, creating how it appears from instant to instant. This idea is prevalent in Sufism, and according to the Sufi philosopher, Ibn Arabi:

> *Creation* as the "rule of being" is the pre-eternal and continuous movement by which being is manifested at *every instant* in a new cloak. The *Creative Being* is the pre-eternal and post-eternal essence or substance which is manifested at every instant in the innumerable forms of beings; when He hides in one, He manifests Himself in another. *Created Being* is the *manifested*, diversified, successive, and evanescent forms, which have their substance not in their fictitious autonomy but in the Being that is manifested in them and by them. (Corbin, 1969, p. 200)

This means that everything that we see is the manifestation of Being, which is completely inseparable from Being, because it is Being itself manifesting itself in the various forms that we see. So God is not something that creates the world; God is the world when we recognize it in its unity. Quoting Ibn Arabi again, he says:

> And His Creation springs, not from nothingness, from something other than Himself, from a not-Him, but from His fundamental being, from the potencies and virtualities latent in His own unrevealed being. . . . The Creation is essentially the revelation of the Divine Being, first to himself, a luminescence occurring within Him, it is a theophany *(tajalli ilahi)*. (Corbin, 1969, p. 185)

The latter quote points to the third way of experiencing the Holy Law. This is the experience that reality is inherently and constantly self-revealing. So everything that we see is nothing but the revelation of Being, the true reality of the universe. This self-revelation highlights the inherent creativity of Being, the fact that it is spontaneously creative, and that this creativity is continuously revealing its richness and its treasures. From this angle, all movements and transformations are seen as the spontaneous self-revealing creativity of Being. The focus here, then, is on the spontaneous magical unfolding and flowering, which is pure appearing.

More exactly, creation or the flow of Being is basically replacement: One unified appearance is replaced by another unified appearance. The word *creation* might make you think that something new and different is being created, but from the perspective of self-revelation, Being is simply revealing itself through the innumerable manifestations of objects, beings, and events that we experience. So by seeing this flow as a self-revelation, we see that there is no distinction between what is created and what is creating.

Here, then, the continuity of Being is its self-revelation, through which we are able to perceive it. As long as there is perception of Being, it is always perceived through the forms it manifests. When you perceive Being without any form, there is no perception. This is the divine coma, the cessation of experience. The forms through which we perceive it are the manifestations of Being itself, so it is not as though Being is manifesting us. Being is manifesting itself, and we are part of that Being.

So we have seen Holy Law as a flow of Being, a creativity, and a self-revelation. Experientially, there is a different flavor to each of these perceptions, and they are progressively more subtle. The self-revelation has more of a magical quality: The whole of reality is Being, magically displaying its qualities and potentialities by making them appear just like that, out of nothing. But that appearance is Being itself, not something separate.

This sense of the flow as a magical unfoldment is close to the fourth, even more subtle way of experiencing Holy Law, in which everything is experienced as a manifestation of Being. This perception is described by Longchenpa, in the following quote:

> All that is has me—universal creativity, pure and total
> presence—as its root.
> How things appear is my being.
> How things arise is my manifestation.
> (Longchenpa, 1987, p. 32)

"How things appear" points to the Beingness, and "how things arise" points to the unfoldment, to the flow, the manifestation. So Holy Law here is the magical manifestation of the mystery. It is the spontaneous self-arising of all appearance. Everything, then, is seen as spontaneously arising, with no creator and no created. What is arising is nothing but the presence itself manifesting itself. This is the complete coemergence of Being and functioning. Longchenpa continues:

> [Because all buddhas, sentient beings, appearances,
> Existences, environments, and inhabitants]
> Arise from the quintessential state of pure and total
> presence,
> One is beyond duality.
> . . .
> Because all phenomena do not exist apart from me,
> One is beyond duality. I fashion everything.
> (Longchenpa, 1987, p. 35)

Each of the ways of perceiving Holy Law adds a slightly different subtlety. Together, they provide a more complete perception of Holy Law. The difference between self-revelation and manifestation may appear very small when discussing it, but experientially, the difference is considerable. In self-revelation, Being is revealing whatever is in it, while in manifestation, Being is the unending spontaneous manifestation. This subtlety has a very different feel experientially.

A fifth way of experiencing Holy Law takes the last quote still further. This is the perception that everything occurs according to one universal will. In other words, there is one reality whose will manifests through all events, movements, and changes. This perception is the closest to the notion of a creator God with a Divine Will. But here, we see that this God is not an entity separate from what is created, so the created and the inner nature of the created are experienced as inseparable. In addition to this inseparability, there is the sense of one unified will moving everything, the sense that Beingness with its own will is transforming itself.

Through the sixth way of experiencing Holy Law, we gain a more complete understanding of it. Here, we experience Being as an inherently dynamic presence. The dynamism is completely inseparable from Being, so it is not as though there is Being and it has a creative quality. From the beginning, Being is constantly dynamic. So it is not only pure presence, but this presence by its very nature is dynamic, energetic, and in a constant state of aliveness and renewal. It is always transforming its appearance, without there being a transformed one and a transforming one. So Being is a living, seething, dynamic, energetic presence, whose dynamism and movement never detract from its stillness. To see the aspect of self-revelation of Being is to appreciate intimately the depth of awareness that appears as the forms of manifestation, to perceive that the Divine Awareness is never left as form arises.

In the experiences of the Holy Law as the revelation or manifestation of Being, there is some sense of you being a witness in the experience, perceiving things unfolding. In the experience of the inherent dynamism of Being, you are not experiencing that things are manifesting; you are yourself in a constant dynamism. There is no distinction between the witness and the revelation or the manifestation. Witnessing itself is part of the dynamism. The dynamism, then, is inherently self-aware.

To understand that the totality of the universe is constantly renewing itself radically changes our notion of death. Personal death is simply Being manifesting at one moment with a particular person as part of the picture, and in the next moment without that person. From this perspective, all the issues about death change character. Death disappears into the continual flow of unfolding, self-arising change.

There are many other ways of experiencing Holy Law; we are mentioning just a few of them here. This is the most difficult Idea to understand intellectually, as well as to grasp experientially, because the entirety of our lives is based on a completely different perspective.

Harmonious Flow

Holy Harmony, the second name or nuance of this Holy Idea, points to two primary insights regarding Holy Law. It refers to Holy Law, but focuses on certain things about it. The first insight is that because everything happens as one action, as one unified flow, the pattern of this flow is experienced as the complete harmony of all the various happenings contained within it. The perception of this harmony is that it is beauty, it is love, it is grace, it is luminosity, it is abundance and fullness. So all movements, changes, and actions form a unified and harmonious patterned flow. This flow is aesthetically and absolutely appealing and satisfying, and on a practical level, is totally fulfilling. There are no incongruities, no inconsistencies, no contradictions between the various local changes and occurrences because they are not separate from each other. Contradictions can only exist from the perspective of an individual who sees one thing happen and then sees another thing happen, which she thinks is contradictory to the first thing. But if there is only one unified unfolding, how can there be inconsistencies? What we call disharmonies and inconsistencies are part of the harmony when seen from this larger perspective.

Another insight that Holy Harmony reveals is the perception that this unified functioning has an inherent intelligence which gives it an *optimizing thrust*. In other words, this dynamic flow and creativity is not haphazard, erratic, or accidental, but rather, is a harmony that reveals an intrinsic intelligence. This intelligence manifests in the fact that the thrust of this flow and creativity is optimizing, in the sense that it spontaneously tends toward the revelation of this primordial and self-existing harmony. In other words, if we perceive the flow, if we perceive Holy Law, we also can perceive that this flow has an intrinsic intelligence, which can be seen in the fact that this flow is optimizing. It is optimizing in the sense that it is always moving in such a way that it reveals its truth. So the dynamism of Being is like a gravitational pull that always tends to pull our perception toward the revelation of its truth, toward seeing its harmony.

From the point of view of the end of the journey, the state of egolessness, the perception of Holy Harmony is that the creative flow is always a harmony, in harmony, and revealing harmony. The harmony is self-existent and is always present. Its existence is not the result of someone advancing on a path; only the perception of it results from spiritual work. From the point of view of one traveling the path, the perception is that the creative flow manifests as an optimizing thrust, pushing one toward harmony. That is, if we let reality unfold without interfering with it, we see that our experience of it evolves spontaneously toward harmony and the awareness of harmony. The optimizing thrust of reality will move our experience of ourselves and the world toward the enlightened state, which is the perception of, and the abiding in, objective reality, as revealed in the nine Holy Ideas.

We can see this Idea of Holy Harmony either from the perspective of the enlightened state or from that of moving toward it. From the enlightened state, we realize that the unfoldment of reality is always a harmony; one harmony is being continuously replaced by another harmony. From the perspective of the path, we realize that there is an unfoldment occurring. If we really attune ourselves to the dynamism of Being, instead of trying to take things into our own hands, we realize that the dynamism of Being has its own inherent optimizing thrust that will guide us and lead us toward the implicit harmony.

This perception and understanding of Holy Harmony manifesting as an optimizing thrust can be seen as inner guidance, the guidance of Being, or as divine guidance or inspiration. Reality, then, is inherently moving our consciousness toward perceiving it as it is. It is always pointing toward its truth. When the ego is not informing our experience, reality is not only pointing toward its truth, but the pointing itself is the truth.

Within ego, you perceive Being acting upon your consciousness in such a way as to draw you toward it. But when the veils of separation are gone, you see that nothing is acting on or guiding anything; the whole thing is Being revealing itself. So while the perspective from the path is a limited point of view of reality, that limited point of view is part of the whole, too.

So we have described Holy Law and Holy Harmony. Holy Hope has two meanings. The first is that the very fact of universal and harmonious functioning is the true hope. The optimizing thrust inherent in this functioning is our hope. The fact that there is a harmony that is always drawing us closer to itself is the real hope. Hope here is not a feeling—it is a perception of the truth. The word *hope* is used as it is when saying to the Divine, "You are my hope." The dynamism of Being is seen as our true hope. Whether you recognize it or not, this dynamism is the hope for any human being of living in the truth, in harmony with objective reality.

Objective Optimism

The second meaning of Holy Hope is the effect on the soul of seeing and understanding Holy Law and Holy Harmony. This, then, is hope in the sense of the theological virtue. It is the realization that Reality "does itself," independent of our imaginary autonomy, and that this doing is a harmonious flow, which, most importantly, guides us spontaneously toward the harmony of enlightenment. This perception transforms the soul through impacting it in the specific way that we call Holy Hope.

Again, this is not hope in the sense of hoping that things will get better. It is a sense that you might be experiencing right now if you have understood Holy Law and Holy Harmony. It is a state of trust that everything will be okay, which is slightly different than Holy Faith. Here, it is a feeling of optimism, an attitude of joyous openness and trusting receptivity to what the unfolding of Being presents to us. A trust in the dynamics of Being naturally makes us feel optimistic. If you recognize that Being is a harmony, that it always functions in a harmonious way, and that it is always optimizing our experience when we don't interfere with it, an optimism about experience in general will arise. You will have an openness to whatever happens; whatever God or the universe presents you with, you will welcome happily because you know that everything is moving naturally toward harmony. This is not something that you conceptualize, nor is it about anything in particular that occurs. It is a general, open-ended optimism about life in general.

The difference between Holy Faith and Holy Hope is that faith is a trust in the fact of the presence of Being, while hope is trust in the creative flow of the functioning of that presence. So faith gives you the sense of being supported and taken care of by the universe, while hope gives you the sense that as things unfold, everything is and will be fine. Holy Hope, then, is an openness, a curiosity, a receptivity, and an optimism about how things are going to reveal themselves, because you are certain that the optimizing thrust of reality moves toward harmony and fulfillment. Even putting it in this way makes the hope sound too specific—it is just an open optimism about life.

It is obvious how this kind of hope is helpful and necessary on the path, since it is needed to allow the unfoldment of the soul to progress without feeling the need to interfere with it or direct it. We know that it is inherently guided, and this knowing is not an idea in our minds, nor the result of reasoning, nor a logical certainty. It is an experiential transformation of the soul that makes the soul progressively more open and happily optimistic, trusting that everything will transpire in the best way, beyond our preconceived ideas of what we think is best. It is not a hope for something specific, as we have said. If it were, it would be egoic hope based on judgments and preconceptions about what we think ought to happen, and on rejection of the present. It is, rather, the growing and deepening certainty that whatever happens will be part of the optimizing thrust of reality and its guidance. It is complete openness to the unfoldment.

Many of us have had experiences in which we felt a sense of unfoldment that has happened naturally, without manipulation, or have had a sense of being guided. These experiences can help us understand this Holy Idea, in that this Idea is a larger, non-specific version of these experiences. To understand this connection will also confront our egoic view about functioning and unfoldment, which is necessary to expose our ego-based convictions.

As we learn about the Holy Ideas, we might judge ourselves harshly because we don't experience them. But believing that we should be experiencing from these enlightened perspectives is based on a judgmental comparison, which is not part of the Holy Ideas. It is the delusion of ennea-type One, as we have seen. There is nothing in the Holy Ideas that judges whether you are experiencing it that way or not. From the perspective of the view of reality that the Holy Ideas describe, there is no judgment and there are no comparisons. In fact, because it is the dynamism of Being, Holy Law includes and allows egoic experience. This, also, is the functioning of Being. You are not creating it, even though it might seem that way. Being allows itself to be experienced accurately and it allows itself to be experienced inaccurately, in both cases with complete compassion.

The Separate Doer

The absence of the Holy Idea that we have been discussing leads to the *specific delusion* of ennea-type Three. It is the belief in a separate and independent doer. We have seen that the delusion of ennea-type Five is the belief in a separate existence, the delusion of ennea-type Two is the belief in a separate will and choice, and the delusion of ennea-type Four is the belief in a separate identity. Here, it is the belief in separate functioning. It is the conviction that one can act independently from the rest of the universe, operating as a separate functional unity. This is an obvious consequence of not perceiving Holy Law, not seeing that everything is the unified functioning of Being. So it is not only the delusion that things happen separately and in isolation in the universe, but specifically, that you are a separate and independent doer, that you can function and accomplish things on your own.

In the absence of Holy Law, you perceive things as separate and functioning separately, and so you believe that events happen in isolation. You also see human beings as separate and functioning separately, which means that you believe that you are doing things on your own, independent of everyone and everything else. So the delusion here is not just that everything functions separately, but specifically, that you are an independent doer, that you, as a separate individual, are a source of action.

When we say that you are not an independent doer, this does not mean that in the objective view, there is no feeling of functioning happening through you—it is not that you don't feel you are moving your arms or talking, nor is it the sense that someone or something else is moving you. It is a different perception in which you see that all functioning, all doing, all activity is happening as one thing. What you are doing and what everyone else is doing is all part of the same movement, so there is no isolated functioning separate from that one flow of activity.

When you are driving your car and you see others driving their cars, instead of perceiving that each of you is engaged in a separate activity, from this perspective, you would see that you and everyone else you pass on the road are all manifestations of the same thing. There are not separate individuals at this level. At a still deeper level, you realize that not only are you and everyone else manifestations of the same reality, but the cars are also manifestations of that reality, and the road itself. The car and you and the driving itself are all the functioning of Being, and so in reality there is no one driving a car. Then you realize that you have never driven from one place to another, that reality has simply manifested in such a way that it appears as if you have driven a car on a road.

When you watch a movie and see someone in it driving a car, is that person really driving a car from one place to another? If you forget that you are sitting in a theater, watching an image on a screen, you believe that someone is really driving. But in reality, what is happening is that one frame of film after another is being projected onto the screen, creating the illusion that someone is driving. Our situation is analogous to this. Your experience of time is part of this belief that you go from one place to another, or that things move from one time to another, but in reality, the pattern of the universe just keeps moving and changing.

So in our analogy, the delusion of ennea-type Three is that the movie is reality and our actions are not part of a larger picture beyond the movie. It is said that ennea-type Three is trying to take God's place by being a little independent god, making up his own laws. This is due to the delusion at the heart of this ennea-type that God is not the only doer. In the old theological language, this belief that you are like a little god, functioning according to your own independent laws, is called the "sin of vanity."

The loss or inadequacy of holding in childhood, reflected through this delusion of vanity, leads to the *specific difficulty* of ennea-type Three. The *specific difficulty*, as we have seen with each ennea-type, is how the environmental inadequacy in holding in early childhood is reflected in one's personal experience. Here, there is the belief that one is a separate and independent doer, and at the same time, the experience that the environment is inadequate and unsupportive. You feel abandoned, rather than held and supported, and you have the sense that no one is taking care of you adequately. While feeling the deficiency, difficulty, and suffering of your experience, there is the growing conviction that you are a doer, that you can act. In other words, the inadequacy of the environment cuts you off from the experience that everything is occurring harmoniously without having to do anything yourself, while at the same time, you begin to believe in yourself as a separate doer. You take the inadequacy in the environment on yourself, believing that you should be able to take care of yourself, since through the delusion, you take yourself to be a center of action. So instead of seeing that the inadequacy is in the environment, you come to believe that it is within yourself. Since you aren't able to provide for and take care of yourself, you not only take it to mean that you can't do these things on your own, but you also take it as a failure, and feel unable, inadequate, and incompetent. If you did not believe that you are an independent doer, it wouldn't make sense to believe that you are inadequate or a failure.

Ego Helplessness and Striving

So the painful emotional state of abandonment and isolation is compounded by feelings of inadequacy, incompetence, ineptness, and failure, all of which crystallizes during the first five or six years of life. The core of this complex of painful emotions is the *specific difficulty* itself, the very difficult feeling of helplessness. The sense of incompetence and failure is the helplessness characterized by self-judgment. Without this characterization, the helplessness is simply the existential predicament resulting from inadequate holding, filtered through this delusion. Without judgment, you wouldn't feel like a failure, but simply helpless.

This sense of helplessness is different from other states of helplessness that result when you cannot do something because of opposition in the environment: when you want to do something and you can't. This helplessness is not specific to one incident, but is inherent in egoic experience. It is true of any ego, whether one is aware of it or not, and is the felt sense of oneself when one is subscribing to the delusion of independent doership. It is a deep inner feeling of helplessness that arises not because the situation is not right, but because you recognize that you just can't do in a much more intrinsic and fundamental way. It becomes especially obvious and severe when the environment is not holding the individual, as happens in early childhood. However, this helplessness is nonsensical if one does not believe that one is an independent doer.

The loss of basic trust is reflected in the mirror of vanity as the *specific reaction* of ennea-type Three. You feel abandoned, no one is taking care of you, and you feel that it is all up to you. Since you believe that you are an independent doer, the *specific reaction* is activity—the activity of the ego, both inner and outer. This activity is agitated, desperate, reactive, and also defensive, since it serves to cover up the *specific difficulty* of helplessness as well as its derivatives: the sense of inadequacy, ineptness, and failure. A good name for this reactive and agitated activity is striving. It manifests as an efforting, a pushing, a constant, obsessive and compulsive need to be active, achieving, doing, and succeeding.

This striving is a reaction formation to the sense of helplessness, and at the same time, it is an imitation of the energetic dynamism of Being. Rather than being intimately connected to Being, however, it is an expression of, and a defense against, the deep sense of helplessness and emptiness experienced as inadequacy. So the striving is both an expression of the disconnection from Being and an activity that cuts one off from Being. It is the activity of the ego which does not trust that Being or God is doing everything, will do everything, and, if one surrenders to it, its optimizing thrust will spontaneously deliver us. This striving embodies egoic hope, as opposed to the flow that expresses the optimism of Holy Hope. Egoic hope makes us react and disconnect from our experience, while Holy Hope makes us relax and open up to the unfolding that is carrying us harmoniously to fulfillment.

True holding comes from the truth itself, from Being. The holding environment in a sense represents reality, whether it is manifesting in a real way—governed by truth, or in a false way—governed by egoic delusion. If it is manifesting in a real way, we experience holding. In the course of our development, the early environment becomes projected onto the totality of existence, so we tend to believe that all of existence is characterized by the lack of holding we experienced in childhood. This makes it difficult for us to see how Being, which is the totality of all of existence, can actually function to hold us.

The more we have the experience of being held by reality, the more the sense of inadequacy will be healed. Such experiences generate more trust and help us understand more completely what holding is about. Initially, such experiences might expose previously unconscious memories of inadequate holding, which is part of the process of working through, and letting go of, those memories. In a sense, we have to re-experience the difficulties in the holding that we had—and feel their impact on us—in order to let them go.

The more you understand the view of reality as seen through the Holy Ideas, the more you realize that the whole universe is holding you. The more you see that, the more you will trust, which in turn allows you to let go of more of your positions of deficiency. To really experience fundamental basic trust is not easy. Each of us already has some trust, so it is a matter of deepening and strengthening it, which requires confronting some difficult parts of ourselves.

As with all of the nine specific reactions, the *specific reaction* of ennea-type Three exists to support the delusion. If you stop striving, you have to give up the delusion that you are a separate and independent doer. So, to prove to yourself that you are an independent doer, you have to always be engaged in activity, regardless of what it is about. Many people think that the most important thing to people of this ennea-type is success, but really, the most important thing is doing itself. Ennea-type Threes may be successful at meeting one goal and not successful at meeting another, but what characterizes them is that they are always striving. They don't rest. So while success is important, it is not as fundamental as the striving itself. They are always generating their identity through activity. This striving is true of everyone living from the egoic perspective—it takes the form of control (ennea-type Four) and willfulness (ennea-type Two), for example—but is exemplified most clearly by those of this ennea-type.

Ego activity always has a goal, whether the activity is internal or external. At some point, you see that even when the goals disappear, the striving continues, finding another goal to attach itself to. The goal itself, then, is not as important as the activity, because we see that the goals change while the activity persists.

Eventually, when we see that the goals keep changing, we might recognize that the point was always the striving, not the goal. But the solution is not to *try* to stop striving, as this simply becomes another act of striving. To stop striving, we need only to fully realize the truth of the situation. This means we must first see how striving is constantly manifesting in our life and then see the reactive and defensive quality of it, how it is a response to our sense of helplessness.

Ceasing to strive happens through accepting your helplessness. This helplessness is existential because in reality, you are not one who can do. This is the innate helplessness of the human being. In traditional religious terminology, awareness of this helplessness is described as "humility," the recognition that only God is almighty. So recognizing your helplessness is, in a sense, recognizing that God is the one who is all-powerful and all-doing. This is why many spiritual traditions emphasize recognizing, feeling, and accepting your smallness and helplessness.

This could be threatening or it might be quite comforting. To see that everything is being done regardless of you, and that things are happening in a harmonious way, can be quite a relief. If, on the other hand, you are trying to preserve your sense of identity, then the thought of giving up the sense of yourself as someone who does can be quite threatening.

So accepting your helplessness is really a spiritual surrender. If you truly accept it, you know that it is really not up to you, and you are free. But if you believe it is all up to you, you will always be busy doing one thing or another and there will be no surrender. So the understanding and acceptance of objective helplessness is an entry into surrender to Being.

Whether we feel threatened by this view of reality or not, it is how things really are. It might be alarming to begin to glimpse how things really are, but it is more alarming to realize that you have not been seeing reality as it is. You see that you have been interpreting what you perceive through various beliefs and concepts, and that these are delusions. If you do not interpret things through the filter of the delusions, you recognize that the world described by the Holy Ideas is the same world, but now without those limiting lenses. When you see that you have not had the vaguest idea about what reality is really like, you experience what is called "the fear of God." Beyond this point, when you see the objective view in operation and let go of who you have taken yourself to be, the view is not only comforting, but very beautiful as well.

Freedom from the Separate Self

A good way to get a glimpse of the view of functioning elucidated by Holy Law is to look at transitional or intermediate experiences of it in which one perceives the functioning of reality, but without the complete loss of the boundaries that define most people's experience. For example, you might experience it when you are in the midst of doing something and you realize that there is no striving—there is a sense of ease, a smoothness to the action that is like a slippery flow.

Physical reality is the most difficult to perceive as part of a whole unfolding pattern. We usually think of physical reality as static, clunky objects outside of ourselves and we have the sense that time passes— both are very difficult perceptions to get beyond. But when observing your inner experience, it is easier to see that there is always an unfolding occurring that you are not making happen. Your sensations, thoughts, and feelings are unfolding and manifesting constantly. In fact, they are unfolding regardless of what you do. Can you stop your thoughts? There is a continual renewal of inner experience going on all the time. It is easy to see that it is not as though our inner experience is happening inside the body while time passes outside it. In reality, our body feels different in each moment. When you become aware of this, you begin to perceive the inner unfoldment of the soul. You might even experience the substance of the soul itself as a dynamic flow with an energetic aliveness. This is close to the sense of the overall unfoldment of reality, in which the flow is not happening just inside of you but everywhere.

Another transitional experience that can move us toward an expanded view of reality is experiencing the soul as an effulgence, a flow. When you experience this fully, you might see that you cannot separate your soul from your body; they are one thing. Seeing this, you can experience the whole of your body as a flow that is continually renewing itself. You perceive, then, that your body is being recreated in every instant.

As these types of experiences deepen over time, and the sense of boundaries dissolves, you begin to see that what you have experienced within yourself is happening all around you. Then you recognize that these are not experiences, but peeks or glimpses of what is happening all the time. Having this kind of perception reveals Holy Hope. When you recognize through your helplessness that you are not the mover, that you are not really making things happen, things begin to happen in a different way. When you realize that you don't have to do it all, there is a sense of release and relief, and you can allow things to unfold by themselves.

For the soul to be free basically means freedom from the separate and individual self. This separate and individual self, in its attempts to support, protect, and enhance itself, accounts for all emotional suffering. This is an important reason to explore the view of objective reality illuminated by the Holy Ideas: As long as we look at spiritual experience from the perspective of the separate self, this freedom will elude us because we will still be identified with the self that needs to be supported, protected, and enhanced. It is all too possible to have all kinds of spiritual experiences and realizations that are contained within, and therefore do not fundamentally challenge, the perspective of the egoic self. The view of reality shows how reality is when there is no egoic self; it shows how reality looks when it is free from that self-centeredness.

It might take us a very long time to realize that this self-centeredness is really the cause of all suffering, and we might continue to believe for a very long time that we will be happier if we support that self, and enhance and protect it. If we don't see that we need to be free of that self, we might use all of our understanding and experience in the spiritual realm to feed that self, which will only add to our problems. These problems are the problems of the self. If there is no self, we don't have problems.

Each of the Holy Ideas challenges and exposes one of the principles that is a foundation for that self—these are the *specific delusions*. Here, we are challenging the delusion that you are a separate and independent center of doing, action, and activity. The striving which supports that identity is pure suffering—there is no peace in it. We are usually not aware of the painful agitation of the striving as we are busily acting it out in our lives, believing that it will bring us something good. If we really saw the inner nature of this agitated, compulsive activity, we might not be so convinced that it will lead us to any sort of peace, happiness, or fulfillment.

Working with Helplessness

So we have explored the delusion of vanity and the striving that is the activity of the ego based on this delusion, and we will now focus more deeply on the *specific difficulty* of helplessness, which as we have seen, may appear as a sense of inability or inadequacy to do what is needed on one's own. One thing we need to understand is that the sense of inadequacy is general and universal to ego. It is not as though some people are inadequate and others are not, nor is it that sometimes you are inadequate and at other times you are not. Nor is this inadequacy just a feeling: Ego, by its very nature, is inadequate. This inadequacy is what I have called elsewhere *ego deficiency*, and we have seen its origin as the lack of contact with the capacities of Being. (For an in-depth discussion of ego deficiency, see *The Pearl Beyond Price*.) The moment you take yourself to be a separate entity, you cut yourself off from your ground, from your support, from Being itself. As a result, you don't have available to you the strength, the power, the will, the intelligence, and all of the other capacities that are inherent in Being. In this sense, the ego not only feels inadequate, but is indeed inadequate.

At a more subtle level, we see that the inadequacy is due to the presence of ego boundaries. The fact that you believe you are a separate entity makes you feel unsupported and not held by Being, and leaves you with this sense of inadequacy. For a long time in spiritual work, when someone tells you that you need to look into your belief that you are a separate identity, you might feel that the person is trying to take away from you your most valued possession. In time, you see that it is really the other way around, that the person is acting compassionately, trying to release you from your suffering. It is an illusion that your sense of self is a good thing, and hopefully, your work will help you see that.

So we have seen two levels of inadequacy or ego deficiency: the disconnection from Being and the fact of boundedness itself, which makes one unable to experience the support and the holding of Being. In working with the present Holy Idea, we can understand this phenomenon even more accurately as the lack of harmony with the unity of functioning, due to vanity—the conviction that one is an independent and separate doer. So the belief that one has autonomous functional capacity separate from the rest of existence is the deepest cause of the sense of lack. The fact that we believe we are separate doers puts us in a state of helplessness, which is experienced as inadequacy.

When you feel the helplessness fully, without resisting it, you might feel that you are so helpless that you can't even raise a finger. This experience is getting down to the truth of the delusion. It does not mean that you are an individual who is feeling inadequate when you could be feeling adequate, nor is there a judgment about the fact that you feel that way. If you experience the helplessness as a failure, it is because you believe that you should be able to be adequate, and since you're not, you are ashamed and have a self-judgment about feeling that way. However, if you see that the helplessness is just an existential fact that is part and parcel of being an ordinary egoic human being, you realize that it is not something to judge and reject yourself for. Rather, it is something to accept with humility and surrender. It is a chance for you to finally see your condition accurately.

So to experience the helplessness without judgment and rejection is to accept our existential situation when we are not in the condition of enlightenment. It is the acceptance that, by the mere fact of being a human individual, you are helpless. This is analogous to the religious notion that it is only God who is mighty and capable, and the experience is similar to being genuinely immersed in prayer. If you really pray, you are acknowledging that there is a much larger force than you as a separate individual. The acceptance of your helplessness has the same sense of surrender and humility, and is in this sense a kind of prayer. Accepting and feeling your helplessness is seeing that you cannot free yourself, nor can you take away anyone else's suffering. As long as you take yourself to be a separate doer, whatever you do is not going to make a difference, and helplessness is your objective condition.

Until you know yourself to be completely Being, you are objectively helpless; taking that prayerful attitude of acknowledging your helplessness in the face of the immensity of Being is not only useful—it also reflects the truth. The attitude of humility and helplessness is accurate as long as there is any remnant of self. From the perspective of pure Being, that prayerful attitude helps to expose the egoic self and to acknowledge its real situation. Then this acceptance of helplessness, without defense, without judgment, without striving, becomes the point of entry into Being and its dynamism.

If you refrain from doing when you have the urge to strive, and merely accept the true condition of the ego, Being naturally acts through its optimizing thrust. Through your striving, you prevent, you block and oppose this optimizing thrust of Being. Striving for happiness or striving to attain any other goal is taking matters into your own hands instead of allowing the optimizing thrust of Being to make things happen. So accepting your helplessness is, in a sense, an invitation for the action of the optimizing thrust.

We are seeing that allowing and understanding this helplessness is vitally important for spiritual development. Often, when we initially contact our sense of helplessness, it is the emotional helplessness that is the result of limitations in the environment—past, present, and imagined. This is the sense of helplessness we have when we are ill and feel helpless to move, or when we want a day off but have to work. It is also a regressive helplessness, shaped by memories of infancy when our capacity to do and to act were indeed limited and dependent. As we have said, this emotional helplessness is not the existential one that comes from merely having a sense of self. As long as you can find a reason for your helplessness, it is still not the fundamental helplessness. When you finally feel that your helplessness is not caused by someone holding you back, or by your lack of strength, or your smallness, or by any other specific circumstance, you will feel the existential helplessness that is present simply as part of the situation of being human.

When we first feel it, this helplessness is a very painful state, one of profound vulnerability, fragility, inadequacy, and weakness. Allowing this level of vulnerability can be scary, especially in the harsh world we live in these days. But whether society supports it or not, those of us who are working to realize our true nature have no alternative. In time, the feeling of vulnerability is something that you can handle even in difficult situations, but in the beginning, you might need a particular environment in which you feel that you are not going to be attacked for being helpless. So we need to be intelligent and not expose our vulnerability in situations where it would hurt us rather than help us. This is why groups like those in our School are important. They provide a time and place where you can feel safe to go deeply into these areas within yourself. When you are by yourself, you need to find your own safe time and place to explore yourself. The concern about safety also reflects our early experiences when the environment was not empathic, gentle, and holding, in the face of our helplessness.

This existential helplessness does not make sense unless you believe yourself to be a separate doer, or believe you are supposed to be able to do. As we feel this sense of helplessness and accept it, we are no longer trying to uphold the delusion that we can do. If we stay with the experience, we can penetrate this delusion. It may seem difficult to stay with because the state may initially be filled with pain and the fear that no one is going to take care of you and you are helpless. We have to remember not to completely believe these fears because believing them might cause us to react by defending against the sense of helplessness. Although it is painful, at some point we see that feeling the helplessness has a sincerity and truthfulness because we are no longer lying to ourselves. We are being authentic. This realization by itself can bring about an egoless state without our doing anything. The helplessness, then, opens the door to the action of Being itself.

Most of us don't let ourselves deeply feel this helplessness because we think it is a bad thing—that it means that there is something wrong with us personally. So we judge it, are ashamed of it, and don't let ourselves feel it. But when you recognize that the helplessness is not about you personally, but is just the human condition, and that if you completely accept it, it becomes a positive state since it ushers you into Being, then you will welcome it whenever it arises.

When you accept the helplessness, it means that you have stopped the efforting. When you see through the striving, you might become aware of how tired your heart is, how tired your mind is, how tired your body is, how tired your soul is. You feel a very old tiredness that exists because you have been trying for years and years and years to do something that you cannot do. The striving has been exhausting in a way you could never let yourself acknowledge before.

The more you get in touch with the helplessness, the more you might also get in touch with a specific physical blockage against it, which is the same thing as holding on to the delusion of vanity, of separate doership. This blockage is a specific holding at the anterior fontanel (at the front of the head) which blocks the channel of Living Daylight. When we see through this delusion and surrender our striving and our belief in it, this channel opens up. Then we can experience the beginning of real holding, the beginning of blessing as a descent of light that is love. This loving light expresses the action of Being as it melts the rigidities and fixations of the soul.

When this occurs, we see that vanity is the specific blockage against the channel of Living Daylight, because in believing in yourself as a separate doer, you are taking God's place. In other words, vanity and striving are reflections of the position that one does not need real holding. You feel that you can do it on your own and so you don't need nourishment—whether human or divine. It also means that you believe that you do not need grace, and therefore block it. Grace is the descent of Living Daylight, specifically in regard to dissolving boundaries, so it allows us to be held by the universe and to trust in it. When you connect with this level of reality, the degree of holding in the environment ceases to be an issue. The environment that allows us to dissolve is Being itself, and when we connect with that dimension of reality, we feel held no matter what situation we are in.

This last Holy Idea is important in the Diamond Approach for two reasons. First, it is important because our approach recognizes and relies on the truth of the optimizing thrust of reality. This optimizing thrust is seen in our approach to spiritual work as the conjunction of understanding and unfoldment, which is a guided flow. Also, the open-minded and open-hearted optimism that is Holy Hope is reflected in our stance of allowing all that unfolds—within and without us—with an attitude of curiosity. This optimism is present in our work in our allowing of the presentations of Being's dynamism, the openness to whatever happens, with an inquiring and a celebrative attitude. Understanding, which is the primary method in our work, needs this open welcoming of whatever arises; this both facilitates the unfoldment and is itself a product of that unfoldment.

Relaxing into Being's Unfoldment

We have explored the nine *specific delusions* that describe the points of view that underlie and support the structure of the ego. This can help us to understand whether what motivates us is coming from a deluded perspective or from an objective view of reality. It should be obvious that most of us act in alignment with the delusions, and that these in turn generate the nine painful states that are the *specific difficulties* of the nine points. We have also seen how we characteristically try to resolve these painful states through the *specific reactions*, and how pointless this is since they are based on mistaken views of reality. We typically believe that by engaging in, and identifying with, these reactions, we will not feel our suffering. Through the course of our exploration, we have seen that these defensive reactions do not resolve the *specific difficulties*. Their resolution will happen only through letting go of the delusions underlying them. This means, first of all, that we must recognize the delusions we are operating from, and then we need to realize that they are the real cause of our suffering. In other words, they need to become ego alien, and we need to see that they constitute and maintain the egoic self.

It is important for our spiritual development that we really understand what the deluded view of the ego is, and what the real view is as elucidated by the Holy Ideas. It is important that we do not deceive ourselves into taking a deluded way of seeing things to be what is objectively true. If you do not understand the view of reality, you will take your experience for granted as an unquestionable and unchanging, concrete reality.

For example, most people have a difficult time because they believe that they don't have enough money, or they don't have enough love or enough security or enough of one thing or another. Most of these concerns are not realistic but are simply supports for the ego. How many friends you have, how many people admire you, how much financial security you have—this whole level of concern needs to be looked at and explored, rather than assumed to be true and acted upon. When you look at your life from the perspective of the objective view, you realize everything that happens is guided by an intelligence greater than your own. As long as you maintain that you want it to happen a certain way, you are striving toward an egically determined outcome and you remain entrenched in suffering.

Understanding the view of the Holy Ideas will create an attitude that is more open and more welcoming to the unfoldment. Holding on to the egoic view gives you a closed attitude, one that is narrow rather than expanded, inward looking rather than outward looking. The attitude of openness that the view of reality creates does not involve a judgment about the egoic view, since the moment you become judgmental and rejecting, you are again stuck in delusion.

The attitude that arises through understanding the Holy Ideas is characterized by Holy Hope, the open-hearted optimism about how things happen. The more you develop this attitude, and the more the attitude is itself informed and supported by the view, the less concerned you will be about trying to change your state or fixing this or that inside or outside of you. You will become less concerned about tinkering with your mind or body, about doing this or that technique or method. There are many kinds of techniques and methods, and it is not that they are not useful, but the more you understand the objective view, the less you will rely on them. You will see more clearly what you really need, and will rely less on this or that method to open yourself up, amuse yourself, or change your state. People whose perception is very close to the view of reality don't really do much. They just relax. This does not mean that they *do* anything to relax, since the moment you do something in order to relax, that becomes striving. But the more you simply relax, the more you find that you are open to what happens and have less judgment about whether it is good or bad. Over time, there will be less and less reflection of any kind on your experience.

The attitude that comes from the view of the Holy Ideas is what is really needed to be able to trust the unfoldment of your soul, since it opens you up to Being with its optimizing thrust. This is what unfolds your experience and transforms it.

CONCLUSION

In this chapter we will summarize the understanding of the Holy Ideas we have explored in this book, look at how Point Nine is seminal in this process, and consider how the Holy Ideas point us toward the mirror-like awareness of the soul.

We began with the exploration of basic trust—the unconditional, nonconceptual trust that the soul can have to a greater or lesser degree. We explored how both the development and the disturbance of basic trust are affected by the child's early holding environment. Elaborating on the exploration of basic trust, we worked with the quality of Being that is needed for the human soul to trust. When experiencing Living Daylight or Loving Light and the basic trust it evokes, the soul naturally begins to perceive the unity of the universe manifesting in one of nine different forms called the Holy Ideas. The loss or absence of this experience disrupts the perception of unity, particularly the unity of the human and the divine. Without this perception, the soul is impacted in very specific ways that can be delineated for each of the nine Points. This impact consists of a core complex made up of a *specific delusion*, a *specific difficulty*, and a *specific reaction*, all related to a specific Holy Idea. By looking at these elements, we have defined very precisely the issues regarding basic trust for each type. As we have already explored these four elements in the context of each Point, it will be useful in summarizing our work, to view them as four separate but closely related Enneagrams.

Traditionally, Point Nine is seen as the seminal Point in the Enneagram map, in that the other eight Points can be seen as different variations growing out of the experience of Point Nine. In other words, all other Points have implicit within them the ground of Point Nine. Now that we have explored in detail each of the Holy Ideas and core complexes, it is possible for us to see how this centrality of Point Nine exists in these four Enneagrams.

The perspective of the Enneagram of Holy Ideas is the perspective of the correct, objective view of reality. We discussed how reality is perceived when perception is completely undistorted, how each Idea reveals a specific facet of the overall perspective. Point Nine as Holy Love reveals the fundamental heart experience of the unity of reality, the experience that all of reality is good, is loving and lovable, and nothing can be without or separate from that love. This perception evokes love in the human soul, thus aligning it with reality, motivating it toward reality, and relaxing it in reality. From this perspective each other Holy Idea can be seen as a complement to, and a clarification of, this Idea. Point One is Holy Perfection; Point Two is Holy Will; Point Three is Holy Law, Hope, and Harmony; Point Four is Holy Origin; Point Five is Holy Omniscience; Point Six is Holy Faith and Strength; Point Seven is Holy Wisdom, Work, and Plan; and Point Eight is Holy Truth. Each can be seen as a discrimination of the indivisible goodness and unity of reality of which the soul is an inseparable element.

Enneagram of Holy Ideas

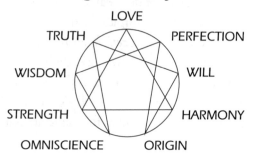

LOVE
TRUTH   PERFECTION
WISDOM   WILL
STRENGTH   HARMONY
OMNISCIENCE   ORIGIN

These objective perspectives on reality are contrasted with the nine perspectives of ego. The latter are the *specific delusions*, the way in which ego views and understands reality, having lost the perception of unity. The nine delusions are universal principles of ego, out of which the difficulties and reactions arise. By studying the delusions of each Point, we have done a thorough exploration of the principles that are responsible for the existence, structure, and activity of ego life.

The Enneagram of Specific Delusions is grounded in the delusion of Point Nine: that love and goodness are local phenomena. In other words, each of the other eight delusions can be seen as based on, or arising out of, this fundamental delusion. The other delusions are Point One, reality is split between good and bad; Point Two, I have a separate personal will; Point Three, I am a separate doer; Point Four, I have a separate identity; Point Five, I am a separate self; Point Six, I have no true nature; Point Seven, I have a separate personal unfoldment; Point Eight, reality is dual and conflictual. Each of these delusions is an expression of the loss of the unity of goodness.

We have seen how each *specific delusion*, which reflects the loss, absence, or distortion of the Holy Idea of that Point, manifests in the life of the soul in the experience of the *specific difficulty* and the *specific reaction*. We have related the *specific difficulty* to the nine ways of experiencing the inadequacy of the original holding environment. So each type or fixation will tend to experience the inadequacy of holding as one *specific difficulty* to which it will have one *specific reaction*

Enneagram of Specific Delusions

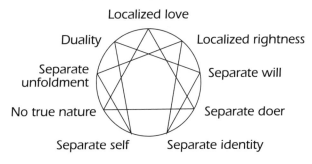

© 1998 A-Hameed Ali

based on its own delusion. Since the inadequacy of holding results in the disturbance of basic trust, the nine reactions we have explored can be understood as expressions of distrust.

In some sense, your *specific difficulty* cannot be completely understood or resolved until you resolve the *specific difficulty* of Point Nine: feeling a sense of inferiority, accompanied by shame about yourself, and a sense that you are not lovable. This is *the* basic difficulty; if you really believe that you are lovable, the *specific difficulties* of the other points will not appear. So a specific foundation for all the specific difficulties is the belief, the feeling, the conviction, that you are unlovable, that there is something inferior or intrinsically distorted about your soul. The Enneagram of Specific Difficulties are all particular flavors added to this sense of inferiority. Point One is feeling there is something wrong with you; Point Two is feeling castrated and humiliated; Point Three is feeling helpless; Point Four is feeling abandoned by or disconnected from reality; Point Five is feeling painful isolation; Point Six is feeling fearful insecurity; Point Seven is feeling lost and not knowing what to do; Point Eight is feeling guilt and badness.

Similarly, your *specific reaction* cannot be worked through fully until you resolve the Point Nine reaction, which is that of falling asleep. This reaction is the basis of all of the nine reactions. Remember, the *specific reactions* are expressions of distrust. The basic expression of distrust is falling asleep, not being present to your experience. The

Enneagram of Specific Difficulties

Enneagram of Specific Reactions arises out of this, starting from Point One: trying to make yourself better; Point Two: trying to get your own way; Point Three: striving; Point Four: controlling; Point Five: withdrawing or hiding; Point Six: suspiciously defending yourself; Point Seven: planning; Point Eight: blaming. All these are ways of expressing distrust, and they all involve falling asleep by functioning in reactive and defensive ways.

Basically, the distrust makes the soul not want to be awake to how reality is. When you do not trust reality, you don't want to see it, you don't want to look it in the face. You don't want to see things as they are. You want to see things in a way that will make you feel safe. You want to protect yourself from the dangers and the pains and the various difficulties because you don't trust that reality can take care of you. You don't trust that there is love. So unconsciousness and falling asleep is the primary foundation of all the reactions. The condition of sleep, of unconsciousness, of lack of awakening, is pervasive in all egos. It is basic to ego. Ego is an expression of a lack of direct awareness of what is. It is the expression of not seeing things as they are.

The process of the soul's disconnection from its essential nature begins happening very early in life, even before birth. As the disconnection happens, the soul loses its central, most basic, most primary, most primal quality—clear knowingness, clear luminous awareness. It loses its capacity to see clearly. It loses its transparency, clarity, and luminosity, and becomes dull and thick.

Enneagram of Specific Reactions

Falling asleep

Blaming — Improving

Planning — Manipulating

Suspiciously defending — Striving

Withdrawing — Controlling

© 1998 A-Hameed Ali

This primal quality—the most original, intrinsic nature of the soul—is pure clarity, transparency, luminosity, awareness. Thus, the soul is primarily an organ of perception with the capacity to see things as they are. You could say that Being perceives through the soul. How does God see? Through the soul. How does Being experience? Through the soul.

This basic quality of the soul is sometimes called "mirror-like awareness." It is mirror-like in the sense that it functions in the way a mirror functions. A mirror reflects things exactly as they are with no distortion. Part of the normal development of ego in the context of inadequacies in the holding environment is the loss of this mirror-like awareness, a loss that is both a result of the reactions based on distrust and a factor causing the reactions. This loss is the loss of the capacity for objectivity, for seeing things without subjective filters.

This loss is very basic to the loss of the Holy Ideas, the loss of the capacity to perceive reality as it is. The inadequacies of the holding environment distort your perception of how things actually are. Either your environment affected you in ways that warped your perception of reality, or it affected you such that you don't want to see reality. So that transparency, that pure clarity of the open and relaxed soul, is what suffered most in the course of your ego development. This loss of clarity and transparency manifests in the soul as falling asleep. So all the *specific reactions* are ways of expressing the state of being asleep, being unawake: They express it, support it, and perpetuate it. So if we want to be awake, we need to become aware of all these reactions and learn to disengage from them.

In the course of spiritual development, as the soul begins to understand the truth and to develop through contact with Essence, it becomes clearer and purer. Eventually, it can be completely purified. The Sufi notion of the Perfect or Complete Soul is the completely developed soul, the completely purified soul. The Sufis say that the completely purified soul is colorless, completely transparent and clear. Thus, the soul has regained through purification its original essential nature of pure luminosity or pure awareness of how things are. At the same time, the soul has developed through maturity a discriminating awareness of reality that includes its nature, its environment, and everything else. The soul can thus have a mirror-like awareness that is transparent and without distortion, as well as a capacity for discrimination and understanding.

So the simplest, most elemental nature of the soul is complete transparency without any qualities, just the fact of its awareness, perception, transparency, luminosity. This is the soul's most basic nature. It is also what is called "primordial awareness."

The quality of mirror-like awareness is what makes it possible to perceive objective reality. Working with, understanding, and realizing the Holy Ideas, brings us closer to that mirror-like awareness as the view of reality expands to include the whole of reality, rather than being oriented around the delusion of a separate sense of self. The view of objective reality of the Holy Ideas makes it possible for the soul to correct the distortions of perception that dominate the egoic view of the self and the world, thus clarifying the soul's awareness, or "polishing the mirror" of the soul. The clear awareness of the human soul, then, perceives the objective view of the patterns of creation with an understanding of the place of the human being in this creation. This understanding awakens the soul to its own unfolding as the expression of Being, and its own participation in the greater pattern of unfolding whose nature is wholeness, dynamism, intelligence, and openness.

REFERENCES

Aurobindo, Sri, *Last Poems*, Pondicherry: Sri Aurobindo Ashram, 1952.

Bleibreu, John, ed., *Interviews with Oscar Ichazo*, New York: Arica Institute Press, 1982.

Castaneda, Carlos, *The Power of Silence: Further Lessons of don Juan*, New York: Pocket Books, 1987.

Corbin, Henry, *Creative Imagination in the Sufism of Ibn Arabi*, Princeton: Princeton University Press, 1969.

Ichazo, Oscar, "The Arica Psycho-catalyzers/Holy Ideas/Mind Catalyzers," handout with Holy Idea definitions, Dobbs Ferry, NY: Arica Institute, 1972.

Jung, C.G., *The Archetypes and the Collective Unconscious* Princeton: Princeton University Press, Second Edition, 1959.

Jung, C.G., *The Basic Writings of C.G. Jung*, ed. Violet Staub De Laszlo, New York: The Modern Library, 1959.

Lilly, John C., and Joseph E. Hart, "The Arica Training," in Charles T. Tart, *Transpersonal Psychologies,* New York: Harper Colophon Books, 1977.

Longchenpa, *You Are the Eyes of the World*, trans. by Kennard Lipman & Merrill Peterson, Novato: Lotsawa, 1987.

Mahler, Margaret, Fred Pine and Anni Bergman, *The Psychological Birth of the Human Infant: Symbiosis and Individuation*, New York: Basic Books, Inc., 1975.

Naranjo, Claudio, *Ennea-type Structures: Self-Analysis for the Seeker*, Nevada City: Gateways/IDHHB, Inc., 1990.

Palmer, Helen, *The Enneagram,* San Francisco: Harper & Row, Publishers, 1988.

Riso, Don Richard, and Russ Hudson, *Personality Types,* Revised Edition, Boston: Houghton Mifflin Company, 1996.

Schwartz-Salant, Nathan, *Narcissism and Character Transformation,* Toronto: Inner City Books, 1982.

Shabistari, Mahmud, *The Secret Garden,* translated by Johnson Pasha, London: Octagon Press, 1969.

Tarthang Tulku, *Time, Space and Knowledge: A New Vision of Reality,* Berkeley: Dharma Publishing, 1977.

Winnicott, D.W., *Maturational Processes and the Facilitating Environment: Studies in the Theory of Emotional Development,* Madison: International Universities Press, Inc., 1965.

The Diamond Approach is taught by Ridhwan teachers, certified by the Ridhwan Foundation. Ridhwan teachers are also ordained ministers of the Ridhwan Foundation. They are trained by DHAT Institute, the educational arm of the Ridhwan Foundation, through an extensive seven-year program, which is in addition to their work and participation as students of the Diamond Approach. The certification process ensures that each person has a good working understanding of the Diamond Approach and a sufficient capacity to teach it before being ordained and authorized to be a Ridhwan teacher.

The Diamond Approach described in this book is taught in group and private settings in California and Colorado by Ridhwan teachers.

For information, write:

> Ridhwan
> P.O. Box 10114
> Berkeley, California 94709-5114

> Ridhwan School
> P.O. Box 18166
> Boulder, Colorado 80308–8166

Satellite groups operate in other national and international locations. For information about these groups, or to explore starting a group in your area, taught by certified Ridhwan teachers, write:

> Ridhwan
> P.O. Box 10114
> Berkeley, California 94709-5114

Diamond Approach is a registered service mark of the Ridhwan Foundation.